Over Ancient Ways

A Portrait of St Peter's School, York

Over Ancient Ways

A Portrait of St Peter's School, York

Edited by Richard Drysdale

III THIRD MILLENNIUM
PUBLISHING, LONDON

*This book is dedicated to all members of the extended St Peter's family who
have contributed to the remarkable history the School has enjoyed.*

OVER ANCIENT WAYS: A PORTRAIT OF ST PETER'S SCHOOL, YORK

© St Peter's School, York and Third Millennium Publishing Limited

First published in 2007 by
Third Millennium Publishing Limited,
a subsidiary of Third Millennium Information Limited.

2–5 Benjamin Street
London
United Kingdom
EC1M 5QL
www.tmiltd.com

ISBN: 978 1 903942 62 8

British Library Cataloguing in Publication Data
A CIP catalogue record for this book is available from the
British Library.

Edited by Richard Drysdale
Designed by Susan Pugsley
Production by Bonnie Murray

Reprographics by Asia Graphic Printing Ltd
Printed by 1010 Printing International Ltd

Contents

PREFACE   **6**

INTRODUCTION   **8**

THE HISTORY OF THE SCHOOL   **9**

The First Twelve Centuries: 627–1844   10

The Guy Fawkes Connection   16

Early Years in Clifton 1844–1913   18

Charles Wright's Letters Home 1854–58   24

The First World War, the 1920s and the Depression:
the Toyne Era 1913–1936   26

Bankruptcy and Closure ? Aubrey Price 1936–37   33

Rescue, Recovery and Consolidation: Dronfield 1937–67   34

Dronfield's First Years 1937–44   38

The War Years 1939–45   42

The Baedecker Raid, 29 April 1942   46

Liberalization and Modernization:
Peter Gardiner 1967–79   47

The Arrival of Girls   51

The Science Renaissance: Peter Hughes 1979–84   52

The Interregnum: David Cummin 1984–85   53

Co-education and Consolidation: Robin Pittman 1985–95   54

Towards the Millennium: Andrew Trotman 1995–2004   59

ST OLAVE'S AND CLIFTON PRE-PREP   **63**

The History of Clifton Pre-preparatory School   64

A Brief History of St Olave's 1876–1969   67

The Memoirs of an Olavite in the 1930s   71

St Olave's under John Rayson 1969–90   75

St Olave's School 1990–2005   78

LIFE AT SCHOOL   **81**

Academic Perspectives: Change and Continuity   82

Boarding 1969–2001   90

Crimes and Misdemeanours   93

The Alcuin Library   96

'The Peterite'   100

The Careers Department   102

The Early Days of the CCF: 1860–1948   104

The Debating Society 1937–90   108

Community Service   110

THE SPIRITUAL LIFE OF THE SCHOOL   **111**

The School Chapel Today   112

Three Chaplains Remember   114

CREATIVE ARTS   **117**

Music 1986–2006   118

Art   122

Design and Technology   125

'The play's the thing …'   126

My Sister's Sixth Form Boyfriend Fancied Me   130

EXPEDITIONS   **131**

World Challenge: Expeditions 2001–2005   132

The First World War Battlefields Trips 1987–2006   134

The Duke of Edinburgh Award Scheme   135

Yr Hafod: Winter Hill Walking and
Mountaineering 1986–2002   136

The Sahara Expeditions 1978–93   138

SPORTS   **139**

Girls' Games 1976–2005   140

Cricket 1945–2005   144

Rugby 1846–2005   147

The Boat Club 1990–2006   150

Hockey 1897–2005   153

GOVERNANCE   **155**

Governors' Tales   156

The Foundation   158

The Non-teaching Staff   160

THE OLD PETERITES   **161**

The History of the Old Peterite Club   162

Famous Old Peterites   165

Rolls of Honour   170

Old Peterite Anecdotes   172

ADDENDA   **177**

Long-serving Members of Staff   178

Rugby, Cricket and Boating Honours   180

LIST OF SUBSCRIBERS   **182**

INDEX   **188**

Preface

RICHARD DRYSDALE

This book is a portrait of the School with particular emphasis on the last four decades. Angelo Raine's book The History of St Peter's *(1926) is a useful introduction.* The Recent History of St Peter's School *(1967) by Freddie Wiseman takes the story up to the end of the Dronfield era. I have drawn on much that is in both books. Although the early history is covered in this book, it has been done briefly. The purpose of the book, therefore, is not to write an exhaustive history of the recent past, but to try to give a broad portrait of the school over the last few decades.*

I am conscious that I have not been able to cover all aspects of the School's life. The approach has necessarily been a selective one and it has been impossible to mention all the many people who have contributed to the School's development. For this I apologize. All the material submitted which I have been unable to use will be placed in the archives for future generations.

The School has gone from times of virtual bankruptcy and closure in 1844, 1899 and 1936 to the achievements of today. History shows that success was not always guaranteed. There were times when the School's fortunes faded and times when they were bright. What makes the success of recent years so remarkable is its breadth across the curriculum; from the academic to the sporting and extracurricular.

Lastly, I have thoroughly enjoyed working on this project and I have learnt much about the School. I am especially grateful to the many colleagues, OPs and friends of the school who have contributed sections or chapters. The project would not have been possible without the vision and support of Richard Smyth. I am also especially grateful to Avril Pedley, the Archivist, who has given me so much vital help and has in effect been the co-editor (although she was too modest to accept the title); to David Morris for his unstinting help with the photographs; to Keith and Margaret Coulthard, who answered numerous questions about the Dronfield era; to John Armstrong for his ICT support and, lastly, to my wife, Jean, whose comments have been helpful. The team at Third Millennium have all been more supportive than I could have wished. Julian Platt, Chris Fagg, Neil Burkey, Susan Pugsley, Lindsey Shaw-Miller and Michael Jackson have all made my task much easier and for this I thank them.

6

Introduction

RICHARD SMYTH

The last history of St Peter's to have been written appeared in 1967. It is timely, after nearly 40 years, to take a fresh look at the rich past of the School. We are very fortunate that the recently retired head of History, Richard Drysdale, and the retired librarian and present archivist of the School, Avril Pedley, have embraced the challenge with such enthusiasm. They both bring to the task long and valued experience of the School. Old Peterites, present and retired staff, Governors and Fellows have all been asked to contribute their view of the present and recent past. Their varied memories and insights enrich our understanding and appreciation of the School's history. They help us to grasp the essence of what makes St Peter's unique.

A school must always move forward aided by vision and strategic planning, endeavouring to improve the education of its pupils. However, from time to time it is important to look back, so that we may both gain a better understanding of the present and plan more effectively for the future. Only by doing so can a school value the progress made, examine what is really important and appreciate the individuals who have contributed to its development.

After nearly fourteen centuries, and arguably the longest history of any school in Western Europe, St Peter's has much to celebrate. It should be proud of its past and move forward with confidence as its pupils and teachers write the next decades of its history.

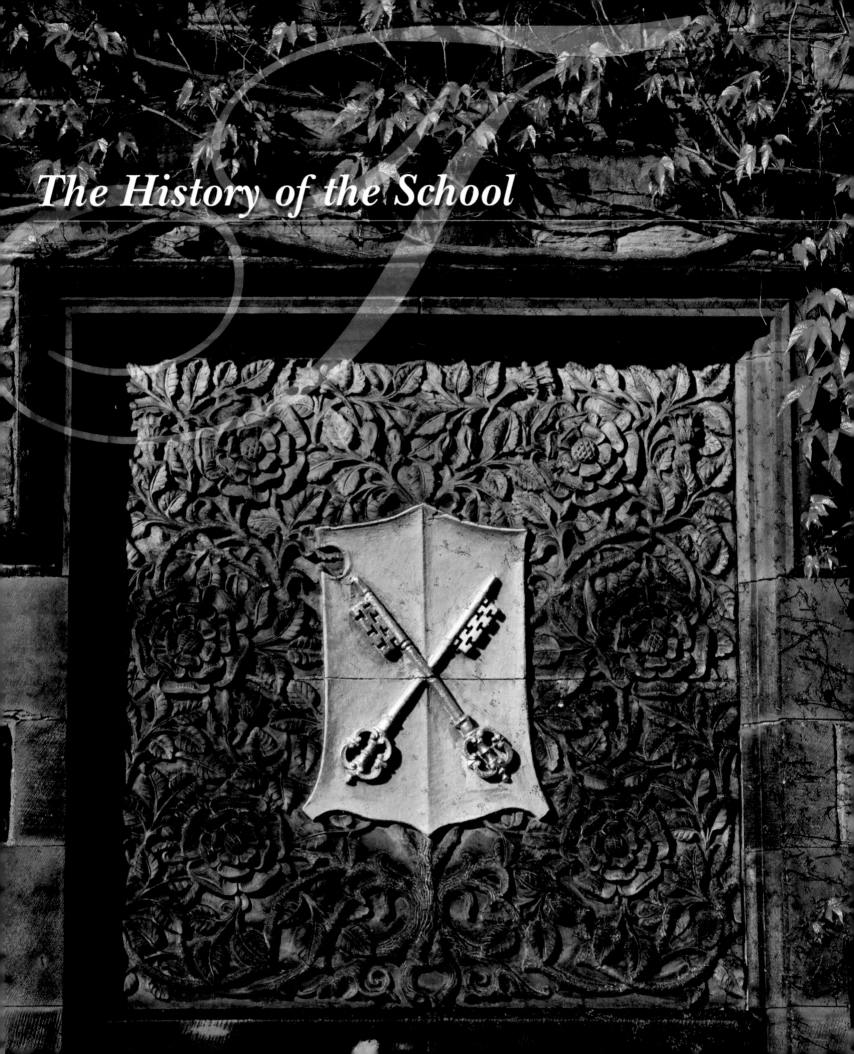

The First Twelve Centuries: 627–1844

AVRIL PEDLEY

'Older than the House of Commons, older than the Universities, older than the House of Lords, older even than the throne or the nation itself.' In 1892 the educational historian A.F. Leach described St Peter's School in these sonorous terms. At the time he was supporting our claim to be the oldest school in the country – several schools vie for the title – and, while Leach later decided against us in the contest, he never disputed our actual age.

We know that in AD 627 St Paulinus built the first wooden church on the site of the present York Minster and founded the Grammar School and the Minster Song School. Records tell us that princes and noblemen gave their sons to be educated and that the school was firmly established when St John of Beverley became Head Master, AD 705. During the eighth century the fame of the School spread to Europe, and the number of pupils increased rapidly. Bishop Maurice Harland of Durham (OP), when opening Dronfield House in 1964, pointed out that the Venerable Bede made one of his very rare excursions from his monastery in 733[1] and may well have visited the School, but in 741 both the Minster and the School burnt down. It fell to Archbishop Albert [Aelberht] to rebuild both, and this event was described by his most famous pupil, Alcuin, who in 778 himself became Head Master. Alcuin was one of the most influential men of his century – indeed of the entire first millennium, and one of York's most illustrious sons. His great learning, acquired here in York, led to his becoming chief adviser to the Emperor Charlemagne, and founding schools in Europe following the York pattern.

Alcuin described York's situation as a commercial, religious and educational centre. He tells us of Archbishop Albert's search for rare books during his travels on the continent and his use of them to establish a curriculum at York, which gave the School a pre-eminent educational position at that time. The boys studied Latin grammar, rhetoric (the art of correct expression and argument in Latin), time-reckoning, logic, astronomy, geometry, arithmetic and, possibly, history and natural history. In a letter to the canons of York written about 793, Alcuin referred to his time at school in York both as a boy and a master: 'You nourished my tender years of childhood with a mother's love, you endured with pious patience the frolics of my boyhood, and with the discipline of fatherly chastisements educated me till I was grown up, and strengthened me with the learning of holy rules'.

After this period of high success, little is known about the School until the Norman Conquest, when William I destroyed the city and the famous library. He then appointed Thomas of Bayeux as Archbishop, under whom the School flourished on the site of the nave of the present Minster. In 1289, at the time of Edward I, another short move took place to a house near the Minster's present east end. It is said that William Rufus had directed that pupils should live in the School, and 50 boys eventually were housed in St Mary's Abbey. Arguments rumbled on between various sections of the clergy, with claims that the School Master ought to be present at divine service in the Minster and, on the other side, 'that the Chancellor or his deputy ought to be continually in residence and lecture in his theological school, but does not'. The Black Death, which visited the city in 1348–49 and 1368, compounded the problems, with the School Master almost certainly being a victim of the disease on each occasion. In a will of 23 May 1369[2] a bequest was made to 60 poor clerks of the Grammar School, of good behaviour, to receive 2d to say psalms and pray for the soul of Richard of Beckyngham, advocate of the court of York, at his funeral. The recipients were to be selected by the Head Master, and if he could choose 60 there must have been a fair number more.

A few years later, in 1375, the Chancellor, Thomas de Farnilaw, tried to suppress a rival Grammar School which had been occupying premises at St Leonard's Hospital for some years. He complained to the Chapter that,

Although the appointment to Grammar Schools and particularly in York itself, belonged to the Chancellor, and no one can keep a school without his permission, nevertheless Master Nicholas de Ferriby dares to have a Grammar School in the City of York, within the Chancellor's jurisdiction, to the grave hurt of the Chancellor and of Master John of York, Master of the York Grammar School, and by so doing furnishes a most pernicious example and causes scandal to many persons.

The attempt at suppressing the opposition seems to have failed, but in 1377, poll tax returns show the School to be doing well. Teenage boys were doing the sort of things that teenage boys still do; a report survives of skirmishes between the boys and bargees on the Ouse, one boy being carried off on a barge. Some Peterites retaliated by pushing a bargee into the river where he sadly drowned; the Head Master made the boys pay for his funeral.

In 1413 Pope John granted a dispensation to John Everingham (who may very well have been one of our pupils) to take holy orders, despite defective eyesight: 'We understand that once on a time you went out at night, in company with other boys, to capture birds, and you were accidentally struck in the left eye and have not been able to open it since, though you have not completely lost your eyesight.' Such small snippets of information continue: 1535 finds 50 poor scholars 'lodging in the mansion called Conclave or the Clee, near the outer gate of

11

Bedern Hall, the only remaining part of the buildings where the School was housed 1644–1730.

Alcuin and Charlemagne, Tiffany Window, Pennsylvania.

The School was situated in the Bagnio between 1730–35.

the monastery, and attending the Minster Grammar School…kept on the broken victuals of the convent'. Also in 1535 Richard Oliver, the rector of All Saints', North Street, York, died and mentioned the School in his will. From this it is clear that there were at least two schoolmasters. Oliver left 20d for repair of the lavatory at the Clee, and also gave the pupils an ale pot to drink to his memory. He expressed the hope that the assistant master or 'usher' might be allowed to bring the boys to his burial at Holy Trinity Priory.

In 1552 Archbishop Holgate warned that deacons who did not attend the grammar school daily, after three warnings, 'Not applienge there bookes for there better advauncement in lernynge, be expulsed, and other called to ther rowme[room] and office'.

In April 1557, in the reign of Philip and Mary, the School was given a Royal Charter and new premises just outside the City walls. The King and Queen

> *do found and establish a Grammar School for the number of fifty boys, if the rents of such school be sufficient for that purpose, to be taught and instructed by a school master and Usher within our House lately called the Hospital of the Blessed Mary without Bothome Bar in the City of Yorke commonly called the Horsefair … We will also and declare that the aforesaid School shall in future depend upon the Cathedral Church.*[3]

Initially the hospital building was ruinous, but for the first time we have the smallest indication of what the School might have looked like. A city map of 1610 marks the 'Free Schole in the Horsefair' and shows a building that seems to have chimneys at either end. Sadly, this is almost certainly only a generic building,

rather than any attempt at a true representation. We do, however, once again have an indication of the activities of the pupils. In the 1560s we learn

> *Against Christopher Dobson and Oswald Atkinson [Charged] that they have plaied at the foote ball within this Cathedrall Church of Yorke. To which they answeringe confessed that the foote ball was broughte into the Churche by Dobson and thereupon Oswald Atkinson did take the ball from him in the churche and there was but one stroke striken at the same in the Churche. Wherefore the Commissioners did order that Oswald Atkinson shal be sett in the Stocks at the churche side upon Sonday nexte at nyne of the clocke before nowne and ther to sitt in the stocke by the space of one whole houre and the houre ende be tayken furthe[r] and laid over the stocke and have six yerts [strikes] with a byrchen rod upon his buttocke and that Chris. Dobson shall have lykewise six yerts upon his buttocke.*

The School remained at the Horsefair for nearly 90 years and James I does not seem to have resented unduly the Gunpowder Plotters' education here: in 1621 he confirmed by Letters Patent the possessions of the hospital to the Dean and Chapter in trust for the School.

The next change of premises was brought about when the Horsefair buildings were destroyed during the Siege of York in the spring and early summer of 1644. (It was at this period that a group of pupils was discovered riding out to see the Battle of Marston Moor, 2 July 1644, a few miles away to the west, and had to be brought home by George Wandesforde, the older brother of one of the party, Christopher Wandesforde.) As a result of the siege, the boys moved back inside the City walls and the School continued in Bedern, in a building that had been built originally as a refectory and dormitory for the Minster clergy. It remained there for the next 86 years, although precisely where in the complex of buildings the School was housed it is impossible to say. Today only the chapel remains.

During the Commonwealth period the School was taken over by the City Council, but its close links with the Minster were renewed at the Restoration. A period of stability occurred with the Headmastership of William Thomlinson, who held that office for more than 30 years from 1679 to his death in 1711. In 1730 the School moved yet again, for a five-year period, to the Bagnio, a former Turkish bath on Coney Street.[4] (After the Bagnio's failure in its original purpose, the School was only one of a variety of enterprises, mainly commercial, to occupy the site.)

Maladministration of the School's endowment had begun in the early seventeenth century and was now a serious problem. Charles I, on a visit to York in 1633, had reprimanded the Dean

12

1833.
St. Peter's School, York.

EVERY BOY who is admitted to the Royal School of St. Peter, at York, is to pay Annually, 10 Guineas for Tuition. On the 1st of May in each Year, there will be an Examination of such Boys as choose to offer themselves, and who are between 13 and 15 years of age; of whom, if sufficiently qualified, a number not exceeding Eight at any one Election, will be admitted on the Foundation for Four Years.

On the 1st of September in each Year, there will be a Second Examination of the *Foundation* Scholars who offer themselves; and to *one or more* of the best qualified Boys, Exhibitions of £50. a Year will be granted, during Three Years, provided he, or they, shall be so long resident Members of the Universities of Oxford or Cambridge.

This Second Examination is open to those Foundation Scholars who are superannuated in the same Year; but in particular Cases an especial permission will be granted to the successful Candidate to remain at the School for another Year.

The unsuccessful Candidates will not be charged for the Tuition of the Quarter in which the Examination takes place.

The Greek and Latin Classics; Writing and Arithmetic; Geography; Mathematics, (that is to say, Euclid, Trigonometry, and Algebra, as far as Quadratic Equations, and problems derived from these,) are taught in the regular course of Education.

Religious Instruction is likewise given daily; and Examination on Religious Subjects, will form a part in both Competitions.

Boarders are received under Regulations made by the Dean and Chapter, at £45. a Year.

The Rev. S. CREYKE, *Head Master.*
The Rev. THOS. RICHARDSON, *Second Master.*
The Rev. RT. DANIEL, *Mathematical Master.*

By Order of the Dean and Chapter.

A Quarter's Notice of the removal of any Boy is required, or the charge for a Quarter's Tuition must be paid.

The Old Residence Occupied in 1828 by Rev Stephen Creyke, Rev Henson.

The Door that leads into Nokes' Dancing Room.

Public House called the Lettice Inn which was since then pulled down.

1828~33
NOKES' DANCING ROOM (19th Century sketch)

An enclosure with the letter goes on:

> *By an inquisition taken at the Castle of York the 25th September 1667 before G. Marwood, J. Hewley Knights, etc. the Free School was found to be endowed as follows:*
> *First with the Rectory of Stillingfleet and its Rights, members and appurtenances then valued by the jury at £100 per annum to be let. Dean Marsh and the Chapter let the lease of Stillingfleet to Mr. Moyser for £70, out of which they kept themselves £50 and gave to Mr. Langley, then Master, £20.*
> *… Item with a Close where the Free School stood before the Civil Wars let now from year to year for £7.10, valued then by the jury at £9 but cannot now be let for more than £7.10 …*

The list went on in this vein and the financial problems continued until 1820.

In 1735 an advertisement appeared in the York Courant Newspaper on June 3: 'This is to give Notice That the Free Grammar School being remov'd from the Bagnio and settled in a large commodious Room in St Andrewgate Church, all Persons may have their Children admitted, and carefully taught Latin, Greek and Hebrew, according to the Westminster, or Lilly's Grammar, at Reasonable rates, by Z Blake.' Zachariah Blake was

and Chapter for the abuse of their position, as the practice of granting long leases of the lands and rights of the School at very low rents to friends and kinsmen of the trustees was already notorious, and must in large part have been responsible for the low fortunes of the School in the 17th and 18th centuries. A letter from Cuthbert Harrison of Acaster Selby to the Archbishop in February 1697 complained:

> *This great Charity hath long been neglected and abused by leasing the land, particularly in Knapton, at a very low rent, viz. £30 per annum, whereas they really to my knowledge are of the annual value of £230 per annum and upwards, and converting the fines to the Trustees own use though it is very apparent from ye donation and letters patent that the same ought to have been let for ye most improved value and the profits thereof converted to the maintenance of as many poor children as possible: but on the contrary a competent maintenance is reserved for the Schoolmaster, and the poor are utterly defeated of the Charity.*

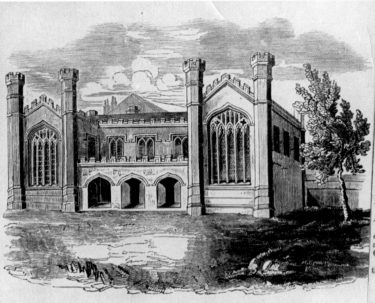

St Peter's 1833–44 now the Minster School.

*York Herald Advertisement
10th August 1844.*

succeeded as Head Master by his son, John, from 1757 to 1784, the only example of a father and son in charge of the School.

The School remained at St Andrew's until 1828, but in a survey of education in 1819 the School had only 20 pupils. The two other grammar schools in the city were doing equally badly: the Haughton School in Pavement also had 20 boys, and Archbishop Holgate's had only four. Some financial reorganization was able to take place in 1820 when a long lease of the tithes of Stillingfleet fell in. These, which had formerly brought in a yearly rent of only £50, were now let at £1,200. These changes were consolidated when, in 1827, Stephen Creyke, a contemporary of the famous Dr Arnold at Rugby, was appointed Head Master at the early age of 31. At this period, the School was still frequently referred to as the Horsefair School, even after the long interval of years and various intervening removals. Annual tuition fees were £10.00 and the ten best scholars annually (after examination) were to be admitted to the Foundation for four years and receive their education free. The salary of the Head Master was set at £200 per year and for the first 100 boys £6 each, so bringing his salary to £500 (£800 if there were 100 boys, and so on, with subsequent possible numbers on a sliding scale of £3 per boy). The Assistant Master received a fixed salary of £100 and further assistants were to teach writing, French, arithmetic, and so on. 'If Drawing, Fencing or Dancing Masters be required they must be paid by the Parents of the Boys.'

As a temporary measure the School moved yet again to an upper room in what had been Mr Nokes's Dancing Academy, adjoining the Old Residence in the Minster Yard,[5] until a brand new building (now the Minster School) was opened in 1833. The York Gazette of 19th July 1828 remarked,

We do not exactly approve of converting the close of a Cathedral into the site of a school. The beautiful painted glass in the windows may be exposed to risk, and the venerable matrons who reside in the confines of the Minster Yard will be in danger of being pushed or upset in their daily passage to and from church in the course of the sport of the schoolboys.

Under Creyke the School prospered and many fine scholars were produced (one FHM Blaydes was later called 'the most eminent Greek scholar of the century'). The number of pupils rose steadily and at Creyke's departure the School was truly flourishing, with two boarding houses, one in the Head Master's own house, the other at 69 Lower Petergate, run by the Reverend James Butler.

Sadly, this upward trend was halted when the cantankerous Reverend William Hewson became Head Master in 1838, beginning an unhappy period of quarrels between the Dean and Chapter and teaching staff, with numbers falling right back. Even Foundation Scholars who had free tuition were removed from the School. The School was about to be plunged into one of its most serious crises, which was ultimately to lead to its relocation on its present site.

1. Whitelock, D., ed., *English Historical Documents* (Eyre and Spottiswode, 1979) Vol.1, c500–1042.

2. Full references for most sources cited are given in Leach, A.F., ed., *Early Yorkshire Schools*, Vol. 1, Yorkshire Archaeological Society, 1899.

3. *Letters Patent of the Dean and Chapter of York*, York Minster Archives, St Peter's School, P2, Box X.

4. The Bagnio was behind no. 12 Coney Street. It was demolished in 1924.

5. It was demolished when Deangate was constructed.

York Proprietary School c1842.

The front of the School today.

The Guy Fawkes Connection

AVRIL PEDLEY

Everyone knows that Guy Fawkes was a pupil at St Peter's, but exactly how we know is a mystery. Nothing remains to us of Guy Fawkes' time at the School, although our modern buildings are on land once owned by him. St Peter's in the late 16th Century was a very different place. 'Ye free schole in ye Horsefair' was in a building at the corner of Gillygate and Lord Mayor's Walk, on land now occupied by part of York St John College. Less than 40 years after the Plot, York became a centre of Royalist activity in the English Civil War. During the Siege of York in 1644 the School buildings were completely destroyed and the boys and their teachers had to find new accommodation within the safety of the walls. We can only assume that either then, or on one of the frequent occasions thereafter when the School moved premises, records were destroyed or abandoned.

There are no School Registers of the period, therefore, but we do know that this was a respected place of education. A letter from the then Archbishop of York to the Chief Judge of the Queen's Exchequer Court,[1] dated 1589, says that 'two hundred scholars or thereabouts' attended the School, and that it was 'the only good schole in this great Cytie'. It was the obvious place for a boy from a solid York family to go. The Head Master was John Pulleyn and although he must have been discreet in order to keep his job in the prevailing Protestant climate under Queen Elizabeth, he was almost certainly a secret Roman Catholic. The previous Head, John Fletcher, had actually been imprisoned for 20 years because of his adherence to the Catholic faith.

Guy was born in 1570 and his ancestors included Lord Mayors and Sheriffs. His father died in 1578 and when his mother, Edith, remarried, it was to Dionis Bainbridge, a Catholic who was connected to the strongly Catholic Pulleyn and Percy families. The seeds of Guy's later career were well and truly sown in his boyhood.

At school Guy would have had another Gunpowder plotter, Christopher Wright, as a contemporary. He and his plotter brother, John, lived at Patrington and presumably were boarders. Their mother was imprisoned for her beliefs and their aunt was possibly Margaret Clitherow, the canonized

Guy Fawkes by Sue Ker (copyright St Peter's School Foundation).

The Gunpowder Plotters.

16

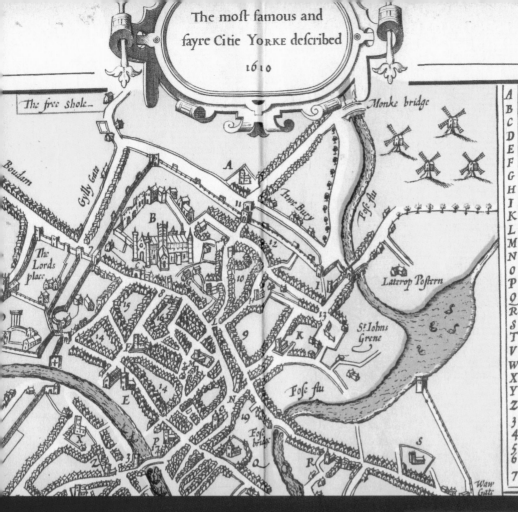

The most famous and fayre Citie YORKE described 1610

A	St. Mauris
B	St. Peters
C	Bellfrey Church
D	S. Maryes Abbey
E	St. Martines
F	St. Helens
G	Trinite Church
H	St. Andrewes
I	St. Cuthberts
K	St. Saviours
L	Chrifts Church
M	St. Sampfons
N	Croufe Church
O	Alhallowes
P	St. Michaels
Q	St. Maryes
R	St Denis
S	St Margarets
T	St. Georges
V	St. Laurence
W	St Nicholas
X	Alhallowes
Y	Trinity Abbey
Z	St Iohns
3	St. Loyes
4	St. Martines
5	St Mary Bifhop E
6	St Mary Bifhop Y
7	Boudam Baxe

Left: Map of York 1610.

Below: Mrs Pankhurst on the Bonfire 1913.

17

York martyr who at one time hid two priests, both Old Peterites, in her house. Oswald Tessimond, known as 'Father Greenway', was also a Peterite. He became a Jesuit and is thought to have been the first priest to learn of the plot. Edward Oldcorne, another priest, was also said by the government to have been involved and was tortured and executed like Guy himself in 1606. A few years before the plot, Robert Middleton, Old Peterite, who was the same age as Guy, converted to Catholicism and became a priest. He did not live to take part in the events of 1605–6, but was executed in Lancaster in 1601. Certainly, the School on the Horsefair at this period nurtured a notable group of dissidents. It also nurtured Bishop Thomas Moreton, who remarked in his autobiography that he was a schoolfellow of the notorious Guy.

The story of the plot itself is very well known and after all the celebrations of 2005 needs no retelling. Antonia Fraser's book *The Gunpowder Plot: terror and faith in 1605* gives a very good account and James Travers's 2005 book, *Gunpowder: the players behind the Plot*, produced by the National Archives to mark the 400th anniversary of the plot, is excellent and beautifully illustrated.

Knowledge and tradition will always link St Peter's and its notorious son. A former Head Boy was once asked for his views on Mr Fawkes and said that while we quite like him, we do not regard him as a role model. The school has a bonfire on 5 November but does not burn a Guy – another established tradition. Is it just that we cannot decently burn an Old Boy?

Patrick Dronfield tells us that his father, when asked the reason, replied magisterially that 'We do not celebrate failures'. The only reliable photograph of a bonfire at the School crowned with a Guy is dated 1913. Further examination showed the figure to be Mrs Pankhurst, who perhaps, in the long run, had more effect on the government of the country than Guy himself.

1. Diocesan Register.

Early Years in Clifton 1844–1914

RICHARD DRYSDALE

In 1842 an inquiry was established by the Dean to examine difficulties in the School. The problems were serious. The roll had declined from 78 to 39. 'There is a want of efficient moral discipline … defective methods of instruction are evident … exercises are not up to the standard of attainment to be expected in the higher class of a good classical school and it would seem that the powers of the pupils are not fully called forth', the inquiry reported. The problems seemed almost insurmountable.

The Revd. Elwyn, Head Master 1864–72.

In January 1843 the following resolution was placed before the Dean and Chapter: 'That the Grammar School of St Peter has declined to such a state of inefficiency as no longer to possess a character of utility answerable to its endowment or justifying the actual expenditure of its funds.' The Chapter wanted the Head Master, Hewson, to resign, yet initially he refused to do this, despite the pressure.

The Minster Archives hold a damning indictment of him in the evidence given in May 1844 to the Chapter by Thomas Richardson, Second Master:

> *During the whole time Mr Creyke was Head Master the school was in a most flourishing condition, having risen from 11 at the time he entered and increased from that to 70 and 80 and being 69 when he left. Since the appointment of the present Head Master the School has very considerably decreased, the number of scholars being only 26 [these were principally in the very top classes, which were not taken by Hewson] and that he seemed not to have such an authority over them as to command respect. A very great change for the worse almost invariably took place on a boy or a class being moved into the upper School, which department as regards classical tuition is solely under the care of the Head Master.*

Ultimately Hewson had no alternative but to resign, and the Dean and Chapter started to address the deep-seated problems. Tuition fees were fixed at £747.[1] Eight scholars were to be selected by competition, two for each year, and were to be taught,

lodged and boarded free for four years. The Head was to be paid £33,600 per year with an additional £224 per entrant once there were more than 50 pupils in the school. The Second Master was to be paid £18,680 per year and receive £149 for every entrant over 50 pupils. The Third Master, who taught Maths and Geography, was paid £11,200 per year. There was even a master appointed to be in charge of writing.

In the summer of 1844 St Peter's amalgamated with the Proprietary School (also known as the Collegiate School), which had been founded in 1838 by local business and professional people. It was the President and Directors of the Collegiate School who chose the Clifton site. They employed an architect called Harper to design and build the central part of the structure at a cost of £195,000. Tuition fees had risen to £723 per year with boarding costing £2,279 per year. The school had only 40 pupils when it opened. Relations between the pupils and the townies were poor and fighting often broke out among them. Smoking was regarded as a serious offence and the breath of likely offenders was regularly checked.

The amalgamation suited both schools. The Proprietary School had plenty of pupils (about 55) but was in financial difficulty, while St Peter's had endowments but few boys (about 18). The Trustees of the Collegiate School were therefore willing to transfer to the Dean and Chapter their premises and land. Numbers quickly increased after the amalgamation and by the summer of 1844 had reached 101 pupils. The School must have been helped by the development of the railway system. York was

Above: Canon Owen,
Head Master 1900–13.

Left: The Royal School of
St Peter's c1900 showing on the
left the stone screen and open
yard before the 1905 extension.

linked to Newcastle in 1841, to Scarborough in 1845 and by 1848 the journey to London, which took 14 hours in 1840, had been reduced to as little as 6 hours.

William Hey, the Head Master from 1844 to 1864, had been a Scholar and Fellow of King's College, Cambridge. As an academic he left a strong imprint on learning in the school. He is described as humble, unpretentious, sincere, affectionate, with a happy, sunny disposition that won the hearts of the boys. The quality of the staff at this time was remarked by one observer, who said 'There have been so many assistant masters who, beyond being revered for their learning and skill in teaching have won a permanent place in the hearts of their pupils and thus have influenced their characters for life. I do not think for its size any school in England has been so fortunate as St Peter's in this respect.'

By 1856 there were 138 pupils, nine teaching staff and five ancillary staff who taught drawing, dancing, fencing, gym and, lastly, drill. The three boarding houses, set up in 1853 and 1857, were each run by a member of the academic staff. The third boarding house for the juniors was at Clifton Green. The punishments included £3 for going to the tuck shop after hours and £1.50 for standing at or outside the school gates. No boy was allowed to have in his possession gunpowder or firearms.

The famous 'Tommy Card' dates from this era. The Reverend Thomas Richardson, who served the school for 43 years, had a card five inches by three inches. On one side was a myriad of scriptural facts, while on the other, facts about Greek and Roman history prevailed. The pupils had to learn the information on the card by rote. So thoroughly were all the facts learnt that many OPs could recite them decades later.

The Civil and Military Department was set up in 1856 to prepare pupils for a career in either the army or the civil service. The curriculum consisted of Engineering, Arithmetic, Theoretical and Practical Maths (Surveying, Fortification and Navigation), History, Geography, Latin, Modern Languages, Chemistry and Natural Philosophy. By 1865 there were 44 pupils in the Department (or about 25 per cent of the school), but only ten of them were prepared for the exam. The remainder were there because their parents preferred what seemed to be a more modern method of instruction. There were, however, problems. The pupils were taught by one master and, as there was a considerable age range, it was inevitable that their levels of attainment differed widely. There was, too, a sense that the Department was separate from the general organization of the School and it was closed in 1889.

The School's academic success was exemplified by the 108 honours gained at universities between 1845 and 1865, seven of which were wranglerships and fellowships. In 1890 *Pall Mall Gazette* recorded that St Peter's came ninth out of 89 schools for Open Awards at Oxford and Cambridge, while in 1891 it came 13th out of 95.

Worship used to be held at St Olave's Church until the Chapel was built between 1861 and 1862. The intention was that the Chapel could also be used for the wider community and so pews were let out at a small annual rent. Chapel was to be central to the

Outdoor lesson c1905.

life of the School in the decades that followed. As one commentator wrote, 'The part that the Chapel has played in the life of the School cannot be measured for its influence and is among the deep things out of sight'. Succeeding generations of Peterites, whether of religious inclination or not, have appreciated the spiritual atmosphere of the building.

Games during this time centred on football and cricket. The rules of football were printed by the school in 1856 and revised again in 1873. It was legitimate to trip players up, but 'attempts to throttle them or strangle them were not allowed'. It was also not permissible to pick up the ball 'after the first bound for any purpose whatever'. Cricket was popular and played on the present 1st XI pitch, which was properly levelled in 1873. The School played Pocklington in 1853 for the first time, Leeds Grammar School for the first time in 1856 and the OPs in 1861, even though there was no formal organization of an OP club until 1886. Rowing started in the 1850s, but there is no record of any racing until 1859.

20

Enlarging the cricket pitch 1905.

Hey resigned in 1864. To many he is regarded as the father and founder of the School as we know it today. He was succeeded by Canon Elwyn, who was a Fellow of Trinity College, Cambridge and a deeply religious man. He was highly regarded by the pupils because of his personal touch. Pupils felt he had a genuine concern for their well-being, and on his retirement in 1872 he personally shook hands with each pupil as he made his way through the School.

The numbers in 1866 were 196, of which 91 were day boarders and 105 were boarders. The School was highly regarded and, according to one source, 'destined to become the model High School of the County'. It was also highly regarded in York itself, yet by 1872 the numbers had declined to 176.

The Reverend Stephenson became Head Master in 1872. He was educated at Christ's College, Cambridge, where he had been a Scholar and a Fellow. The picture of him in the Stephenson Room with his stern, severe gaze seems indicative of the man. He did not suffer fools gladly and was not generally popular. He was, however, a hard worker and a quiet, unselfish person who was kind underneath his stern exterior. There is no doubt that he was a disciplinarian. In 1879 a visiting examiner reported that St Peter's would 'rank high among the schools of the kingdom in Maths'. The demand for a classical education, on the other hand, was beginning to falter as numbers declined.

One of Stephenson's major changes was to the format of the school year, which went from a four- to a three-term year. Summer holidays now started at the end of July rather than from mid-June. The Old Peterite Club, the Debating Society and *The Peterite* all emerged during these years.

Between 1880 and 1900 it was clear that there was a lack of capital to finance expansion. The School had never had large endowments upon which to draw. This was a problem that was to prove to be a continual thread in the School's history, which we can trace in the boom-and-bust cycle in the School's finances.

The Reverend Handford took over from Stephenson in 1887 and held the position for 13 years. Handford had also been a Scholar at Christ's, where he had gained a First Class degree in Classics. The numbers in the School by this time never went beyond 130, and although the atmosphere was friendly, Angelo Raine's comment that St Peter's was essentially marking time during these years, is an accurate one.[2]

Raine's view was that the school was in an unhealthy condition and in need of invigoration at the end of a chapter in its life. The School's debts were increasing. The chemistry lab was a small, poorly equipped wooden shed. There was no physics lab or any workshops. The one major building project during these years was the building of the gym funded by an anonymous OP, soon discovered to be the Reverend Herbert Bloomfield. Classes in the

The Revd. Walker, teacher of drawing, carpentry and English in costume for the York Pageant 1909.

gym, started in 1895 and in 1897 the OP club gave £4,160 for panelling, on which the names of School teams in cricket, rugby and boats were to be listed.

In the late 1880s the Dean and Chapter realized that the School had to modernize, but were uncertain where to acquire the money for such a plan. The Charity Commissioners were approached and they told the Dean that as the School was a royal foundation they could assume control to develop it. This, however, meant that the Dean and Chapter would have to relinquish control, something they would not accept. They therefore started to look for proof that the School was indeed a cathedral foundation, in which case the Ecclesiastical Commissioners would have to find funds for the School's

21

development. When proof was found the Ecclesiastical Commissioners rejected it, but finally, at the end of a heated debate, they gave £22,500 as a token gesture. In return, the Dean and Chapter had to allow representatives of the County on to the Board of Governors. The influence of the Church on the new governing body, which took charge in January 1898, was thus reduced.

When Handford left in the summer of 1900 there were only 65 pupils on the roll and the school had debts of over £360,000. Fee income in 1900–1901, together with money from the endowment, came to £176,400. The curriculum had been firmly biased towards a classical education, but the numbers were too few to make much of an impact, either in the academic or sporting world. Without a marked change in leadership and funding, the school would struggle to survive. Modernize or die would have been an appropriate way of looking at the situation. Raine goes so far as to say, 'St Peter's had literally been dying from ancient methods'.

When the Reverend Owen took over in 1900, the School entered the first phase of its modern development. There was need for new premises for boarding, science and art, and more space was needed for playing fields. In 1901 St Olave's was acquired and moved from its location in Bootham to Clifton Garth in 1910. An appeal for a science block for £234,000 was launched in 1902 and the building was opened in June, 1903, by Professor Clifford Allbutt, FRS and Regius Professor of Physic at Cambridge. The bias towards classics and maths was now beginning to tilt in favour of the sciences.

School House washrooms c1910.

The first Government Inspection of the School took place in 1903. This was not an inspection of teaching and learning but rather of the organisation of the establishment. It drew attention to the inadequate boarding accommodation, and the ensuing bad publicity lost the School many prospective boarders. The School did, however, secure some government funds through the direct grant scheme recently established, whereby it was obliged to recruit 10 per cent of its entrants from the Local Education Authorities in return for a government grant of £13,700. Of the total fee income of £202,000, however, this was hardly a significant amount.

Despite these difficult times, the School orchestra was formed in 1901 and a miniature rifle range was opened in 1903. The organ was purchased in 1907 for £32,000. Games, however, suffered between 1900 and 1913 because of the low numbers.

Natural History Society excursion 1910.

Owen's tenure ended when he was appointed to the Headship of King William's, Isle of Man, and he did not try to hide the fact that St Peter's had been going through difficult times. There were only 84 pupils in the School in 1910–11 and the financial future looked insecure. Toyne's arrival as Head Master was to change this situation as numbers quickly increased by 28 pupils in his first year.

1. *All monetary values in the chapter are of 2005.*
2. *A. Raine, The History of St Peter's (Bell, 1926).*

Left: George F. Tendall (music teacher and Housemaster of The Grove) with the starter's pistol, Sports Day c 1912.

23

The Day Boys in 1911 with George Yeld (centre) the longest-serving Master who served the School for 52 years from 1868 to 1919.

Charles Wright's Letters Home 1854–58

RICHARD DRYSDALE

Charles Wright was the fourth of 13 children of a Wakefield GP, five of whom died in childhood. Charles came to St Peter's at the age of 12 and left at 16. He was to go on to a distinguished career as Professor of Midwifery in Leeds and Lecturer in Obstetrics in the Leeds School of Medicine. The correspondence is not complete. There are no letters in the archive for 1857. Nonetheless, these writings give a unique insight into the School at the time from a pupil's perspective. What is recorded is a tantalizingly narrow glimpse of school life but an invaluable one nevertheless. Charles' punctuation is somewhat erratic.

From a homesick child in his early days there is a change of tone as he enters adolescence and becomes more confident and mature in his views and perceptions. Much that he writes about is very similar to what a boarder might communicate today: progress in work, food, family members, his contemporaries and outings from School. The language and tone are, of course, different. The open affection and terms of endearment suggest that the Victorians were not quite as repressed emotionally as they are portrayed. There is real and genuine affection and respect expressed for his parents. The letters are addressed to 'My very dear papa,' or even, 'My very, very, dear papa' and signed 'Your most fond and affectionate Charlie', or even 'Your ever very affectionate son, CJ Wright'.

The wretchedness of homesickness is the main topic of his letter of 17 April 1855, the second day of term. Anyone who has suffered from homesickness will readily identify with his feelings.

Here I am again at school, I am very unhappy and desolate, I could scarcely get to sleep last night and I awoke when it was just light this morning and was crying till I got up which was about half past six and then I could scarcely do any lessons in school and I could scarcely eat any dinner or breakfast and have been shedding tears most of the afternoon I am so unhappy I do not know how it is but I cannot help crying; it seems a week or more since I last saw you last although it was only last night.

His father obviously wrote back by return, only to receive another letter from Charles dated 21 April in the same tone of wretchedness.

…as I have no news except unhappiness as an unhappy schoolboy never has…I could tell you a great many more sorrows but they would take such a time writing…

On the academic side, it might surprise the present generation of Peterites to know that there were many more orders than today. There were daily, weekly, monthly and termly orders. Each pupil was given a position in each of the orders. This gives a new meaning to the term 'continual assessment'. In his letter of 5 May he writes with an air of pride,

I was first for the week last week and I have never been higher than sixth before. I don't know what I am for this week. My ranks during the week, for the day have been Monday fourth, Tuesday first, Wednesday first, Thursday fifth, Friday first and Saturday first.

His concern for his class position is a regular theme of his letters and occasionally, when he has done especially well, he writes a short note to tell his father. He confessed to finding Caesar rather difficult and complained 'I have no Papa to help like some of the day boys have'. There is some indication of the textbooks he used. He asked for his prayer book to be sent, 'because I want one for school'. He asks his father if he can buy Kennedy's Latin Grammar and Scott's Geography of Palestine, Cornwell's Geography and Caesar as well as Markham's History of England. One must presume his father acquiesced. Occasionally, there are requests about news from the Crimean War or later the Indian Mutiny. Food was, as always, a major consideration for a boarder. In one letter Charles reports that he bought 'a pennyworth of shrimps of a man at the door yesterday but they were not very good'. In his letter of 17 August 1855, the second day of the new academic year he writes,

I have finished all my pasties, nuts and gingerbread, I have still a pot of preserves and the cake left which I shall cut into tomorrow; I had a herring yesterday it is about the best pennyworth.

Food parcels were a useful way of supplementing the school diet. On 3 September 1855 he received a parcel that delighted him and impressed his fellow pupils. 'All the boys say it is a regular stunner, but I say a great deal more … I like the grub very much and the boys approve of it equally … I have just had a bit of the strawberry preserve to my bread and butter and it is jolly.' He ends by asking his father to excuse his writing because the letter had been written with a quill pen. In a letter written on 7 February he records that they had pancakes to dinner but 'they weren't jolly.'

The tone of his letters has understandably changed by the age of 16. The letter written on 7 February gives us a flavour of this different tone. Like many a pupil over time he is struggling to find something to tell his parents.

> I might as well give you a scribble although I don't know of what it will be concocted In primus dear Guv' let me wish you very many happy returns of the day … I have looked anxiously for several mornings past for a letter …

The letter of 1 April 1858 suggests a slightly rebellious streak is emerging, although the tone is not necessarily disrespectful. The address is headed: 'St Peter's Hole, Eboracium' [sic] and starts confidently

> Well, dear guv'ner, here I is at school again … O my eyes, I don't think this is worth reading and I can say no more … Your most jolly progeny, Jemm.

There was then the issue of money. What follows is a letter that practically every parent will have received at one time or another. The letter is not dated but was probably written at some point in 1856 and is the last letter in the archive to his father.

> My very dear Father,
> I scarcely dare ask you what I am about to, as I am afraid it will displease you, but my funds have got so low lately, and I am getting so out of pocket that I shall be obliged to make a petition for some more tip [cash] as I want to go out for the day on the holiday next week as most of the coves are going to do. Don't think I have spent rashly what you gave me, dear Papa.

Charles then lists all his expenses and ends by saying that of the 12/6d he was given he only has 1/- left. As in all letters of this nature there then follows some pleading.

> And as this is the last opportunity of sending me anything to school I don't think you will refuse to send me a post-office order for something, dear papa, but don't if you think I shall misuse it which of course you don't … hoping you will not be vexed but will comply with my request. Believe me dear Guv'ner
> Your affectionate son
> Carolus.

His last letter in the archive, dated 8 May 1858, is to his sister. In it he speaks of writing 'a stodging long letter the other day' to one of his other sisters. He goes on to describe a presentation to his housemaster of 'two spoons (table or dessert or something of the sort) however they were beautiful silver ones lined with gold and beautifully marked and raised … You don't know how proud he is of them. He has shown them to no end of people; and he thinks the more of it because it is the first thing of the kind done to any of the masters by the fellows …' This is the first recorded presentation of a gift to a housemaster.

The First World War, the 1920s and the Depression: the Toyne era 1913–36

RICHARD DRYSDALE

Few Head Masters have been at the helm during such immense trauma as that of the First World War, and later the Depression. The far-reaching economic, political and social consequences of some of the most difficult years of the twentieth century defined 'Sam' Toyne's headship.

Sam Toyne Head Master 1913–36.

Toyne must be regarded as one of the School's great Head Masters. He was the first layman to be appointed since John Pulleyn at the time of Guy Fawkes. Toyne was educated at Haileybury and took a Classical Exhibition at Hertford College, Oxford. In his book, *The History of St Peter's School*, Wiseman describes him as a scholar/athlete. On the scholarly side, he was made a Fellow of the Royal Historical Society in 1919. In sports he played county cricket for Hampshire, captained Hertfordshire at Hockey and went with the English Squash team to the USA. He played a central role in the everyday life of the School well beyond the confines of headmastering and was active in coaching teams, helping and acting in plays and in teaching. He even played on the wing for the 1st XV against Club opponents. In short, if there was anyone capable of leading the School through the storms of the period 1913–36 it was Sam Toyne.

The School's financial situation was not strong when he took over. There were about 80 pupils in the School and its indebtedness was higher than it should have been. Not for the first, nor the last time in its history, the School was at a turning point, with closure a real possibility. Fortunately Toyne was the man to resolve the very real difficulties and set the School on an upward trend. Yet, still to come were the difficult days of the First World War and the dark days of the Depression, which were to plunge the School into yet another financial crisis and near bankruptcy.

Army cadets on parade c1914 outside the Big Hall before it was extended after the Second World War.

THE FIRST WORLD WAR (1914–18)

The growing tensions in Europe before the outbreak of the First World War meant that few were surprised when war was declared in August 1914. Some 540 OPs served with the Armed Forces in the First World War and of those 75 were killed. This represents 14 per cent mortality, as against 13 per cent of those who enlisted nationally. There is no reference to those who were wounded in mind or body, but one may assume a figure of around 30 per cent, in correspondence with the national figure. In total about 44 per cent of OPs who enlisted were killed or injured. This represents 188 casualties. The 1st XV of 1913 ultimately lost five members of the original team on the battlefield. The impact of the war on the School is difficult to overstate.

1st XV 1913, five of whom were killed in the First World War.

The idea of an OTC (Officers' Training Corps) at the School had been suggested in December 1913. The only military possession the School had before that was a miniature rifle range. The Government required a guarantee of £9,600[1] in funds, at least 80 boys over the age of 15 and two officers if they were to agree to the establishment of an OTC at the School. These conditions were quickly met. Toyne took command of the contingent. Initially, the OTC was attached to the 11th battalion of the Yorkshire and Lancashire regiment. By July 1914 there were 87 members. The deteriorating situation in Europe, together with a strident patriotism, aided recruitment. In addition, it was not possible to take a commission or to enter the Officer Cadet Battalions direct from School without membership

of the OTC, so it came to play a central part in the life of the School. Two parades were held each week. Summer camps and field days at places like Stillington and Ampleforth became integral to the OTC, where consciousness of matters military was supreme. The ten-and-a-half miles' march to Stillington was long remembered.

The national state of tension and suspicion was such that invasion was expected and a hysteria about spies prevailed. It was at Stillington that a poor, unfortunate local was arrested when he refused to answer the summons of a sentry, only to be released after an apology was given. One of the OTC's tasks was to help defend the coast in the event of an invasion. The editorial of

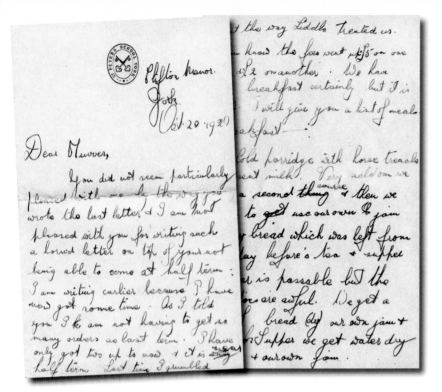

A letter from Alfred Milne (The Manor, 1920–22).

The Peterite in 1915 reported, 'Here in the upper part of the School there are people who can talk of little else but trenches, pickets and night attacks. They are waiting for the time when they can take over commissions.' There was a feeling that those who were going off to war were the lucky ones, and indeed, they were envied.

News that CSM French, who had helped to set up the OTC, had distinguished himself by killing 'yards of Germans' was greeted with approval. 'May he continue in the same pursuit and with the same luck as he has at present', commented *The Peterite*. In June 1915, a lecture on the progress of the war entitled *The Road to Calais* was well received by pupils, who went away with 'a strong idea of the huge numbers of German losses'. The militarization of School and society was inevitable. At this point the full horrors of the Western Front were not yet suspected.

The School was also urged to raise funds for the Public Schools' Hospital, run for the wounded by the Red Cross at Boulogne. By the end of the war over £1,432 had been raised. The School also participated in the War Savings Association, and by February 1918 its 133 members had raised over £49,641 for the war effort.

By early 1915, the gym, a form room and the fives courts had been occupied by the Army Pay Corps, while the 6th West Yorkshire regiment occupied the shooting range and some of the playing fields. The OTC had a field day with the York Citizen Defence Force and the whole School participated in Military Sunday for the first time. This involved the OTC, which marched to the Minster as part of the armed services led by the School band. By this stage the OTC included bayonet fighting as part of its training. The links between the OTC and the York Defence Company led to certain members of the OTC being detached as cyclists for special duty. *The Peterite* reported that details of these could not be published as they were secret, a fact which must have given the participants a sense of self-importance and pride at being part of the war effort

By July 1916, the jingoism of 1914 had been replaced by a more sombre national mood. The war, far from being over by Christmas 1914, showed no sign of coming to an end and casualty figures were mounting horrendously. Little wonder that the crowd of sightseers for Military Sunday in July 1916 was largely silent. One woman in the crowd was heard to exclaim, 'They are going to the front and they are only boy scouts'. However, the importance of the OTC was underlined when it had to provide the guard of honour for the Australian Premier when he visited York in 1916, and for the visit of the Prime Minister of New Zealand some time later. The band played at the Memorial Service in the Minster for Lord Kitchener after his death in 1916.

The first obituaries of OP casualties appeared in *The Peterite* of June 1915. The edition of October 1915 reprinted a piece entitled *Love of Country* from the St Peter's *Journal* (the predecessor of *The Peterite*), in which it said 'The dying soldier when he reflects that it is for his country that he bleeds, gladly resigns himself to his fate and feels an inward satisfaction when he reviews his conduct'. Thus were the horrors of the carnage on the Western Front glossed over. It was only nine months later when the British army suffered its heaviest loss of casualties in one day: over 20,000 soldiers were killed on the first day of the Somme offensive of July 1916 and a further 40,000 were injured. It is hard to imagine that the words of *Love of Country* would have reflected the views of those troops or their families, despite the different mores of the times, although it was not until later in the war that the British were fully aware of the appalling casualties their own troops were suffering.

The Manor c1919.

28

The sense of God on our side was nontheless evident, whether in church sermons or speeches at Commemoration. There is no doubt that Prussian militarism was seen as the villain of the piece. At Commemoration in July 1917, the Dean of York attributed Great Britain's supremacy to the national conviction that our system of administration, government, education and culture was not only the best for us, but for the rest of the world too.

By 1916 the War Office gave the OTC the opportunity of training Army Recruits Class B before their groups were called up. In this, the OTC was helped by the Voluntary Training Corps; soon there was a company of 160. These were the so-called Derby recruits, who volunteered before conscription had to be introduced in January 1916. What is significant is that 361 OPs, out of the total of 540 who eventually fought in the conflict, had joined up before conscription was introduced. It was a reflection of the mood of the School that more than 78 per cent of OPs joined up voluntarily.

The Pavilion, built in 1914.

The Rise c1920.

In July 1916 *The Peterite* editorial echoed the national mood of growing war weariness. 'The war has hit the School hard so far as outward and visible signs can show, for the average age has considerably lessened …' Games teams were affected. Pupils had to replace staff who had gone off to the war. Bell-ringing, sweeping, scrubbing, the distribution of pens and paper were all now done by pupils. A punishment of the time was removing weeds from the grounds.

The war was, of course, affecting education generally. In his Speech Day address of 1916 Toyne stated, 'Dangers assailed education on all sides, for no sooner had the seriousness of war begun to force itself upon the most placid of our educationalists than the floodgates of crankdom were thrown wide open … The war is bringing home to boys, parents and schoolmasters the demands which the citizenship in the British Empire must make …' Nonetheless, Toyne argued that to leave School too soon was an unpatriotic act, as it could rob the nation of useful officer material.

The July 1917 edition of *The Peterite* devoted 12 out of its 59 pages to listing serving OPs: the wounded, appointments, promotions, decorations and killed. No one could now doubt the terrible toll the war was taking on a whole generation of young men. By the end of the year proposals for a war memorial were put forward. There were to be three parts to it: the decoration of the chapel and an oak sanctuary, with the names of those who had fallen in battle; the oak panelling and seating for the Big Hall with a scroll bearing the names of all who had served, to create a hall worthy of the School and capable of accommodating increasing numbers; thirdly, the foundation of a scholarship for sons of OPs, with a preference for the sons of the fallen. The target was to raise £149,300. The War Memorial was finally completed by Commemoration of July 1921, with some minor modifications.

York was not immune to Zeppelin Raids. Each night the School had a look-out in the tower to send pupils to the cellars in the event of an air raid. York was raided twice, in May and November of 1916, and on one of these occasions searchlights picked up a Zeppelin to the north of the School. Guns opened up on the target and fired across the School. The excitement tempted the boys who had gone down to the cellars to look out. The Zeppelin was hit to the great cheering of the pupils and citizens who had left their shelters. It was later to crash on the Norfolk coast. One pupil was hit by a piece of shrapnel. So ended one of the most exciting nights the School had experienced.

When the war was over the School was finally able to count its war dead and mourn the appalling loss of life. The tally of war decorations is clear evidence that OPs acquitted themselves with courage and bravery. Between them they were awarded one KCB, two CBs, two CMGs, nine DSOs, twenty-six MCs, one CBE and

29

GAMES COMMITTEE.

At a Games Committee meeting held on December 2nd, certain proposals concerning a rearrangement of the colours were submitted for discussion and the following resolutions were finally passed :—

I. (a) CAPS. (i). *The School Cap* shall be plain Chocolate with White Cross Keys.

(ii). *School Colours (i.e.* 1st XV., 1st XI., 1st IV., Hockey XI. and Boxing, Squash and Gym. representatives of the School against outsiders) and *Monitors* shall wear a plain Chocolate cap, with White Cross Keys and a Crown.

(iii). All other distinctive Walking out caps are abolished.

(iv). The following other caps may be worn :—
1st XV. Tassel Cap.
1st XI. Fielding Cap.
1st XI. Hockey Tassel Cap.
1st IV. Cap.
2nd IV. (White with Chocolate Cross Oars, no letters).

(b) STRAW HAT BANDS :—
(i). The School Hat band shall be Chocolate with White Cross Keys.
(ii). Monitors and School Colours wear a blue-white-blue band.
(iii). All other hat bands abolished.

II. BLAZERS. (i). *The School Blazer* shall be plain Chocolate with White Cross Keys.
(ii). *The 1st XV.* Plain Chocolate, White braid on pocket Cross Keys, Crown and Dates.
(iii). *The 1st XI.* Blue and White Stripes.
(iv). *The 1st IV.* White, Chocolate braid, on pocket Cross Oars and lettering.
(v). *Hockey XI.* Blue, White braid, White Cross Keys (N.B. The Colour as now worn is too light).
(vi). *2nd XI., 2nd XV., 2nd IV., Boxing, Squash, etc.,* Plain blue blazer, White Cross Keys.

III. MUFFLERS AND SCARVES :—
(i). 1st XV. } a plain Chocolate Muffler.
1st IV. }
(ii). 1st XI. A blue and White Scarf.
(iii). Hockey XI. }
2nd XV. }
2nd XI. } A plain blue Muffler.
2nd IV. }
Boxing, etc., }

IV. TIES. (i). *School Tie.* Plain Chocolate or black.
(ii). *1st XV.* Chocolate and White.
(iii). *1st XI.* Blue and White.
(iv). *Joint 1st IV. and Hockey XI.* Design not submitted.

V. HOUSE COLOURS (Knitted Ties) :—
(i). *School House.*—Blue and Black.
Clifton Grove.—Red and White.
Clifton Rise.—Black and White.
Clifton Manor.—Black and Yellow.
Day boys.—Black and Green.
(ii). Boating Mufflers in House Colours are forbidden.
(iii). Stripes down the sides of boating bags are forbidden.
(iv). House Boating Vests may be worn by those IV.'s during races and by House Boating Colours at other times.

VI. SWEATER BANDS :—
1st XV. } Plain Chocolate Band.
1st IV. }
1st XI. } Plain Blue Band.
Hockey XI. }

three MBEs. In addition, 31 were mentioned in dispatches. One OP was nominated for a posthumous VC. Some 14 per cent of OPs who served were thus recognized through decorations or mentions for their bravery or service to the war effort. *The Peterite* of December 1918 included stirring tales of how some of these decorations came to be awarded.

The sense of national relief at the end of the conflict was immense, with rejoicing and thanksgiving throughout the land. The end of the War was commemorated in the Chapel service of November 1918, in a long and moving address by Toyne. 'Let us

discipline ourselves to God's ways … let us as Peterites never betray the trust of those beloved and honoured sons of the School who have laid down their lives in this mighty conflict.' He ended by reciting Rupert Brooke's poem *The Dead*, followed by a reading out of the names of those who had died. It was one of the most moving services held in the Chapel. The names of the fallen were also read out at the Commemoration service of July 1919.

A letter from the War Office in March 1919 thanked the OTC for all the work it had carried out during the war. Re-adjustment to peacetime and reconstruction were not going to be easy. Toyne asked rhetorically, 'Have boys ever lived through such stirring times?'

The War Memorial cost £81,000. Some £7,300 was allocated to the scholarship fund, £58,400 to the Hall and £13,800 to the Chapel. The words on the memorial, in Greek, state:

> *If to die nobly is life's greatest test,*
> *To us of all her boons fate gave her best.*
> *Eager to crown her land with liberty,*
> *We died and won a praise which cannot die.*

THE 1920S

Toyne's reputation as Head Master was formidable. This was shown in the report of the Board of Inspectors of Christmas, 1925. 'The progress of the School is reflected in the energy and capacity of the Head and had it not been for the confidence inspired by his personality the developments which have taken place under circumstances of considerable difficulty would not have been possible.' Toyne continued to be active in a whole range of sporting and cultural activities, both inside the School and outside it. He coached cricket and hockey to School teams and played rugby against the 2nd XV when he was 48. In the summer of 1923 he scored more than a thousand runs for York Cricket Club. He also captained the Yorkshire Squash Racquets Club in the same year. In April 1923 he took a School party to Norway. His energy was prodigious. Toyne and his family were well integrated into both the life of the School and the life of the city, and there is little doubt that he was a respected and popular Head Master in both contexts.

Consideration was given to a plan in 1923 to move the School to Kirby Hall, an eighteenth-century country house near Boroughbridge. The City Council heard of the plan and a deputation went to see Toyne. The plan was ultimately rejected, both for financial reasons and in principle; St Peter's had always been an integral part of the life of York. To have moved would have cut this important link, even if the temptation to move was strong. It would have given the School more space in which to expand and would have ended the practice of having to adapt

G.E. Cutforth in uniform c1927.

The opening of the Library block 1929.

private homes for the use of boarding houses. Space was temporarily increased by the purchase of huts bought from the army. One hut was converted for use as a common room to be used by Grove, while the other provided two form rooms and an art room.

Toyne's Headship was thus marked by an expansion in numbers and the acquisition of properties, which enabled the School to break out from its cramped confines. In 1914 the shooting range and the pavilion were built and Clifton Grove was opened as a boarding house. Clifton Rise and Clifton Manor were acquired as additional boarding houses 1918–19. The outdoor swimming pool opened in 1922 and cost £50,900. It was in use for 43 years before being roofed and heated. In 1925 the School acquired the 11 acres that were to make up the riverside pitches. Up to this point the School had had only one rugby pitch in Water Lane. A permanent boat-house replaced the temporary one in 1927. Two second-hand clinker fours were bought from Oxford University and the slipway was enlarged.

Nonetheless, financial difficulties were never far beneath the surface. By 1922 the Board of Education had become concerned by the School's high level of debt and had ordered the Board of Governors to repay the Midland Bank £224,000 per year, to reduce the unsecured debt of £2.6m with the aim of eliminating it in 12 years. The School also had £2.5m of secured debts, of which two thirds were to the Midland Bank and one third to a York Friendly Society. The Governors were ordered to repay £60,200 per year to reduce the debt to the Midland Bank and £39,270 to the Friendly Society. The School's overdraft had increased between 1924 and 1925. The Board of Education was rightly concerned. The Governors realized they needed to increase income from £748,000 to £890,00 p.a. The fact that the School roll fell from 315 to 271, and that salaries had increased, made the task of achieving financial security more difficult.

Economy measures were, therefore, introduced to deal with the situation. Expenditure was to be reduced by the equivalent of one master's salary, the Finance Committee was set up to monitor the situation and fees were increased. If these difficulties seemed severe, worse was to follow in the mid-1930s.

To celebrate the 1,300th anniversary of the School a new building, designed by F.T. Penty in 1926, was to house the library, music and art rooms, common rooms and a sixth-form room on the upper floor. It was estimated that it would cost £5,000 but eventually cost less. The plans had to be revised slightly when someone noticed there was no door to exit the rooms on the second floor. This was rectified and the building was opened in July 1929. Later the new block with twin towers, that today contains Queen's and the subject areas of religious studies, geography, history and classics, was added.

There was academic progress too. The sixth form had expanded from four pupils to twenty over a ten-year period. Advanced courses, the forerunner of A levels, were offered in four groups: classics, history, maths and sciences. The first of the triennial Science Exhibitions was held in 1924 and these were soon to become events of national standing. One of the novelties at the Exhibition was a wireless demonstration.

The long-running argument about which school was the oldest in England was settled by a rugby match in 1927 with King's School, Canterbury. In a gripping, hard-fought match watched by pupils from King's in their boaters and with snow falling, St Peter's won narrowly by 13–9. The matter had thus been settled beyond all doubt.

The new classroom block 1935.

THE DEPRESSION 1929–36

The 1920s was a period of major readjustment to a peace-time economy and as the decade progressed prosperity generally increased. The Wall Street Crash of October 1929, however, was a symptom of the Depression that was to grip the world economy until the Second World War broke out in September 1939. It is not surprising, therefore, that the fortunes of the School during these years mirrored broader national and international economic trends. The advent of the Depression led to difficult times for the School, but this was true everywhere and there is no indication that St Peter's fared any worse than schools elsewhere.

In 1927 there were 249 pupils, comprising 125 boarders and 62 day-boarders in the senior School and 22 boarders and 40 day-boarders in St Olave's, thus 147 boarders and 102 day-boarders overall. By 1934 the overall figure was 215 pupils, a drop of almost 14 per cent. Boarding, however, was especially hard hit. In the senior School the boarding numbers were down by almost 38 per cent, while in St Olave's they had fallen by 50 per cent. Day-boarders in the senior School had dropped only slightly by just under 10 per cent, while in St Olave's they had actually increased by 24 per cent. Between 1932 and 1939 the roll remained below 1927 figures. It is scarcely surprising, therefore, that The Manor was closed as a boarding house in 1932 (re-opened 1942) and the Grove in 1935 (re-opened 1948).

The School community was made well aware of the economic difficulties of the time. Unemployment was 21.9 per cent of the workforce in 1932 and, although this declined, it was still 13 per cent in 1936. The staff had no alternative but to take a 10 per cent pay cut. The awareness of the problems and suffering in the wider world were forcefully brought home one Sunday evening in 1936, just before the chapel service, when the Jarrow marchers came down Burtonstone Lane and into Bootham, en route to London in their campaign for employment.

In the March 1934 issue of *The Peterite*, Colonel Scott, the Secretary of the OP Club, wrote that the Depression had seriously affected the School. Some boys had had to leave early, the loans for the science block had not been fully repaid and money for scholarships had run out. He proposed an endowment appeal to help the scholarship fund, but also to avoid the sale of any School land. It was decided to complete the set of buildings to finish the library block. The cost was to be about £520,000 and although the appeal was £123,000 short in July 1935, the building was officially opened by Lord Halifax, Secretary of State for War and later Foreign Secretary under Baldwin. Archbishop Temple, the Archbishop of York, and Lord Halifax had managed to get royal patronage for the scheme and a telegram arrived from the Duke of York congratulating all concerned with the project.

The School's academic and sporting successes during these years were reflected in the large number of scholarships and exhibitions to Oxford and Cambridge. Several OPs were awarded Blues. Toyne firmly believed that a smaller public school allowed more frequent and closer contact between staff and pupils, which was integral to the successful running and ethos of the School. Discipline was strict yet there was a friendly informality. Punishments, when they had to be meted out, were quickly forgotten in the knowledge that bygones were bygones.

Toyne decided to retire, unexpectedly, in 1936 at the age of 55, on health grounds. He had been Head Master since 1913 (a total of 23 years) and seen the School through difficult times. His announcement took everyone by surprise but, as he commented, Heads tend to stay on too long. His tenure of 23 years had been one of distinction, love and respect. *The Peterite* of April 1936 applauded Toyne's vigour and foresight during a period of rapid growth and referred to a time of remarkable achievement in the history of the School. 'There cannot be a school anywhere in the country where the family spirit is developed to a higher degree. No interest of the School has been too insignificant of his support and encouragement. Here was a Headmaster, who taught to a high level, played and coached games, who acted and produced plays and whose directing hand helped in every School activity.' The Valete went on to refer to the Saturday evening activities organized and shared by Toyne, whether in the gym, the hall or outings for picnics and skating.

Toyne himself found it a wrench to leave, and after one presentation hurriedly left the room, filled with emotion. It was immediately clear how popular he and his wife had been in the School community. Mrs Toyne had played an active role as Head Master's wife, whether in drama productions or evening entertainments in the drawing room. Her kindness and interest in everyone made her well liked. There was a genuine sense of loss with their departure.

1. All monetary values in the chapter are of 2005.

Bankruptcy and Closure? Aubrey Price 1936–37

RICHARD DRYSDALE

The full story of Aubrey Price's headship is difficult to ascertain as evidence is fragmentary. According to one member of staff at the time, Price had been appointed primarily because the Chairman of Governors, the Dean of York, had wanted him as he was a member of the Oxford Movement and would, therefore, develop the spiritual side of the school. When appointed, Price tried to implement his ideas and quickly ran into difficulties with the staff, who opposed his approach to the point that they all handed in their resignations. The number of expulsions also caused concern, especially in a time of falling numbers. Probably by that time Price had decided that his position was untenable.

In his first report to the Governors in the Christmas term he stated, 'The standard of work in the school was low and the boys had got into slack habits. The games were good considering the numbers in the senior school were small and, lastly, the spiritual side of the school was at a low ebb with the boys showing lack of reverence and respect.' By the end of the Christmas term, Price told the Governors that he had taken advice and decided that he should hand in his resignation. He handed in his notice at the Governors' meeting in February 1937 and told them he had applied for another post. At the same meeting he had supposedly recommended that the Senior School should be closed and the Junior School amalgamated with Archbishop Holgate's Grammar School. Some Governors agreed with this proposal. According to the Governors' minutes of the meeting, the Chairman stated that he was very much displeased with the Head Master's decision to leave as he had hoped that the courage and vigour of Mr Price would enable the school to pull round.

Towards the end of 1936 the School's overdraft was £861,000 and the School's bank had been asked to increase this to £996,000. The actual deficit for the 1936 school year was £54,300. The fact that there were only 218 boys in the School was an indication of the seriousness of the situation. It is probable that Price thought the School's financial situation was so dire that there was little chance of preventing closure. He was later appointed to the headship of Queen's College, Taunton, where evidence suggests he enjoyed a successful tenure.

With hindsight, it is easy to see how near the School was to closure. The Governors then approached John Dronfield, a housemaster at Worksop who had been the runner-up when Price had been appointed, to ask if he would accept the job. He did.

33

Left: Aubrey Price, Head Master 1936–37.

Rescue, Recovery and Consolidation: Dronfield 1937–67

John Dronfield's huge influence during 31 years was fundamental to the School's survival and development. There is no doubt that he ranks as a great Head Master. He was held in awe by pupils and staff alike and it seems significant that he was known to pupils by the nickname of 'The Man'. Like many strong characters who know their mind, however, he was not always an easy person to work for. He is quoted as remarking that the most effective committee is one consisting of two people, one absent. To describe him as a benevolent autocrat would not be short of the mark. A former colleague wrote, 'Dronfield was indeed an authoritarian and a disciplinarian, but he belonged to a very different breed of Head Master in that he felt responsible for every aspect of the School and for every person involved with it'. He knew not just the pupils and teaching staff, but all employees, including ground staff, kitchen staff, cleaners and office staff. He kept a close eye on school finances, which was especially difficult in the 1930s and the post-war period, and believed that expenditure should be firmly controlled. It was Dronfield who gave the School the leadership it needed, leaving it in a strong position to face the turmoil of the late 1960s and early 1970s.

John Dronfield, Head Master 1937–67.

The School roll gives a clear picture of development during the Dronfield years. In 1937 there were 218 pupils in St Peter's and St Olave's, 30 of whom would have been removed through loss of confidence in the School had Dronfield not been appointed. Numbers rose steadily in the coming years to 264 in 1940, 371 in 1944, 521 in 1952, 614 in 1957 and finally 645 in 1967. The latter figure represents an almost 300 per cent rise. The number of boarding houses increased from two in 1937 to five in 1967. This dramatic increase in numbers is a reflection of Dronfield's success and stature as Head Master.

Dronfield's links with the City of York were also remarkable for such a busy Head Master. In 1971 he was awarded an OBE for his services to the York community. He had been a magistrate for 28 years and chairman of the bench for 8 years. For 20 years he was Chairman of the York Probation Committee and was credited with the success of the probation system in the city. In addition, he served as Secretary of the Minster Appeal Fund and was Chairman of the North Riding Agricultural Wages Board. He found time to be a lay reader, Chairman of the Northern Division of the HMC and in 1952 he became a member of the Northern Regional Council of the BBC. His wife, Dr Sheila Dronfield, was a practising GP who had set up the first family planning clinic in the city. She was also very active in York as a magistrate, but still had time to become fully involved in the life of the school. She gave vital support, for example, during the flu epidemics of 1955 and 1958 when the school, in effect, became a hospital.

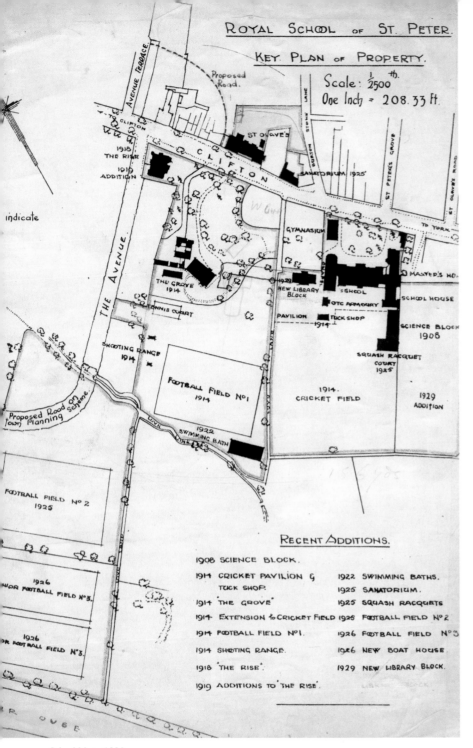

ROYAL SCHOOL OF ST. PETER.

KEY PLAN OF PROPERTY.

Scale: 1/2500 th.
One Inch = 208.33 Ft.

RECENT ADDITIONS.

1908 SCIENCE BLOCK.

1914 CRICKET PAVILION &   1922 SWIMMING BATHS.
TUCK SHOP.   1925 SANATORIUM.

1914 'THE GROVE'   1925 SQUASH RACQUETS.

1914 EXTENSION to CRICKET FIELD 1925 FOOTBALL FIELD Nº2

1914 FOOTBALL FIELD Nº1.   1926 FOOTBALL FIELD Nº3.

1914 SHOOTING RANGE.   1926 NEW BOAT HOUSE.

1918 'THE RISE'.   1929 NEW LIBRARY BLOCK.

1919 ADDITIONS to 'THE RISE'.

School Map c1930.

Together, John and Sheila Dronfield were a formidable couple. It was their joint leadership, both in the community and in the School, that so strengthened the image of St Peter's during these years.

Acquisition and development of property were at the heart of Dronfield's plan. Several properties were purchased for the School, including Wentworth House (1937), The Grove (1942), 1 St Peter's Grove and 24 Clifton (the Manor), St Catherine's (1945) and 7 St Peter's Grove (1946). The construction of the new dining hall and kitchen for the senior School, as well as the extension of the Big Hall, dedicated in 1960, were of major importance in the School's development. Boarding capacity was

helped by the opening of Dronfield House in 1963, while the purchase of more property enabled the creation of the music school. The new covered and heated swimming pool opened in 1964, ending the horrors of the open one. In 1966 the bridge over the main road was constructed, despite initial hostility from the City Council. The pace of development was thus unrivalled in the School's history until the recent reconfiguration.

Fund-raising appeals for the new buildings were constant. The first one after the war raised £388,960[1] by mid-1948, including one significant donation of £182,300 from the Wolstonholme bequest, to help re-build The Rise after the bomb damage of 1942. The 1955 appeal reached a total of £351,000 in its first year, underlining the support for Dronfield's development schemes. A third appeal was started in 1962 and within eighteen months had raised £1.5m.

The examination system changed from the School Leaving Certificate to O and A levels in 1949. Dronfield's welcome for the new system was qualified, as he felt that it would lower educational standards and was concerned for the abolition of credits and distinctions. These doubts are clear in his report to parents in the same year: 'The observation that we are living relentlessly in days of swift and remorseless change is commonplace … it is especially true in education … reforms are being initiated of which the outcome cannot be seen'. The first O- and A-level results came out in the late summer of 1952, and Dronfield expressed his satisfaction with the School's performance.

The academic results were not always what Dronfield would have liked them to be. A confidential memorandum was sent to the staff on the 1959 O-level results, which were, according to Dronfield, 'the worst the School has ever had'. Urgent action was called for and 37 fifth-formers were asked to repeat the year rather than move up into sixth form. Heads of department were asked to let the Head Master have their comments on their particular subjects within a week. The examination results, which were not graded as they are today, were indeed weak. The pass rates were: English Language 64 per cent, English Literature 39 per cent, History 40 per cent, Geography 35 per cent, Maths 63 per cent, Physics 48 per cent, French 68 per cent. The average pass rate in that year was 55 per cent. By 1961 the results had improved significantly with an overall pass rate of 74 per cent.

35

End of term spirits, December 1937.

Temple House in 1939 – the Day Boys House.

The A-level results for 1962 were very different from those of today. Only 20 per cent achieved A or B grades while 29 per cent were outright failures. Of the 119 A level subjects taken, only eight were awarded at grade A. There is no doubt that exams were more demanding at that time. The problem today is one of grade inflation and lack of sufficient differentiation. This is not to decry the excellent exam results of recent years, but the focus on exams and the importance of results have become critical nowadays. It is, however, also true that the exam papers have become more accessible, in as much as one can generalize. Equally, there is no doubt that the pupils of recent years have been hard-working and focused on academic success in a way that was unnecessary when A-level results were not so important, as only 8 per cent of the year-group nationally went on to higher education, compared with 40 per cent today.

Dronfield warned of the danger of teaching exam technique. In his report at Commemoration in 1963 he said, 'Sometimes we think that the teaching of exam technique can be successful at the expense of real educational training'. While exam results were always important, they did not hold the overwhelming position of importance that they do today. By 1962, 80 per cent of pupils were staying for the sixth form and about 50 per cent of those continued to university. Dronfield broadened the curriculum by introducing Woodwork and Metalwork in 1962. A General Studies course was introduced for sixth-formers, whereby scientists had to keep up a language and arts students a science subject.

The financial plight of the School was indeed serious in the 1930s, when it was losing money every year. The School did not start breaking even until after the war years. Dronfield was always mindful of the need to balance the books and to avoid over-spending, and when fees had to be increased he was careful to justify the rise to parents. Very unusually, there were two consecutive years (1952 and 1953) when the fees did not increase at all.

In 1938, Captain Riley-Smith, an industrialist from the West Riding, offered to give the School £213,000. Unfortunately, because of a typing error made by his secretary, it was understood that he was going to donate £213,000 each year for a seven-year period. What he actually meant was that he would donate £213,000 spread over seven years. The incident caused much embarrassment when Dronfield announced to the press that the total donation would be £1.6m. In the end Captain Riley-Smith donated a total of £426,000, and cautioned people to read their letters through carefully before signing them.

Although a man of his time, Dronfield was also ahead of his time in many ways. He introduced the day-boarder scheme, whereby day pupils would spend the whole day at the School, stay for prep and go home to sleep. This meant that it was not unusual for day-boarders to be in the School from 8am until 9pm. It had the advantage of integrating the day-pupils rather more fully into the School, where previously they had been regarded as totally separate. He also abolished the system whereby housemasters had complete financial and administrative control over their domains and lived on what profit they could make – although making a profit was not always possible. Housemasters were no longer to be responsible for feeding the pupils in their houses. This led to better conditions and helped parents build confidence in the School. St Peter's was one of the very first schools to appoint a Careers Master. In this role, Keith Coulthard instituted the successful careers conventions, which played such a central role in education in the decades to come. It was during Dronfield's headship that the Young Farmers' Club was begun, and a walking group was permitted as an alternative afternoon activity to games. It was now that, for the first time, a half-term holiday entered the

36

calendar. Although latterly Dronfield seemed set in his ways and readily admitted as much, he remained open to new ideas and recognized that the future would lead to co-education, even if he was not the person to bring it about.

Links with the Minster and the city were extremely important to him. These years reached a high-water mark of the School's good relations with both bodies. Dean Milner-White, who had been Chairman of the Governors for 22 years from 1941, died in 1963. His contribution to the school was considerable and he did much to draw the School and the Minster together. The part the School played in the Epiphany procession each January was an example of these close ties. Dronfield had worked closely with the Dean and missed his wisdom, advice and support.

There was never any sense of complacency about Dronfield. When a reporter asked him if he had had any failures he replied, 'One is never quite satisfied. I think you have to remember that the success of the School depends on what one does for the average and below average. Anyone can educate a clever boy. Bringing the best out in weaker boys gives me much more satisfaction than helping the clever boy.' In the same article Dronfield spoke of 'trying for years to abolish various fagging systems' and indicated that he had largely succeeded. He went on to say that he had not caned a boy for 25 years, but did not object to corporal punishment, which he thought to be the kindest form in the long run.

In 1964 the Bishop of Durham, Dr Harland, paid tribute to Dronfield on the occasion of the opening of Dronfield House. 'With almost superhuman courage and faith he not only wiped out existing debts, but went on to further building developments and at the same time developed to the highest standard every aspect of life of the School.' It was remarkable that Dronfield should have a house named after him while he was still the Head Master.

Field Marshal Montgomery inspects the CCF 1962.

The Grove and Scott Blocks 1966.

People's memories of him now tend to focus on the immense respect he engendered and his massive achievement, not only in saving the School, but in making it one of the most respected in the north of England. Yet the beginnings of rumblings against the independent sector were growing. In 1965 the Minister for Education and Science had spoken of the Government's intention 'to put an end to the public school as one of the dividing forces of our country'. Ironically, just as the School had survived its most difficult of times and was in a stronger position than ever before, it came under threat from government policy.

In his tribute to Dronfield at his last Commemoration, the Archbishop of York pointed out that the School might well have collapsed but for his arrival, praising his skills as an administrator (one with a careful eye on finance) and his insight into character in his choice of men. In his responding speech, Dronfield alluded to how desperate the situation was when he arrived, and said that it was only through the faith of key members of staff like Kenneth Rhodes and the support of the OPs that the situation was reversed.

The Peterite recorded that Dronfield spent his last week in office seeing every pupil, 'just has he has done for the last thirty years'. It went on to state simply, 'He breathed fresh life into a dying school'. Dronfield had given the School stability, continuity, growth, firm financial foundations and envious prestige. It was never going to be easy for Dronfield's successor to fill the void he had left at the heart of St Peter's.

37

THE ARMS OF ST PETER'S SCHOOL

The School received its Grant of Arms in July 1953. The keys are those of St Peter, the golden one of Heaven, the silver one of Hell. The Ancient Crown denotes the antiquity of the School and also that it is under Royal Charter granted by Philip and Mary in March 1557. The Roses are the Roses of Yorkshire. The Tiara is the cap of St Peter which appears in a number of shields in York Minster.

School Coat of Arms 1953.

1. All monetary values in the chapter are of 2005.

Dronfield's First Years 1937–44

*G*uy King-Reynolds *was a pupil in St Peter's during this key period in the School's history and has given a unique insight into these years.*

The summer term of 1936 was significant; not only for the retirement of the legendary Sam Toyne, who had taught many of our fathers, but also for being the last term for we fifth-form Olavites, who eagerly anticipated a move to the Senior School under a new Head Master, Mr. A.J. Price.

One or two of us can still clearly remember being unimpressed by the man in a tight blue suit who introduced himself as our new Head Master at a series of School, house and form assemblies. He seemed aloof and humourless, very different from the much respected figure of his predecessor.

However, as juniors at St Peter's, we saw little of him in the ensuing two terms, and although we picked up staff and parental mutterings, the crisis arising from the Governors' confrontation with the Head Master about the School's future and identity passed over our heads.

So it was with some surprise that we were addressed by another Head Master, John Dronfield, at the beginning of the summer term in 1937, in a similar series of assemblies. Even at this stage, we sensed a formidable personality.

The papers had reported his age as 38 and yet he was grey-haired, which, with his sallow complexion, made him seem older. Later, we were to find that anger turned his face a whiter shade of pale as his somewhat flat tone of voice became clipped rather than raised.

Dronfield made it clear in his first prospectus that the boarding and day-houses were under his personal supervision, with the housemasters and school monitors answerable to him for the running, good order and discipline in each house. In those days, school monitors had wide responsibilities and authority to use the cane. They also had the privilege of a private study, in which they could smoke after 9.30 pm.

Within the School, it had taken only a few weeks for Dronfield to earn the sobriquet 'The Man'. He had a presence which silenced assemblies, classrooms and corridors, as a warning muted hiss of 'Cave ! The Man !' anticipated his entries. Whilst his reprimands and sarcasm were feared, it was the threat of a caning, regarded in those days as an appropriate penalty for offences and indiscipline throughout the country's schools and sanctioned in the British legal system, which haunted our lives as juniors. However, this

stemmed not from the official regime administered by staff and school monitors, but from the hierarchical tyranny which, by tradition, turned a blind eye on the slipper-beatings carried out by the dormitory captain, the middles (second year), the third-year studyites or house monitors for minor infringements such as failing to knock, to show respect, or for being late into bed.

Fagging was central to the system. School monitors were entitled to a personal fag, which was a preferable role to being in the 'fag pool', at the beck and call of the house monitors and studyites. Nevertheless, a fag's duties were demanding and included preparing tea and toast, cleaning rugby boots, with laces scrubbed white, and blancoing cricket boots; running a bath to the right depth and temperature with a towel kept hot on the pipes. Shoes had to be cleaned before breakfast, the study swept and the coal fire relaid. The school monitor's duties also included ringing the school chapel bell on Sundays.

Whilst corporal punishment administered by the Head Master, housemasters or school monitors (after agreement with housemasters) remained intact, the unofficial tyranny by year groups was progressively purged as we juniors moved up the School and the Head Master made his disapproval clear in very practical ways. To be sent to him to account for an offence was the ultimate deterrent.

For routine and less serious offences, the penalties demanded exercises of hand and brain. This meant the 'date card': learning the dates and copying out 'Discipline defined' from its verso in best writing a certain number of times. The summer term offered alternative chores of rolling cricket pitches or digging plantains, 100 plantains being the usual unit, based on a full box.

While pupils became resigned to detentions, report cards and re-writes of unsatisfactory work, their parents were delighted by the change, which saw School Certificates and Higher School Certificates rise from 20 and 3 respectively in 1936, to the 31 and 6 which Dronfield was able to announce at Speech Day in November 1940. He also confirmed an increase of pupil numbers by 50 per cent since 1937, which led to the re-opening of The Manor after its closure in 1931.

The creation of a day-house commemorating the visit of the Lord Archbishop of York, Dr William Temple, to conduct a service of confirmation in March 1937, did not alter the School's regime in any way. The routine continued to be that of a boarding school and it is surprising, in today's social climate, to realize how the families of day-pupils conformed to the arrangements and regulations as far as was practicable. Thus, school uniform had to be worn by all pupils both in and outside school throughout the term and during the evening hours of prep in the boarding houses. Day-boys were expected to be working at home. Permission to be out, or to miss Sunday chapel services designated for full School attendance, required a parental request and a housemaster's exeat.

Gradually, as a result of the war, the air of pipe-smoking masculinity was diluted and softened by the perfumed presence of female teachers in the senior School, traversing the ancient corridors and sharing the staff common room, an erstwhile male sanctuary apart from a tip-toeing cleaner.

The pupils had been taught art by the only female teacher and supervised by a matron in their boarding houses. Even for day-pupils, contact with the opposite sex was limited to family, since going out with a girl was regarded as soppy and merited mocking. The sister of a day-boy or boarder was regarded as a

sort of 'honorary chap', ready to compete with boys in a way that would be little understood now. It was very much the attitude described in Richmal Crompton's 'Just William'.

There were always a few Lotharios in the upper forms whose assignations in York, particularly with Queen Anne's girls in the appropriately named Love Lane, were firmly dealt with by school monitors. There were no lessons in personal relationships, as feature in schools' curricula today. Matters of sex were rarely mentioned, even in homes, but were occasionally the subject of a talk on male puberty in the boarding houses, to the mutual embarrassment of the housemaster and his audience. The only mention of girls was that they should be respected.

There was the Head Master's gorgeous secretary who, as she walked through the grounds, attracted more watching boys than the new streamlined 'Silver Link' LNER train as it glided out of York Station bound for Scotland. Another femme fatale for

York and Ainsty Hunt 1939.

the pupils was the blonde disciplinarian, Miss Collett, a French teacher. We laboured long over our prep to please her, and listened to her lessons with wrapt attention because, in reality, we were nervous of her irritation.

None of the women appointed to replace the men who had been called for war service had the slightest difficulty with discipline – unlike one or two men holding temporary appointments – and yet, by the end of the 1940s, St Peter's reverted to an all-male staff.

One of the first women to be appointed was the voluminously-draped Mrs Baird, an enthusiastic, no-nonsense Director of Music, who found some difficulty in fitting herself into the Chapel organ loft without a wayward note escaping, much to the delight of the assembled School.

Since the Czech Crisis of 1938 there had been constant rumours of war. We had dug trenches on the west side of the rugby pitch, carried out air raid precautions and exercises in gas masks and yet, in the Lent term of 1939, we were visited by the Harvestehude Hockey Club from Hamburg, which astonished the School's team and spectators by lining its players up on the half-way line of the pitch to give the Nazi salute. As if to underline this sinister portent, the first member of staff to be called up, the veteran soldier of the Territorial Army, Colonel K.G.Chilman, left to take command of the 91st Anti-Aircraft Regiment of the Royal Artillery in London almost on the same day.

However, there were exciting parochial matters to occupy the minds of boys in the spring of 1939. The York and Ainsty Hunt met at the School. The head of School House, J.T. Brockbank, named a new LNER engine of the Green Arrow V2 type 'St Peter's School, York, AD627' at York Station, before an assembly of staff, pupils and parents. The Head Master married his fiancée, Dr Sheila Williams.

The School was on holiday when war was declared in September 1939 and we returned for what was a fairly normal routine, reflecting the inaction in Europe. Air-Raid Patrol exercises were rehearsed and a fire-watching regime had been prepared, but the most notable memory was of the bitter winter when the Ouse froze over and there were many days of skating and sledging in temperatures recalling those of 1895, then quoted as the lowest on record.

When the first air-raid warning of the war sounded in York on 27 January 1940, the day-boys of Temple House had to trudge across the rugby pitch, covered in snow, which almost filled the trenches dug in previous terms as a refuge away from the School buildings. The boarders sought safety in the prepared cellars of The Rise and School House.

The air battle over Britain, which followed the evacuation from Dunkirk and lasted from July to October, largely bypassed York, although there were many alarms to alert those on nightly fire-watching duty, for which there was no shortage of volunteers. We were moved not only by patriotism, but also by the delicious fish and chips often generously financed by the master-in-charge.

Not that the School food was too bad in the first years of the 1940s, though rationing was to become more severe later. A typical Sunday lunch was boiled beef, carrots, onions, onion sauce and large, greasy dumplings followed by a grey, glutinous boiled pudding studded with currants and raisins and full of jam.

In the School tuck shop, Mrs Mackie's mournful Scots mantra of 'Ah canna get stuff' indicated the parlous state of supplies as penny bars of chocolate, packets of biscuits and greasy sausage rolls disappeared from time to time.

Naturally, the significance of the compulsory Junior Training Corps and Air Training Corps had grown as the war progressed and seniors began to think of war service and volunteering, which gave one a choice denied in conscription. At 17 years old, we sixth- formers could join the LDV (Local Defence Volunteers, later re-named the Home Guard). We were issued with an armband (LDV), which was worn over our JTC/ATC uniforms, when on patrol with local units to which we were attached in the Clifton-Wiggington area. No doubt some of us would have made role models for 'young Pike' in the beloved series 'Dad's Army'.

We patrolled the river bank and the Ings in pairs, armed with torch, binoculars and, on occasions, a rifle (empty or with blanks), on the look-out for German parachutists, to the discomfort of many a courting couple ordered to 'Halt!' in some state of undress. But we appreciated the serious side to this, and never more so than when, out on the Ings on a moonless night, a German bomber throbbed overhead, stirring fears of a parachute drop.

An arduous addition to the lower-sixth curriculum was the compulsory 14 days experience of farm work in the autumn term, which turned out to be potato gathering. Urged on by huge bucolic farmers, impatient with our puny efforts, there were many close encounters of the lumbago kind.

It was all very different from the idyllic, over-subscribed harvest camps in the summer holidays, held in the vicinity of the Head Master's country cottage at Coulton, between Brandsby and Hovingham. With luck, we found ourselves working in leisurely fashion alongside the sun-kissed daughters of the farmers and labourers, as well as seeing our Head Master in a jovial, avuncular role as he toured the fields.

Drama was re-vitalized by Leslie Burgess, Head of Classics and director of school plays. Play rehearsals could be dramatic, with Leslie threatening a walk-out if lines were not known. There was one occasion when Dronfield found himself in the unusual position of negotiating the return of Leslie to a subdued and apologetic cast. He established a company of enthusiastic and talented actors, some of whom saw themselves treading the boards as a career after war service. Jimmy Thompson, Rex Langstaffe and Jeffrey Dench fulfilled their ambition; others, equally gifted, chose more secure occupations.

Music, compared with today's status, resources and performance, was in a Cinderella position and, as if reflecting this, the music room was to be found at the back of the library extension, opposite the bike sheds. There was little music outside the choral work in chapel and the Junior Training Corps Band, made up of drums and somewhat dissonant bugles, until the arrival of Mrs Baird, who introduced school concerts and encouraged visits to others held in the city, particularly in the Minster. The much respected and learned Dr B.G. Whitmore presided at recitals of classical records on Sunday afternoons, which he accompanied by talks on the lives and times of the great composers.

The expense and limitations of audio equipment restricted possession, so that schools did not vibrate to the sound of popular music as they do today. One or two of the wealthier school monitors had gramophones and there was a well-husbanded wireless available in the boarding houses. It was the era of the big band, but it was from Hollywood musicals and orchestras such as Glen Miller's that much of our popular music came.

Our peer group was fortunate to have a skilful pianist called John Bulmer. There was an old upright piano in one of the classrooms, and here, surrounded by his fans, he would play his repertoire of 'boogie woogie', then popular in the dance halls. Staff, passing by, did so with facial expressions not unfamiliar to those of us today when assaulted by 'heavy metal'.

The most popular school meetings were those held by the Science Society. There was always an annual excursion and an exhibition every three years, in addition to lectures every term. The Saturday Society, which organised speakers for Saturday evenings, had difficulty in getting speakers because of wartime restrictions on travel. A Mr. 'X' of the Secret Service, who had been engaged to speak, was so secretive that he did not turn up.

So how does one summarize these Proustian reflections about life at St Peter's during Dronfield's first seven years? By any standards, he was a remarkable Head Master, with a natural authority that won the confidence of Governors and parents. He had an enviable gift of staff selection and the ability to get the best out of them, even though, at times, he ruffled feelings. He was regarded as the last of the despots at the Head Masters' Conference, not without a little envy and considerable admiration.

For those of us who spent five years in the School, they were the best and worst of times. There was a buoyant spirit and real sense of purpose, as shown by the response to the bombing in April 1942. The worst of times were mourning the deaths on active service of our maths master, Mr George Stead, and each of the 13 Peterites, a year or more ahead of us, with whom we had shared our life at the School during Dronfield's first seven years.

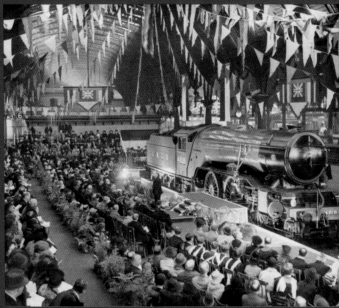

The naming ceremony of the locomotive 'St Peter's School' in 1939.

41

The War Years 1939–45

RICHARD DRYSDALE

When boarders returned at the end of summer of 1939, they were not surprised to find gas-proof cellars to protect them against air raids. The day-pupils were less fortunate and were only provided with trenches near the 1st XV pitch. Protection against bomb blasts and flying splinters was also provided.

Yet in the early stages of the war the School seemed little affected, probably because this was still the calm period of the 'phoney war', which was to last until May 1940. *The Peterite* editorial of January 1940 commented: 'All through the term there have been few things which we could associate with war'. St Peter's, unlike some schools, did not have to relocate. Numbers on the roll remained steady – even increased – and the Christmas term started on time. This situation was not to last and gradually, the School became sucked into the vortex of the war. Initially, changes in the routine seemed slight. Lighting restrictions, for example, meant that the carol service had to be held in the afternoon rather than the evening.

The first members of staff, Messrs Chilman and Stead, were called up. The Officer Training Corps flourished and there were now two parades per week. Eventually, because of the popularity of the OTC, the number of platoons increased from four to five, and by 1940 there were 100 cadets in School, rising to 180 by 1945. In addition to this, the fives courts and a form room were being used by the Pay Corps and the 6th West Yorkshire regiment; thus St Peter's began to have the feel of a military establishment. The gas mask was omnipresent and blackout was strictly enforced. This led to a shortening of morning periods to enable afternoon school to start and finish earlier. Petrol rationing limited away fixtures. Shooting suffered owing to blackout arrangements and it was reported in *The Peterite* that the scoring was rather below the usual standard. Fund-raising for the Five Million Club played a central role in the life of the School during the war, and the funds raised bought recreational facilities for evacuated children in 250 villages. Routine continued much as before.

The first air-raid warning was a salutary indication of what was to come and dispelled any room for complacency. The announcement of the first OP casualty, Flying Officer Hollington, killed on a raid over Germany, was an indication of what lay ahead. His body drifted ashore in Germany, where he was buried. The officiating pastor's words are memorable. 'We do not know whom the waves of the North Sea have carried to our shore but we know there are people who will grieve for him and long for the moment when they can stand at his grave.'

A year after the beginning of the war the editorial in *The Peterite* was still commenting: 'The school life has been remarkably little affected by the war'. Yet incremental changes were becoming more evident. The print size of *The Peterite* in September 1940 was much smaller than usual, to economize on the use of paper. Many of those members of the OTC (later the JTC) over the age of 17 joined the Local Defence Volunteers, or the Home Guard as it was more commonly known. Commemoration in 1940 was abandoned because of the difficulty of travel and the fact that so many OPs were now in the Armed Services: some 133 at this point, but rising to just over 400 by 1945.

In September 1942, *The Peterite* article on the school Home Guard Platoon stated, 'It is not without some tinge of private regret that we record the uneventful passing of the 1942 invasion season … however, the fighting spirit of the platoon was vented as vigorously as possible on straw dummies'.

As the war progressed, so news of OP casualties, missing and prisoners of war were recorded at the front of each edition of *The Peterite*. It makes for poignant reading. The youngest OPs to be killed were both 19 years old. Sergeant Navigator H. Richardson's aircraft was brought down over the sea and his body was washed ashore in 1940 and H. Milburn was killed in action flying over Malta. Pilot Officer R. Lynch's body was found in a

The War Savings Group 1943.

EVEN BOYS ARE BUSY DIGGING TRENCHES

Everywhere digging goes on, and St. Peter's School, York, is no exception. Boys laying duckboards yesterday in one of the trenches being dug in the school field as a precautionary measure against air raids. Right: All busy with their spades.—[N.E.]

Digging Trenches 1938.

rubber dinghy in 1942. He was 21 and his son had just been born. Pilot Officer H. Amor was shot down flying a Typhoon fighter over the Channel and died on 15 December 1942. He was 21 years old. The sense of personal loss when one reads of such young men being killed is overwhelming. One family, the Walters, lost both their sons. By 1945 46 OPs had been killed in all theatres of the war from the Atlantic to the Western Desert, from Burma to the Pacific and from the Mediterranean to Normandy.

Remembrance Day each year now took on a particularly sombre significance. Some 11 per cent of those who served were killed. Reading out the names of OPs who had died also brought the seriousness of war home to the school. Dronfield reported in one Speech Day on the unsettling effect on older pupils, whose plans for the future were uncertain as the war progressed. It is not known what percentage of those OPs who served were wounded. Eighteen OPs were made prisoners of war, while there were always three or four who were missing in action. Of the nine members of staff who joined up, Flight Lieutenant Stead, the former Housemaster of Temple House, was killed in action. Messrs Chilman (who had at one point been in command of the anti-aircraft battery defending Buckingham Palace), Crews, Harding, Waine, Cooper and Le Tocq returned after the war to continue their teaching careers.

The Debating Society's choice of topics reflected the issues of the day. During the particularly cold spell in early 1940, the motion 'It is desirable that periods of cold weather should continue' was discussed. One participant argued that burst pipes could be re-cycled as scrap metal for warships. Not surprisingly, topical issues on the conduct of the war were considered, such as 'This house believes that the Allies should openly intervene on behalf of Finland' (carried by 20 votes to 6), 'This House would approve the policy of purely reprisal raids over Germany'

(carried by 19 votes to 11), 'This House would welcome a return from petrol to oats', a reflection of the shortage of petrol and the need to use horses again. It was carried by 14 votes to 11. The motion 'Propaganda will win the war' was defeated soundly 26–10.

Several visiting speakers came to the School to give talks on war-related subjects. One of the most popular lectures was given by Major Collis; he spoke about the commandos and airborne troops. A talk given to the Science Society by Flight Lieutenant Cribb was entitled 'How a bomber reaches its objective'. Group Captain Trott visited the School in 1940 to speak of opportunities for aircrews. Some 60,000 members of Bomber Command were to lose their lives in the conflict, which gave a certain resonance in this recruitment visit. The talk was, however, especially well received. Speakers from the armed services were a regular feature. In 1942 Pilot Officer Shillitoe gave a talk to pupils about his experience as a fighter pilot.

TERRITORIAL ARMY & AIR FORCE ASSOCIATION of the WEST RIDING of the COUNTY of YORK.

This is to Certify that St. Peter's School, York, furnished a Platoon as part of the 14th West Riding Battalion Home Guard from the date of its inception in May, 1940 until December, 1943.

The following members of the School served –

David Anderson
William Brian Anderson
John Michael Bannister
Robert Derek Sydney Barber
Mark Milton Barker
Stanley Hubert Beetham
Harry Croxton Belchamber
Thomas Babington Boulton
Alan Crawshaw Brown
Frederick Noel Buckler
Edward Peter Bulmer
John Desmond Bulmer
David John Garslee Bramwell Burton
Alexander Calder
John Prestwidge Caley
Peter Francis Cheesewright
Arthur Malcolm Claybourn
Anthony Scott Clephan
Derek Cole
Anthony Paul Coombe
Clifford Anthony Frederick Cookson
John Scott Cooper
John Percival Corry
Denys Kingwell Crews
Eric Pollitt Davison
Guy Wilkinson Denby
Peter George Reginald Dench
David Hill Denholm
John Anthony Denison

George Edward Drake-Brockman
Michael James Dunn
Richard Earle
David Dunston Silian Evans
John Roger Frost
Frank Denison Godsmark
Reginald Brian Goodman
Peter Robert Geoffrey Graham
Richard Henry Hanson
Robert Frederick Harding
Frederick Brian Simpson Hornby
Dennis Martin Hart
Peter Lawrence Hort
James McNaught Inglis
George Frederick Jackson
Edwin Stephen Jeffs
Rex Graham Langstaff
Peter Vance Leigh
Leslie Charles Le Tocq
Philip Anthony Lockwood
Gerald Long
Richard Challenor Lynch
Ronald James McKinlay
Derek George Middleton
Harold Ashton Milburn
Robert Leslie Miller
Gordon Routh Morris
Gordon Curtis Norris
Geoffrey Horace Ogley
Ian Maclay Ormiston

Gordon Henry Oxtoby
Peter Penniston
Andrew Wentworth Ping
William Hugh Wentworth Ping
James Phillips Pulleyn
Derek Lorimer Pryer
Richard Rhodes Lorimer Pryer
David Frank Ruddick
Harold Davison Revill
Guy Edwin King Reynolds
John Cannon Robson
Tom Gordon Robson
Gerald Frederick Ruddock
Peter Henry Ostick Ruddock
Tom Michael John Scott
Edward Alan Shearston
Anthony Allen Short
Frank Fenwick Steele
Dennis Taylor
Hugh Lister Taylor
Peter Frank Tee
Derek Clegg Thompson
Douglas Sidney Tompkins
William Eric Veitch
Gerald William Vero
Richard Scott Foster Webber
Neville Edward Wicks
George Wilson
Albert Leonard Wyman.

Awareness of the war was also raised by the British Ship Adoption Scheme. At the start of the war the School's adopted ship was the *SS Holmpark*. Its Captain and some of its crew sent long letters to the School about their voyages and experiences. They were not, however, allowed to reveal their location for security reasons. One of the crew, Mr Martin, visited the school and gave a graphic account of how his ship had been attacked and bombed in the Battle of the Atlantic. Later in the war the Norwegian ship *Hestmanden* was adopted and Captain Jentoft, who was warmly received, spoke to the School. The addresses of OP prisoners of war in Germany were published in *The Peterite* and it was reckoned that letters would take about four weeks to reach their destination via the Red Cross; so this, too, added a sense of reality to the war.

The Government campaign to increase self-sufficiency in food production and to grow more led to waste land being turned into vegetable patches. By 1940 an allotment of some 300 square yards had been established near the shooting range. In 1941 the School gardeners put more land under cultivation for vegetables for consumption in the dining hall. *The Peterite* reported that people became slimmer.

In the summer of 1942 Dronfield introduced holiday camps to help with the harvest. Some 30–40 pupils helped to bring in what was to be one of the most important harvests in British history. Pupils also helped to lift the potato crop during the autumn term. These camps proved highly successful. The first one was held at Coulton and lasted six weeks; 92 pupils attended, a very high proportion of the School, and put in 7,693 hours of work to help 22 farmers. The harvest camp in 1944 attracted 57 pupils. It lasted four weeks and helped 18 farmers. There was a sense of satisfaction in helping the war effort.

Saving for the war effort was also integral to the school curriculum. In May 1941, York aimed to raise £42m[1] for War Weapons' Week. York schools had a target of £660,000, of which St Peter's raised £83,500, a large sum of money by the standards of the time. Added to this figure was £6,600 raised by the School War Savings Group. The prize-winners of 1941 took a single book as a token prize and donated the balance of the money to their individual war savings accounts. The chief savings event in 1942 was to raise funds for Warships Week. The city raised £1.25m to adopt *HMS York*, of which the school raised £37,000 – again, a considerable achievement. In the Wings for Victory fund-raising the school's target of £30,000 was easily exceeded by a total collection of £67,000. The School, however, beat all records in raising funds for Salute the Soldier week in June 1944, when £101,000 was raised. By 1945 the School had raised £603,274 for the war effort, a truly remarkable sum. Another change, which affected the community in a small way, was the removal of the iron railings at the front of the School, which were sacrificed to the York scrap metal campaign for the war effort.

Morale was as much an issue for the School community as it was for the civilian population. In the September 1940 issue of *The Peterite* a cautionary short story appeared entitled 'The Menace'. It started by saying that the School had had to face many new menaces: air raids, chatterbugs, Lord Haw Haw, blackouts and fifth column activities (although what these were in the context of the School is not specified). It then warned against the dreadful creed of pessimism taking hold. In the story, the flag of optimism wins the day. When Major General Gepp delivered his speech at the 1940 prize-giving, which had replaced Commemoration for the duration of the war, he urged, 'Above all be glad you are alive in these days of high and magnificent endeavour'. There is little doubt that the School rose to the challenge.

Accounts of daring exploits and lucky escapes also found their way into the school magazine. Pilot Officer Whitney's Stirling bomber was caught in searchlights over the Ruhr and hit by anti-aircraft fire. It was then involved in a slight collision with another aircraft before being attacked by a night fighter. Eventually the aircraft had to be ditched eight miles off the Belgian coast. Fortunately, all the crew were picked up alive. Captain Dodd wrote of his experiences as a prisoner of war in *The Peterite* of February 1944. A dramatic rescue of downed aircrew in French

The Baedecker Raid, 29 April 1942

Tony Reynolds OP

The Rise after the Baedecker Raid 1942.

Early in 1942 Hitler decided that he should attack the cathedral cities of England, and it would appear that the list to be subjected to bombing was taken from the old and respected Baedecker guide-book covering the United Kingdom. As a consequence, this period of the air war became known as the Baedecker Raids.

Early in the morning of 29 April 1942, we were awakened by the frightening and unmistakable crump of bombs, followed immediately by the air-raid siren. My mother and I were lucky to have a Morrison steel table shelter, which certainly saved us from serious injury or worse, since many persons were killed and injured in the subsequent devastation of our area. We shall never know the exact number of bombs that fell around us but, judging by the craters, there were certainly in excess of one hundred in a square mile. The rear, and most of the central part of our house was destroyed by a bomb that landed on a concrete path behind the garden. However, the shelter bore the brunt of the debris and we were unharmed. When the wardens, who were particularly brave, released us, it was just before dawn.

Clad only in sooty pyjamas and a dressing gown, I took my mother to Queen Anne School, which had been chosen as a rest-and-relief centre for those made homeless in the event of an air raid.

After ensuring that my mother had been made comfortable, I made my way to St Peter's and was shocked to see that School House was on fire and there was a sinister glow coming from the area of The Rise. Having climbed the fence of the cricket field, I found an enormous crater in the part where we played hockey, into which I narrowly avoided falling. Before reaching the quad outside the Big Hall (smaller in those days than it is now), I saw a spectacle which was both ghastly and gorgeous. The Minster was silhouetted against the pale green of the dawn and was glowing from the surrounding fires. Gazing at the twin towers, still secure, was a huge fillip to morale. The stark beauty of that scene, which had its origin in violence and destruction, made an indelible impression on my memory.

The first person I met in the quad was the Head Master, John Dronfield, and we were joined almost immediately by Kenneth Rhodes, the housemaster of School House. The Head Master asked 'Rhoddy' about the condition of School House and, so far as I can recollect, the reply was that the fire brigade was doing a good job and much of the building would be saved. Then 'Wheeze' Jackson, the housemaster of The Manor, appeared. Dronfield informed us that The Rise was on fire and the four of us ran there to see what could be done. I remember that, at first, the flames seemed to be gaining control. Assisted by the wardens, we rescued as much furniture as we could before the fire brigade arrived and did marvellous work in saving part of the building.

The dawn had presaged a glorious morning and, as we wearily walked back to School House with the sun rising, the Head Master looked at me and asked, 'Why are you dressed like that?' I then had to tell him why I had not had time to dress normally, and that our house was no longer habitable. He and his colleagues could not have been more supportive in resolving our problems. The following night the siren sounded again, but fortunately there was no repeat raid. The happy ending is that we survived a terrible night, but only just …

45

Queen Anne Road after the Baedecker Raid 1942.

York St. Peter's Boys Help with Harvest

Boys of St. Peter's School, York, having their midday break during harvesting on a farm near Hovingham.

Helping with the Harvest 1942.

West Africa by Pilot Officer M. Wall's Sunderland Flying Boat was published in *The Times* of 9 May 1942.

A perceptive series of articles on the air war was published by three Peterites in the school magazine. What is remarkable about these articles is the knowledge that the pupils had of aircraft and general air-war strategy. A visit to the school in March 1945 of 25 Poles liberated from a German prison camp in France also kept the pupils informed about what had been happening, in a way that no newspaper article could hope to achieve. An Austrian pupil at the school wrote confidently in *The Peterite* of September 1940 that Britain would achieve victory. 'England will win this war. Why? The spirit of the population … if we have the will to see it through. We have to show that our spirit is better than that of German youth, and that the English principle of education – to make a gentleman and a sportsman out of a boy – triumphs over the German principle to make a soldier and a brainless follower of Hitler.'

It was, however, the Baedecker raid of 29 April 1942 which thrust the School into national prominence. The city was attacked at 2.30am by 20 German bombers, killing 92 and injuring hundreds, with considerable damage to property. The Germans targeted the railway station and network. Bombing in the Second World War was so inaccurate that it was inevitable that other parts of the city would be hit. Sticks of bombs fell in Queen Anne Road and Sycamore Terrace. The BBC morning news reported that St Peter's had been destroyed. Although much damage had been done, the School was far from destroyed, and a later news bulletin amended the earlier statement to speak of the School being badly damaged. In fact, two School House dormitories, 'the Long' and 'the Incubator', and the front of The Rise were destroyed by fire, causing a temporary loss of boarding accommodation. One high-explosive bomb landed just outside the boundary of the cricket pitch and blasted the squash courts. Another landed on the 1st XV rugger pitch. Few windows in the School were left intact. Even the remote boat-house had its scars to show: eleven oars were destroyed, along with the boat *Sally*, and a clinker was put out of action.

Remarkably, the problems caused by the bombing were overcome in a short time. The examination classes returned to school a week later than usual and the remainder of the School followed a week after that. The acquisition of number 17 Clifton, later to become The Manor, as the third boarding house, helped with accommodation problems. The Rise, which had separate dining facilities, now joined School House for central dining in what had been part of School House.

The end of the war in Europe in May 1945, and in the Far East in August, brought time for reflection on the cost of the conflict in lives lost and injured. The editorial in *The Peterite* spoke of temporary elation, but pointed out that the task of reconstruction would be no less demanding. Some of the staff who had gone to fight in the war returned to teaching with a different perspective.

A new building plan for the School was announced in 1946. It was decided that a new dining hall should be the School's memorial to the war and £830,000 was raised for this purpose. Britain had had a close escape from defeat and occupation. The sense of relief after the war was clearly evident. A holiday was declared on VE day and pupils and staff alike entered into the celebrations and general rejoicing.

Adjusting to peacetime and the re-building of shattered lives would not be done swiftly. Despite this, the School emerged from the war with higher numbers and the prospect of a secure and prosperous future under Dronfield's leadership.

During the length of the war the day-to-day work of the School had continued much as before and the curriculum was largely unaffected. Exams were taken, Higher School and School Certificates awarded, plays like *Julius Caesar* and *The Taming of the Shrew* produced, and some inter-school fixtures played. The attempt to achieve a degree of normality in such abnormal conditions had not been entirely without success. Once the war ended there was a feeling of relief and thankfulness that it was over. There is no doubt that, judging by the number of decorations awarded, OPs acquitted themselves well in the conflict. There were ten DFCs (plus two bars), two DSOs, two DSCs, one BEM, one DSM, two OBEs, one MBE, one KCB and one CBE. The poignancy of the Roll of Honour in the Book of Remembrance in the ante-chapel is a constant reminder of the cost paid, for the freedoms we enjoy today, by a previous generation of OPs.

1. All monetary values in the chapter are of 2005.

46

Liberalization and Modernization:
Peter Gardiner 1967–79

RICHARD DRYSDALE

Peter Gardiner came as Head Master from Charterhouse at the young age of 38. This was a far from easy task, as Dronfield had built a formidable reputation: in the School, in York and in the independent sector, where he was regarded as a leading HMC Head Master. The name of Dronfield was synonymous with St Peter's.

Peter arrived at a time when wider national trends were moving away from authoritarianism and a growing sense of permissiveness pervaded society. The late 1960s are remembered as a time of rapid social change and experimentation with music to match. Long hair was 'de rigueur' amongst young men, norms of behaviour were called into question, authority and convention often rejected or ridiculed. In 1979 David Cummin wrote, 'No Head had so many external influences to consider and of these probably the most worrying was the worldwide student unrest in the early 1970s'. That the School was not detrimentally affected by these wider developments was a tribute to Peter's combination of firmness and adaptability. The resistance to chapel, for example, amongst some pupils was met with these qualities and as a result, chapel remained central to the School's life.

Peter was, by instinct and character, a liberal. Liberalization and modernization were to be central to his headship. He was helped by a small group of experienced and loyal masters, who included Leslie Le Tocq (the Second Master), Kenneth Rhodes, Robert Harding and David Cummin. Not only were the staff expecting changes, they were wanting them. Leslie used to say, 'This is the way we do things Head Master', and then with a twinkle in his eye, 'But you may want to change them'.

It is not surprising that there was opposition to Peter's attempts to modernize, partly from the common room, but also from a minority of OPs for whom Dronfield had represented the pinnacle of headmastering. Anyone who followed could only be a pale imitation in their eyes.

Peter Gardiner, Head Master 1967–79.

ST. PETER'S SCHOOL
YORK

OFFICIAL OPENING

OF THE

SPORTS CENTRE

BY

County Councillor Jack M. Wood

ON

Saturday, 22nd June, 1974

AT 2.0 P.M.

Hockey 1st XI 1973. Hair styles were different then.

Peter had a sharp, scholarly and cultured mind. His concern and care for those in his charge was apparent from the outset and it was not long before he gained the respect of the community, even if there were backwoodsmen sniping from time to time. The school had to adjust to the new style of headship, which offered openness, a spirit of co-operation and a step into a more modern world.

The wearing of the school cap ended. Corporal punishment by monitors was stopped. Eighteen-year-olds were allowed to go into pubs after prep as long as they drank sensibly. In 1971 formal meals in the dining hall were replaced by a cafeteria system. Parents' Meetings were introduced. Links with the wider community were encouraged through the social service group. On one occasion, an exchange was set up for some sixth-formers to spend a week at a comprehensive in Sheffield, whose pupils then came on a return visit. The completion of the sports centre in 1977 added a new dimension to the games programme, while the opening of the new art studio in 1970 raised the profile of art. The science exhibitions, which had been well regarded in academic circles since 1924, continued to attract strong interest and the exhibition of 1971 drew 320 exhibitors into the school. The addition of the Duke of Edinburgh Award Scheme to the extra-curricular programme proved popular.

Disciplinary issues in such a climate could easily become confrontational, but this was mostly avoided. Discussion of issues such as hair length, graffiti and flared trousers took up time at housemasters' meetings. Press attention was attracted when one fifth-former decided to buck the trend and have his hair shaved off. Peter referred to it in *The Evening Press* as an act of disfigurement, and the boy was gated until it grew to a sufficient length. School photos taken at the time show that long hair was the norm, with the proviso that it was not permitted to touch the collar, while sideboards were not allowed below the ears. Smoking led to a £5 fine for cancer relief and brought in a fairly steady income. One pupil even offered £10 on credit before ever being caught.

Peter's strength was that he knew all the boys and girls personally and was always available to them. He continued the merit scheme inaugurated by Dronfield, whereby any good work recommended by a teacher was brought by the pupil for him to see and he was thus able to talk to pupils in a congratulatory rather than disciplinary mode. Peter also laid great emphasis on creativity. In one year he continued a tradition of Dronfield's, which required new pupils to make something and then take it to his study, show it to him, tell him how it was made and how it worked. These personal links with individuals were important to Peter. Pupils responded well to his genuine interest and care for them. In conversation, pupils always felt his concern for them as an individual.

Peter's ability to inspire loyalty in those who worked for him was legendary. His care for the individual was paramount. Meeting a former colleague twenty years after Peter had left the School, he could not only remember the names of the colleague's children, but also a book he had been lent by that colleague over two decades previously.

Peter's speeches at Commemoration were thought-provoking and well-crafted, with a strong bent towards ethical, spiritual and educational issues. Although national examination results were occasionally reported, they were not at the heart of his speeches, as they might be now. The O- and A-level pass rates in 1978, of 70.5

and 75 per cent respectively, were mentioned because they fell short of the School's recent results.

These years were difficult for the independent sector. Much of the press comment was negative and the Labour Party was vociferous in its opposition. When the Labour Party announced that it was prepared to end independent education, Peter responded robustly in his speeches, defending the right of the sector to exist. The HMC was against advertising at this time, and when Peter took out advertising space in a calendar for diplomats, his knuckles were rapped. For a penance he was sent to the NUT conference at Scarborough as the delegate from the HMC. The one idea agreed by all the representatives was that independent schools were an abomination.

Peter had few illusions about the nature of the School he had taken over. On his first speech day he stated unequivocally, 'St Peters is essentially a rugger School'. For better or worse, this has been the image of the School in the wider community for many years. There were a few OPs who judged the success or failure of the school simply on the basis of the 1st XV's results. Peter tried to change this image with a more cultural focus, particularly on drama, which he believed unleashed incredible energies and teamwork without having an 'enemy'. In 1968, for example, there were eight drama productions at both house and school level. The new drama centre, in what had been the gym, was a welcome addition to productions. Not only were the acoustics better, but the audience felt more a part of the proceedings. Memorable productions in Peter's time included a series of Gilbert and Sullivan operettas, involving both senior pupils and St Olave's; *Rosenkrantz* and *Guildenstern are Dead*, one of a lively run of Queen's House plays; *The Crucible*, a collaboration with Queen Anne's Grammar School; and *Woyzek*, an early example of the brilliant productions that Ian Lowe was to present over the next 25 years. In the 1350th anniversary of the school, Robin Walker, OP, a professional composer, was commissioned to write a setting of the Japanese play, *The Birdcatcher from Hell*, for tenor and small instrumental ensemble, with 13- and 14-year-old Peterites acting it out. Sometimes Peter would cajole colleagues to appear with him in short modernistic plays, say by Harold Pinter, for the amusement of any audience who would care to come.

In 1973 the cultural life of the School was also boosted by the introduction of music scholarships, which are so firmly established today. About this time, all sixth-formers were required to pick from a list of books that reflected teachers' enthusiasms, and join in a small, sociable group discussion in an evening with a teacher, in the hope that intellectual horizons might be broadened beyond narrow subject specialization.

The arrival of six girls into the sixth form in September 1976 represented a significant shift in the strongly male ethos and

The Paulinus pageant 1977.

began the move to full co-education. The lack of science facilities in girls' schools was perceived as an advantage in recruiting girls. The Science Society, which already had joint meetings with Queen Margaret's, Escrick, now had female members from St Peter's. It took some adjustment for both sexes to relax in the presence of the other. When Dr Sheila Dronfield gave a talk on birth control, there was a palpable initial reserve as props were passed round before she deftly succeeded in putting the audience at ease.

The 1350th birthday of the School was celebrated in 1977, with a commemorative plate produced by Mulberry Hall. It was the Bursar's idea that every pupil in St Peter's and St Olave's should receive a commemorative mug. There was a special first-day postal cover produced to celebrate the event and the beautiful hanging cross in the chapel, made by John Brown, was installed. David Cummin produced a superb historical pageant, along with many other events to commemorate this special anniversary. A cricket match with King's School, Canterbury, to determine which school was the more ancient, produced a dull draw. The excruciating school song was retrieved from the archives to be given a single performance. It has not been repeated since.

Of supreme importance to the well-being of the School is the relationship between the Head Master and the Governors. In 1967, the Governing Body, said to have been hand-picked by Dronfield, consisted of the local 'great and good'; experienced professionals, retired army officers, ecclesiastics, the bank manager and landed gentry. They agreed school policies but remained detached from the day-to-day running of the School. An important consequence of the inflationary pressures of the mid-1970s, however (24 per cent in 1975), was the influx of businessmen into the Governing Body; good with money and eager to enable the financing of new developments, but more likely to intervene in the running of the School. This could be uncomfortable, and Peter was not at his best in the company of businessmen.

49

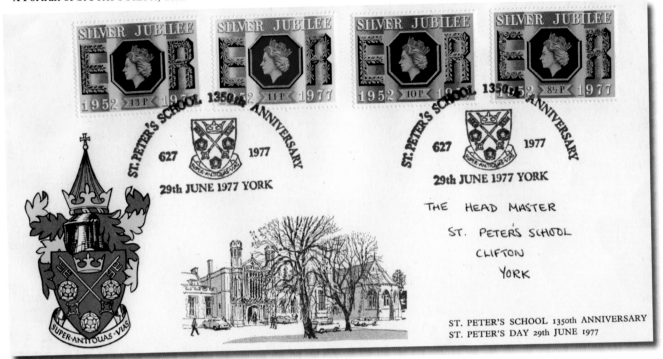

First-day cover 1977 commemorating the School's 1350th anniversary.

The power of the Chairman of the Finance Committee could be seen by the fact that he would meet Peter in advance of Governors' meetings to discuss the agenda. Minutes of the future meeting would then be drafted. Only rarely did these have to be rewritten.

Peter ended the enforced watching of the 1st XV. This did not please everyone, least of all those OPs who judged the success of the school by its rugby results. For Peter, however, pupils could pursue other interests than just watching rugby. Peter also enjoyed teaching and, unlike many Heads, did not desert the classroom. He was never happier than when he was involved in a drama production or teaching. This active involvement in the School's life meant that he could also be found doing duty in boarding houses from time to time and regularly supervised sessions in the sports centre on Sundays for the boarders. Peter was thus involved in the day-to-day life of the School in a way that few Heads either manage or want.

He was discomforted by the lack of space for music and art. The addition of a further floor to the pavilion gave the art department the space it needed. Lack of subject areas was another problem, but this remained unresolved until Robin Pittman's time. The major property development during Peter's tenure, however, was the building of the Sports Centre, which was financed without a prior appeal. It was to prove a remarkable asset over the coming years, with its versatile configurations.

On the curricular side, General Studies was introduced as an A-level subject. There was no syllabus laid down, so teaching was challenging and tended to reflect the interests and enthusiasms of the staff; a course on wine proved to be one of the more popular choices. Part of the course hinged on inviting a wide range of outside speakers to address the sixth form on Saturdays:

poets, sociologists, scientists and architects, among others. General Studies, along with other initiatives such as the annual general knowledge quiz, set by Gordon Craine, enabled sixth-formers to broaden their intellectual horizons.

In interview, Peter was quick to point out that many of the successes of his headship were the result of hard work and initiatives undertaken by colleagues. In this sense, he saw himself as the conductor of an orchestra. This was typical of his modesty.

There was a sense of loss when it was announced that he was leaving the school after 12 years. The Dean of York, then Chairman of the Board of Governors, paid a generous tribute to him at his last Commemoration, when he said, 'Here was a man whose dedication to the School and its well-being was complete. Here was a scholar, in love with his subject and with teaching. Here was a pastor, with a genuine concern for those under his care. Here was a man of culture, interested not only in the arts but also in all manner of things of good report. But above all here was a true Christian gentleman, and that is the highest compliment I can pay.' No one who knew Peter would dispute those words.

The Valete in *The Peterite* was cogent and concise: 'His concern, his culture, his sense of humour, his enthusiasm, his capacity for hard work have been pervading and incalculable influences for good. It is sometimes said that it is impossible to be both a gentleman and a good Head, but at St Peter's that dilemma has not existed. We remember him as both.' Peter had led the School though a difficult time and left it in a good position to make further progress under his successor. In retrospect, there was no other option but to liberalize and to modernize. Peter accomplished this difficult task with a degree of distinction.

The Arrival of Girls

LOUISE DENISON

I started St Peter's with four other new girls in September 1976. Our first appointment was with Mr Gardiner, the Head Master, and a photographer from the local press in front of the Memorial Hall to record the historic moment. I think we were all a little taken aback by the attention we received. After all, we were there to go to school and just wanted to settle in and get on with the day. Chapel was next – and this I do remember, especially the first hymn. I had not given any thought to the difference in pitch between male and female voices and the first few bars were quite unnerving, particularly as I had previously been at an all girls' school. The next hurdle was getting to my first lesson with one of the other girls. What and where was S3 ? A helpful school monitor kindly pointed us in the direction of the Scott Building, although I think we mistook him for a member of staff!

We settled into a routine that was probably not that different from our previous schools. Careful consideration had been given to our welfare and we had a girls' common room above the Rhodes Room, which was fitted with a shower and had chairs, a table, coat pegs and a kettle. It was mainly used as a changing room, but was also a place to which we could retreat if necessary.

Some of the staff were concerned about how we should be addressed in what had been a boys' school, where surnames were the order of the day. I can only ever remember being called by my Christian name. There were also members of staff who were concerned that we might cry if we were told off and were unsure how they would cope if this happened.

An odd number of girls must have posed a slight problem at games. I can remember four of us playing badminton and tennis on a regular basis. Squash was another option, on the courts on the far side of The Avenue. Two of us used to go riding at the Kemp Welch's stables in Wiggington on a Wednesday afternoon, which left three girls at school, not an ideal number for any sport.

I remember being involved in at least two of the School's drama productions. At my previous school I had been very happy to be behind the curtains, but with only five girls at St Peter's we were much in demand for the female roles. We were not keen on the alternative – girls imported from a nearby school. That would have been letting the side down! And so we rose to the challenge; I even sang in one production, and that is a reflection of how desperate they must have been.

The two years passed by incredibly quickly. We were something of a novelty, being the first girls in the School's 1,349 years of history, but I think we did quite enjoy the attention. We were welcomed and made many good friends. Three of us went on to marry fellow pupils. Co-education at St Peter's continues and little did I think, in September 1976, that 30 years later my daughter would be starting her first term at St Peter's.

The arrival of the first girls 1976.

Girl pupil breaks leadership tradition

CLAIRE LOCKEY
Head of house

THE FIRST girl head of house has been appointed at St. Peter's, York, 'which claims to be Britain's oldest public school.

Claire Lockey, 17, a sixth-former, is in charge of eight girls and 50 boys in School House.

Claire, of Prospect Farm, Hessay, near York, is a boarder at the 1,350-year-old school, which numbers Guy Fawkes among its former pupils.

She has responsibility under the housemaster, Mr. Barry Daniel, for maintaining discipline, as well as advising pupils and acting as their representative with staff.

Claire admitted yesterday that she was surprised when Mr. Daniel asked her to take the job.

"I never thought that in a largely male society there would be an opportunity for a girl to become a head of house.

"But I feel I can keep discipline among the boys as well as any senior boy in my position. The boys seem to respect me, and that is a help," she said.

Mr. Daniel said: "I chose Claire for the same reasons as I would pick out any boy.

"She has shown leadership qualities, and she has a positive approach to things and holds definite opinions. She is doing a very good job."

Claire, who is studying A-level history, French and English, hopes to go to university. She is a former pupil of Queen Anne Grammar School, York.

Girls were first admitted to the Sixth Form at St. Peter's School four years ago. There are now 22 girl pupils, and more than 400 boys.

Clare Lockey, first girl to be made Head of House.

51

The Science Renaissance: Peter Hughes 1980–84

RICHARD DRYSDALE

Peter Hughes came to St Peter's from Shrewsbury, where he had been a Deputy Head and Head of Science. He was an energetic, restless person with an incisive intellect. One had the sense, when you were speaking to him, that he had not only worked out what you were going to say as you were saying it, but had framed a suitable response. As a scientist his main focus tended to be in that direction and there is no doubt that the sciences flourished significantly during his headship.

Peter believed that the Head Master's main task was to create the right sort of environment, in which the staff's skills and interests could be used to the best advantage of the pupils of the School. The tone of his headship was set in his first speech day address in October 1980, when he placed a strong emphasis on values and focussed on the importance of truth, self-discipline, integrity and a sense of responsibility, both in the school community and the wider world.

Peter's concern about the quality of exam results was apparent at the outset of his tenure, when, at his first speech day, he reported that the exam results were 'mixed' and voiced his concern 'that too many boys leave the School without the minimum collection of O levels or grade one CSEs'. During his time in the School, solid progress was made on the academic side. In 1982 the School experienced its best-ever A-level results with a 92 per cent pass rate. By 1984 the A-level pass rate had dropped marginally to 89 per cent, with 20 per cent achieving grade A. The O-level results were also encouraging, with an 80 per cent overall pass rate which compared favourably with a national average of around 65 per cent and an HMC average of 72 per cent. These results heralded the beginning of a steady improvement over the next two decades.

Nevertheless, Peter Hughes' headship was not immune to external political and economic influences. The independent sector was, as ever, vulnerable to criticisms from elements of the Labour Party, whose hostility was clear. HMC Heads therefore had little option but to respond, and Peter was no exception. By 1983, the recession, a 10 per cent increase in fee levels and a

declining birth rate were all having an impact on numbers. In 1979–80 there had been 452 pupils in the senior School: 223 boarders and 229 day-pupils. By 1985–86 there were 188 boarders and 266 day-pupils, making a total of 436 pupils, a 3.5 per cent decline overall. More ominously, boarding had declined by 16 per cent. The increase in girls in the sixth form,

Peter Hughes, Head Master 1980–84.

however, was most welcome, and encouraged by Peter, who favoured a change to co-education.

The Governors had given Peter the brief of improving the science facilities and to this end an appeal was started. The money came in slowly and the building eventually had to be funded from other sources, including the sale of No. 8, St Peter's Grove, and money from a previous appeal. The building eventually cost £600,000. It was opened by the Archbishop of York, John Habgood, himself a scientist, in May 1984. The new building represented a quantum leap for the sciences. The Biology, Physics and CDT departments moved into the new block.

The School now had one of the most modern science facilities in the country, yet the project might have floundered over finance, but for the tenaciousness of Peter Hughes.

When Peter was interviewed by two sixth-formers in 1983 for *The Peterite*, he was aware that much remained to be achieved. He

The new Science block.

felt that not enough was being done on the intellectual and cultural side of the School's life. He recognized that art and music needed particular support and he felt that the library was inadequate. These problems were not to be addressed until his successor arrived.

Peter's short reign of four-and-a-half years was a troubled one, and there is no doubt that the disagreements between him and the governing body had spilled into the public domain to the detriment of the School. Differences developed within the governing body at an early stage over Peter's style of leadership, and these tensions made it increasingly difficult for him to carry out his role effectively. Confidence in the School had suffered, despite strong exam results in 1982 and 1983. There is no doubt in the educational world that a house divided amongst itself cannot progress significantly and could even be completely undermined. This point was nearly reached in 1984, and it soon became clear that Peter could not continue in the post without the full-hearted support of the governing body. A sense of crisis was evident. For this reason Peter decided to apply elsewhere and in 1984 he was appointed Head of Science at Westminister School.

Peter Hughes resigned at the end of the academic year. He was given leave of absence for the summer term and David Cummin, the former Second Master, came out of retirement to stand in as Acting Head.

53

The Interregnum: David Cummin 1984–85

It was a brave gesture for David to step in after almost four years of retirement and take over the running of the School. His mission was to steer with a firm grasp until a new appointment was made. It was not intended that there would be new initiatives during the interregnum. They would be the preserve of the new Head. David's wisdom and quiet authority, his firm but fair regime, sailed the School into calmer waters and earned him the respect of staff and pupils alike. The wider community detected that stability had been restored. The debt owed to him by the School in this period of transition was considerable. The Governors wisely changed his title from Acting Head to Head Master, in recognition of his pivotal role at a difficult time.

The appointment of a new Head proved more difficult than expected. Of the six invited for final interview, two were appointed to headships elsewhere, two withdrew and the Governors could not agree on the remaining two candidates.

At this point, Guy King-Reynolds, an OP and Head of Dauntsey's School in Wiltshire, approached Robin Pittman, Head of QEH, Bristol. Robin was interviewed and offered the job in January 1985 and began the following September. He started his tenure in an especially strong position, given the background of his appointment and the fact that the Head Masters' Conference were fully aware of the nature of the circumstances of the departure of the previous two Head Masters. If Robin Pittman ran into problems with the governing body there was a significant chance that St Peter's would no longer be an HMC school. No Governors wanted this to happen.

Co-education and Consolidation: Robin Pittman 1985–95

RICHARD DRYSDALE

Robin Pittman came to St Peter's from Queen Elizabeth Hospital, one of Bristol's independent schools, where he had been Head Master for seven years. The Governors chose a person with experience to take up the challenges that the School now faced. Robin inherited an institution that had been faltering in a number of ways. Numbers had dropped, corporate discipline was not strong and staff morale was at a low ebb. Equally significant was the fact that the School had been standing still while competitors forged ahead. In order to lift the School, Robin had to address a broad range of issues. He was aided in this task by the abolition of the grammar schools in York and the introduction of the Assisted Places Scheme.

The tone of Robin's tenure was established at his first Commemoration, when he quoted Thomas Arnold, the Head Master of Rugby: 'There is nothing so unnatural and convulsive to society as the strain to keep things fixed when all the world is in eternal progress; and the cause of all the evils of the world may be traced to that most natural but most deadly error of human indolence and corruption that our business is to preserve and not improve. It is the ruin and fall alike of individuals, schools and nations.' The years that followed showed that Robin was to remain true to this vision. There were more changes in the first six years of the Pittman era than in the previous two decades.

Central to Robin's goals was to be a change in the ethos of the School. There was an atmosphere of boorishness and alienation amongst some pupils, which Robin quickly sensed when, on saying good morning to a group of sixth-formers before his first term started, he was greeted with blank indifference. This small encounter told him much about the ethos of the place and the difficulty of the task ahead. The improvement of corporate discipline was thus a central plank in his plan.

Robin believed that corporate discipline could best be reinforced in assembly on Saturday mornings, and it quickly became apparent that he was not a person to be trifled with. This was done in small ways, but the message was clear. If there were too much talking as Robin strode through the Memorial Hall at the end of assembly, he would stop and demand silence. The school was thus silenced and the message learnt. If coughing became too frequent or obvious, Robin would demand that it be

Robin Pittman, Head Master 1985–95.

St. PETER'S NEWS

September 1988   St. Peter's School, York YO3 6AB

GIRLS' FIRST YEAR

Co-education has been launched well and there is nothing to make us doubt the wisdom of the decision to take this relevant and significant step forward in the school's further development.

We have just completed the first year of co-education throughout the junior and senior schools. 11 girls joined the middle school of St Peter's and 50 entered the junior school (there have been girls in the sixth form since 1976).

The girls have immediately blended into the school's life as though they had always been part of it.

The smiles say it all. Girls have fitted in well since they joined St Peter's Junior and Middle Schools a year ago.

September 1988 St Peter's News.

The presentation of the St Peter's diesel locomotive plate 1989.

controlled. This was no vain task in the spring term, when growing numbers of pupils succumbed to colds, yet pupils did try hard to stifle coughs that in the past might have gone unmasked. *The Bulletin*, a magazine produced by sixth-formers, picked up on this and produced a cover similar to *Private Eye*. The picture showed the chaplain, a speech bubble appearing from his mouth with the words, 'And the eleventh commandment is that thou shalt not cough.' At the other side of the picture stood Robin pronouncing an 'Amen'.

Other aspects of discipline were tightened, including the dress code and the rules against smoking and drinking. The 'three strikes and you are expelled' rule for smoking and drinking made it clear what pupils who transgressed could expect. The dress code, a topic that took endless hours of discussion in housemasters' meetings, was tightened. Equally important was the fact that the rules were enforced, with staff obliged to patrol the environs of the school to prevent smoking.

Housemasters had no doubt that Robin would support them when it came to dealing with recalcitrant pupils or difficult parents. The last thing that pupils wanted was a visit to Robin to explain their behaviour. His presence around the School also helped in this respect. He made a point, for example, of sitting in lessons to get an impression of what was going on in the classroom. Pupils generally responded well to this new regime, which was so much needed at the time. As staff/pupil relations improved, the strong hand of discipline became less obvious. A certain informal formality was thus created.

Robin's combative leadership style did encounter opposition. He was inclined to be forthright and say exactly what he felt. Initially, he pursued a 'get tough' policy with the common room, to assert his authority. He did, however, respect colleagues who stood their ground and argued a case. One member of staff took his opposition to an extreme conclusion and resigned. His leaving speech to the school, which became part of the folklore, included the exhortation 'Don't let the ******** grind you down'.

Robin did not always find the common room totally amenable to his policies. There was a sense that the changes were happening too quickly and without a full and necessary consultation. Matters came to a head at one common-room meeting when these issues were aired. Robin was probably surprised by the views that were expressed and he listened in silence. One change which emerged from this difficult meeting was the setting up of termly, informal gatherings at St Catherine's. A wide range of issues was discussed with no written agenda. From these meetings Robin was able to take informal soundings of staff opinions and observations. It was here that the idea of a compulsory eucharist each term, for the whole school, was suggested and later successfully adopted.

The tragic death of Barry Daniel in Norway in 1986, while leading a school party across a glacier, stunned the school community. Peter Croft, the Second Master, flew to Norway to help cope with the difficult situation and provide support for the traumatized members of the party. Robin flew back from holiday to see the School through this most difficult of times. The crisis brought out all that is best about the School community. Cindy, Barry's widow, and Gael and Lindsey, his daughters, were supported and nurtured. Barry's name lives on in the Barry Daniel Fund that was set up in his name, to give financial support to Peterites embarking on adventurous travel.

In 1986 Robin decided that the way forward for the School was to go entirely co-educational. The paper he presented to the governing body was well received and, despite pockets of resistance amongst the OPs and from a few of the staff, the policy was implemented in September 1987. Robin remembers feeling a surge of pride on the first day of the new academic year, when he went into chapel and saw girls in the school uniform. Becoming a genuinely co-educational school, however, was not simply achieved by having girls in the School. For the first few years St Peter's remained a boys' school in ethos. That changed in time to become that of a genuine co-educational establishment with girls changing the tone of the School for the better. The boorish behaviour, which could occasionally surface before, largely disappeared. The girls civilized the place. Academic standards rose and the extracurricular programme benefited, notably in music and drama.

The visit of the Duchess of Kent, July 1990, on the occasion of her opening the Chilman Building and visiting the new Alcuin Library.

The worst fears of the games' lobby, that boys' sports would suffer because there would be up to a third fewer boys in any year group from which to choose for teams, went unrealized. In fact, the opposite happened. Far from being marginalized, rugby and cricket were strengthened, and some of the best teams the School has ever produced emerged in the years after co-education was established.

The first girls in this male bastion proved resilient and more than able to cope with the pressures. The ease of social relations between the sexes made for a more pleasant working environment. Inevitably, the boys felt that staff were tougher on them than they were on the girls, while the girls thought that the girls' sports would never receive the emphasis and accolades that boys' sports received. These perceptions have never really changed between 1987 and the present.

Opposition to going co-educational came from some staff, who dreaded the thought of having to cope with the females on a day-to-day basis. One colleague believed that girls would not be able to cope with the pressures of the place and spend too much time in tears. There was also some opposition from a few OPs, who attended Commemoration in June 1986 sporting badges calling for co-education to be resisted. When Robin made mention of the intention to go co-educational, at the OP dinner on the evening of his first Commemoration, one table got up and left the room in disgust. They were in the minority, however, and at the end of the address he received a standing ovation. Once the policy was implemented, opposition died away quickly. Going co-educational was a major factor in the success after 1987.

The intensity and rapidity of change during Robin's few years is, in retrospect, remarkable. Modernization was needed in procedures and systems. Brian Jelbert, the new Bursar, introduced tight financial management with 'cost centres'. Numbers in the school increased after 1985, which enabled expenditure on a whole range of facilities. This financed badly-needed refurbishment of the fabric of the School, which had come to look shabby in places.

An appeal was launched in 1989, with an initial target of £500,000, to finance the building of a new teaching block for St Olave's and the creation of a new library from the old gym, latterly the drama centre. The purchase of the Methodist Church Hall and adjacent rooms resulted in their conversion into a new drama centre and rooms for the music department. In addition, the Scott and Grove blocks were converted into subject areas for maths and languages respectively. The initial target of the appeal was surpassed and the various building schemes proceeded. The Chilman Building and Alcuin Library were opened in 1990 by the Duchess of Kent, with Kenneth Chilman in attendance.

Far left: The Yorvik Festival 1993.

Left: Red Nose Day 1993, the de–waxing.

The new Alcuin Library represented a major step forward for St Peter's. The appointment of Avril Pedley in 1992 as the first full-time librarian gave this important side of the School the prominence it deserved. The School now had a well-stocked, comfortable and inviting library. Robin was spared the embarrassment of showing prospective parents around the dismal accommodation that had preceded the Alcuin Library.

On the academic front there were many changes. A system of annual appraisal was introduced. This opportunity to sit down with Robin was generally welcomed by staff, who now felt that what they were doing received recognition. Heads of departments were held responsible for departmental examination results and had an annual meeting with Robin to discuss them.

Academic standards rose markedly between 1985 and 1994. In 1994, 96 per cent of GCSE candidates achieved A–C grades, of which 44 per cent attained grade A and 15 per cent attained the new A* grade. The A-level results showed a similar improvement, from a 78 per cent pass rate in 1988 to 93 per cent in 1993. Of equal importance, however, was the proportion of top grades, which rose significantly. There were several reasons why this happened. The academic quality of pupils was higher after co-education. Teaching became more focused as academic results assumed a much greater importance within both the School and the national community. League tables were introduced in 1991. The creation of subject areas was instrumental to this improvement and made teaching considerably easier. The School's academic reputation soared and the demand for places rose significantly.

Andrew Wright was appointed Director of Music a year after Robin became Head Master. The development of music was to help moderate the games-playing image of the School in the wider community. Robin, a church organist himself, was keen

that music should develop rapidly and enhance the School's wider reputation. A long missive to Andrew one morning after chapel on the quality of hymn singing was evidence of Robin's close interest in the School's music. The high standard of music performed at Commemoration, in concerts and on tours was ample proof that Robin's goal was being realized. This was to prove one of Robin's most significant and long-lasting legacies. The vital restoration of the chapel organ was a major but necessary expense at this time.

On the science side, the arrival of GCSEs made for intense debate as to whether the Dual Award Science course should be adopted or single science subjects should be taught. The former prevailed. Personal and Social Education became an integral part of the curriculum for the first time. The art department benefited from its move from the cramped space above the cricket pavilion to part of the former School House building. Art, like music, thus enjoyed a greatly enhanced profile. The appointment of an artist-in-residence was also to prove significant for the development of the department. The careers department benefited from greater resources and a much higher profile. It was re-located in September 1994, from its small rooms at the back of the music school to the main block. This not only gave it considerably more space but its location in the centre of the school increased its accessibility.

Outside the academic confines a range of other changes helped in the School's development. The Friends of St Peter's was established and soon made an invaluable contribution to the School's life. An exchange programme with Selborne College and Clarendon in South Africa proved both popular and successful. Marketing received greater prominence, with the creation of a marketing committee. Yet, although numbers in the School rose, the departure of 28 fifth-formers at the end of one year suggested there was no room for complacency.

57

Archbishop Coggan's visit.

58

There is no doubt, too, that the School, like many in the independent sector, benefited from the introduction of the Assisted Places Scheme. This was introduced in 1980 as a means-tested method of enabling parents who could not afford full school fees to receive a government subsidy. Ultimately there were 140 pupils on the Assisted Places Scheme in the School. When Labour came to power in 1997 they made it clear that the scheme would be abolished and this gave concern that a decline in numbers would follow to detrimental effect. The scheme was phased out gradually and fortunately, the worst fears about a dramatic fall in numbers were not realized. By 1995 the School's image as a strongly performing academic school, with strength across the whole curriculum, meant that demand for places remained strong.

Robin made it one of his priorities to improve relations between the staff and the governing body. The difficult times between 1979 and 1985 had left a legacy of mutual suspicion and, sadly, lack of trust. The annual dinner for staff and governors, however, allowed both sides to improve their understanding of one another and to work together. Visits by individual governors to attend classes in subject departments enabled them to acquire a better understanding of educational issues.

Two changes of routine caused some upset in certain quarters. Sunday chapel services were ended for good reasons. The majority welcomed this development, as the Service had become less about corporate worship and more about an act of discipline. More contentious were the alterations to Commemoration at the end of the summer term. This upset some OPs particularly, because part of Commemoration was moved to the start of the September term, which meant it enjoyed a slightly lower profile.

The key development on the boarding side was the opening of Dronfield House as the first girls' boarding house in 1987. Peter and Sue Taylor were to preside over a remarkably happy house for the next nine years. Linton Lodge was purchased in 1993 and the members of School House transferred to the new house in St Peter's Grove. Robin was keen to continue to create a less institutional atmosphere in the boarding houses, something which the boarding Housemasters had long worked towards.

On the pastoral side, all members of staff became house tutors and met with their tutees at least once a week. This eased the load of Housemasters, although pupils continued to regard the housemaster as the most important person to see in the event of a crisis. The creation of Clifton as a new house eased the numbers in the day-houses, which had become unsustainable.

Fund-raising through charity walks became a feature of school life. Robin initiated the idea of these walks and took part in them with Laura, his wife. The first saw the whole school walking the 20 miles across the North Yorkshire Moors from Osmotherley to Helmsley in May 1986. While the school walked in one direction, Robin and Laura would walk in the opposite direction, towards the School, distributing sweets. By the end of one particular walk, Robin had grown weary of being told by Peterites that they had been told by their parents not to accept sweets from strange men. The Peterswalk of 1989 raised £16,000, while the walk of 1993 raised £12,000.

One of the final developments in Robin's term was the acquisition of Miss Meaby's, later known as Clifton Pre-preparatory School, in 1995. This acquisition was achieved in the face of stiff competition. In retrospect it was vital to the future of St Olave's and St Peter's and was a significant development for the future of all three schools, which were eventually to number over a thousand pupils.

With hindsight, it is possible to see that the changes in this period were both far-reaching and, in some cases, overdue. The School was left in a much stronger position in 1995 than it had been in 1985. By 1994 there were 483 pupils in St Peter's, the highest number in a decade, with 169 boarders, the highest number in five years.

Robin Pittman's legacy is a considerable one. There is little doubt that he had helped to lay the foundations for the School's pre-eminent position today. It must also be remembered, however, that he was helped in his task by a highly motivated and committed staff. Andrew Trotman inherited a financially secure, successful school, which had become one of the major schools of the north of England.

Towards the Millennium: Andrew Trotman 1995–2004

RICHARD DRYSDALE

Andrew Trotman came to St Peter's from Edinburgh Academy where he had been Deputy Rector. Appointed at the age of 42, he inherited a school with a growing reputation and sound finances. Andrew was to build on the successes and strong foundations created in the Pittman era. The worst an Edinburgh Academy colleague could say of him was that he could be over-enthusiastic. His strength was his open disposition and his friendly, approachable persona. Good public relations with parents and the wider world were an additional asset. Andrew's leadership style was relaxed and informal. He favoured a culture of praise, which engendered a gentler ethos during his tenure. Pupils found him approachable and empathetic, with a sense of fun. When he appeared in chapel on a 'red nose' fund-raising day as Ozzie Osmond, there was universal applause. His participation in the Beverley Fun Run with other members of staff and his abseiling down the Tyne Bridge (both for charity) demonstrated his will to take an active part in the life of the School.

Andrew Trotman, Head Master 1995–2004.

Prince Andrew's visit to St Olave's.

Andrew was a consultative Head and for this reason a series of committees were set up after his arrival, to examine every aspect of school life and then make recommendations. The resulting reports were translated into a vision-plan document, which was to direct the School forward. That boarding numbers had shown a gentle decline over the years from 222 in 1957 to 140 in 2003, was a particular concern. This was due in part to both national and regional trends. The commitment to boarding remained strong, as it was fundamental to the character of the School, and although day-pupils outnumbered boarders by 72 per cent to 28 per cent in 2003, the ethos of the School remained primarily a boarding one, with all the demands that such an institution makes of its pupils and staff.

By 1998 preparatory schools left in the North East were struggling to hold up, while there were only two prep schools in the North West which were not part of larger senior schools. The concern for boarding numbers led to Andrew's involvement in the York Boarding Schools Group, made up of the heads of

60

schools in and around York. The purpose of the Group was to promote boarding education based in York for pupils both in the UK and abroad. Further commitment to the boarding principle was demonstrated in the building of a new boarding house for St Olave's, which was opened by HRH Prince Andrew.

On the academic side, the school excelled. The advent of national league tables in 1991 had had a major impact across the educational world, since only a slight variation in a School's academic performance could lead to a significant change in its overall position. What is clear is that between 1994, when the School came 227th, and 1997, when its position was 66th out of a total of around 500 independent schools, St Peter's had moved from the third to the first division. This was a remarkable achievement, considering the entrance procedures for the School were not as demanding as those of many schools. Since then St Peter's has remained in the first division. In a press interview Andrew was quick to point out that, although proud of the School's academic success, 'Parents tend to pay too much attention to league tables and they don't tell the whole story. They don't include drama, music, sport and, importantly, the work the School does in the community.'

Thirteen pupils gained Oxbridge places in 2001, another testament to high academic standards, while the 2003 GCSE results were the best the School had achieved. This academic success was quickly perceived in the wider community and demand for places increased, as did numbers. Such an upsurge in demand came at just the right moment, as the last few Assisted Place pupils left in 2004. (There had been 140 pupils on Assisted Places at the height of the scheme.) By 2000–2001 there were 1,003 pupils in all three schools, with 501 in the senior school.

The School's first full 1999 inspection provided an objective assessment of its achievement with most gratifying comments. It reported, 'The level of academic achievement is very high … overall exam results are impressive … pupils are relaxed, articulate, self-confident and well-motivated … they display a strong sense of community and purpose. Pupils are courteous and cheerful … leadership is strong, positive and enlightened …' As is usual, the Inspection team made recommendations for improvement; these were of minor importance in the scheme of things. The Inspection Report of 2004 took a similarly congratulatory tone, 'The School does far better by its pupils than might be expected at both GCSE and A level. At GCSE the results are far above the national average for all maintained schools and are even above the national level for selective schools.' The same was true for the A-level results. The report referred to the richness and variety of activities which enhanced

Above: Preparing for a school photo 2004.

Top left: A problem of identity – too many twins 1997.

Left: The last of the tweed jackets 1997 with the new dark brown uniforms.

and extended the already broad and well-balanced curriculum. It continued, 'The excellent discipline and wide range of intellectual, artistic and sporting activities help the pupils to develop into responsible young people who have the highest standards of behaviour and are very good at learning'. The excellence of pastoral care was also remarked. The School was doing well across the whole spectrum from the academic to the sporting and the extracurricular.

The well-founded perception of the wider community was that the School was an academic success. *The Sunday Times* reported in 1998 that St Peter's was the school most asked about by potential buyers of property in Yorkshire. *The Yorkshire Evening Press* was equally congratulatory in 2000, when their correspondent reported, 'St Peter's, which scored highest of the York schools, is proving to be one of the best schools in the country as far as league tables are concerned and its status is growing every year'. This view was echoed by a local estate agent, who commented that the School went from strength to strength. In 2006 *The Financial Times*, in an article about York, reported that the success of St Peter's was driving house prices up in the area.

New regimes bring a fresh eye to an institution and change generally follows. On the academic front, drama, sports, science and Spanish were added to the curriculum, while General

Studies for the sixth form had to be dropped because of timetable pressures. The new post of Director of Drama was created in 2003, while the modern languages department benefited from the opening of the suite of Colin Shepherd Language Rooms. The school uniform, which had remained the same for many decades, was changed in 1997. Another significant departure from the past was that both Commemoration and prize-giving took place in the Minister in 2000. Although some may have had reservations about this change, in retrospect it was clearly an improvement. The opening of the Whitestone Gallery in 2003 was an important development for the Art Department. It was used to exhibit the work of both students and other artists. Of great import to securing the financial future of the School was setting up the Foundation, which started its operations in 2000. The first Foundation Scholarships were presented in 2002.

The most significant change to the long-term future of the School was the acquisition of the former Queen Anne's School building at Easter 2001 for £4.8m, financed by the sale of Alcuin and the tennis court land behind it. This development, the most important since the School's move to the Clifton site in 1844, gave more space and the chance to re-configure. The School had acquired much needed playing field space as well as extra classrooms, a large hall and an additional sports centre. The re-configuration of the campus followed. St Olave's moved to the Queen Anne site, together with the art and biology departments, while Clifton Pre-preparatory School moved into the Chilman Building. The new St Olave's was opened by the Archbishop of York in September 2001.

61

Linton Boarding House in St Peter's Grove.

Own-clothes day 2004.

The traditional links with the Minster needed to change with the times. Thus major change in the governance of the School took place when the Charity Commissioners agreed that the Dean of the Minster, who might not always be supportive of independent education, would no longer be required to chair the governing body. For a short time after this change, relations with the Minster deteriorated. The School's part in the Epiphany Service was, for example, brought to an end. This historic link has since improved with the instigation of the joint Commemoration and prize-giving ceremony in the Minster.

Fund-raising remained central to the life of the School. The Peterswalk of 1997–98 raised £14,000, the charity fun-run in 2002 £13,500. The 2004 'Peterswalk', however, had a different significance, as it was to raise funds for cancer research in memory of Peter Taylor, the Head of Classics, former housemaster of School and Dronfield Houses and Chairman of the Senior Common Room, who had tragically died in February 2004. The walk raised £16,000.

If there was any concern at this time, it was the fact that the School was becoming an exam factory, with high pressure on pupils and staff alike. In a sense, this was unavoidable and was the ultimate logic of an educational world dominated by league tables. What is remarkable, however, is the wide level of achievement in other areas of the School's life during these years. Music, drama and sport all flourished as rarely before. The under-15 XV won *The Daily Mail* rugby competition in 2002 and the same team went on to reach the final of the same competition at senior level in 2005, only to be beaten after a tense and thrilling match. The spirit of the School was clearly defined by the magnanimous way in which the 1st XV congratulated their victorious opponents and managed to hide what must have been their bitter disappointment. The success of the rowers,

collectively and individually, was formidable, with several competing at national and international levels.

St Peter's was no different from any other school in having to cope with an ever-increasing amount of bureaucracy during these years. The administrative staff grew in number from six in 1979 to 14 in 2005. As recently as 1995 the Second Master was doing work now shared by five members of staff. This was in part the result of the increasing complexity of the demands being made upon management. Vision plans, work schedules, development plans, departmental improvement plans, appraisals and risk assessments all became central to the functioning of any school. The managerial role became more pronounced. The laissez-faire days of earlier decades, when teachers were trusted professionals allowed to find their own way forward, were a dim memory. There was a growing feeling that teaching staff could not be expected to do much more than they were already doing. As one member of staff said, 'I cannot get up any earlier in the morning than I am already doing, nor can I go to bed any later'. These demands were, in the main, externally generated by national policies. Teachers, in common with public and private sector workers, were feeling increasingly besieged by the relentless barrage of initiatives, some of which were re-inventing the wheel and had been tried years before. For pupils the same trend was exemplified in the increasing numbers of examinations. British children were now the most examined in the developed world. It is too easy in this context to lose sight of education at its broadest. To reduce pupils and teachers to a set of statistics produces a deeply flawed view of education.

The increasing pace of change within the School has been a key feature in recent years. There have been more changes within the last four decades than in the previous ten. It is interesting to speculate what the position of the School will be by the end of this millennium. By the end of the Trotman era the School was probably in a stronger position, academically and in extracurricular activities, than at any time in the past and was well-placed for further advances under Richard Smyth, who was appointed Head Master in 2004. From a school roll of 376 in the senior School in 1957 to 499 in 2003, a 30 per cent increase, the numbers were clearly a reflection of the School's popularity and success. One of the other keys to success was adaptability and a sense of direction, while holding on to those values and traditions for which the School has stood over the decades. Despite these considerable successes, everyone involved in the School community realized that there was no room for complacency. The past had shown only too clearly how quickly a strong position could slip away and, once that happens, how difficult it is to re-establish ascendancy. Above all, the ethos of the School was and is a productive, happy one with good relationships at its heart.

The History of Clifton Pre-preparatory School

Greta Spaven

In 1890, Miss Gertrude Singleton, concerned by what she perceived as the lack of suitable educational facilities for the young in York, opened a small academy in Avenue Terrace. Her aim was to teach the three 'r's: reading, writing and arithmetic. The School was so successful, with such steadily increasing numbers, that she had to move to larger premises on the corner of Bootham and Queen Anne's Road.

64

Pupils largely came on foot, but some travelled a greater distance by pony and trap. As far as we know, the girls wore mid-calf-length dresses with white shirts and a bow at the neck, black-buttoned boots and stockings. In addition to the three 'r's, the girls were also taught to 'sew a fine seam', to work cross-stitch samplers, to sing, dance and play the pianoforte. These skills were designed to fit the girls for the marriage market.

At the turn of the century, Gertrude Singleton fell ill and was joined at the school by her sister Susan. The work was too much for Miss Susan Singleton to cope with and numbers began to decline until there were only about ten pupils. At this point, Miss Phyllis Meaby joined them, and under her firm hand and excellent teaching the school began to gain a reputation for providing a well-balanced education. When asked if his daughter was receiving a good education, a local farmer replied 'Ay, she is thet. They're makkin' a lady oot of ower Sarah!'

Miss Meaby was making so much of a success that she took over the running of the School in 1931 and appointed some part-time teachers to help out. The School had achieved such a reputation that it was full and even had a waiting list for places. When the Second World War broke out, the children all came to School with their gas masks but their education continued as before. On the night of 29 April 1942, a Luftwaffe raid on York saw a number of bombs dropped on the railway station, marshalling yards and carriage works. Some of the bombs missed their targets and landed on close-by areas of York, including

Miss Meaby, Headmistress 1931–63.

Clifton Preparatory School. Damage was extensive and much of the equipment was lost. Luckily, Miss Meaby had spent the night in the cellar of the house and so survived the bomb.

She was at a loss to know what to do and feared that the school might have to close. However, the Vicar of St Maurice's Church in Monkgate offered the use of a room at his house. Then, hearing of her plight and of the rather cramped schoolroom, Dr and Mrs Riddolls offered her better premises in New Earswick to tide her over for the immediate future. Miss Meaby's own recollections tell of the great kindness and help of the parents in these difficult times. Some parents helped by cooking the lunches – no mean

Judi Dench as Alice in Wonderland.

CLIFTON SCHOOL,
THE AVENUE, CLIFTON,
YORK.

Miss Meaby wishes to notify Parents that as from the beginning of the Spring Term, 1953, the following scale of School Fees will operate:—

Pupils under 5 years of age, mornings only.	£6 6s. 0d.
Pupils „ 5 „ „ „	£7 7s. 0d.
Pupils „ 6 „ „ „	£8 8s. 0d.
Pupils „ 7 „ „ „	£9 9s. 0d.
Pupils „ 8 „ „ „	£10 10s. 0d.
Pupils „ 10 „ „ „	£12 12s. 0d.
Pupils „ 12 „ „ „	£14 14s. 0d.
Pupils over 12 „ „ „	£16 16s. 0d.

The price for Lunches at School will be raised to 2s. per meal.

Miss Singleton's School 1922.

task in the days of rationing. Mr Julian Bedford, a pupil at the time, remembered the lunches being moderately appetizing. The School, fortunately, continued to flourish and maintain its reputation.

In 1943 Miss Meaby bought a large Edwardian House with a good-sized garden. 13, The Avenue, York offered good-sized rooms for the children and a flat on the top floor for Miss Meaby herself. Staff, parents and children all helped with the move. The School went from strength to strength, educating many of York's boys and girls. Dame Judi Dench, the daughter of a local doctor, started her acting career there as the Mad Hatter in 'Alice in Wonderland'.

In 1957 Miss Ruth Robinson joined the staff. Boys attended from the ages of four until eight. Many of them at this stage went on to St Olave's School and Clifton Preparatory School. 'Miss Meaby's', as it was often known, was considered an excellent preparation for the rigorous entrance examination. Most girls stayed on until the age of 11 when they took the 11+ examinations for the local grammar schools, or entrance to girls' day- or boarding schools.

By this stage the curriculum had widened to include other subjects, including French and science, to prepare the pupils for their next phase of education. Miss Robinson took over as Headmistress in 1963 on the retirement of Miss Meaby. Despite being officially retired, Miss Meaby continued to take an active interest in the School until her death many years later. Miss Robinson carried on the traditions of the School, believing that pupils should receive a good academic education, but that good manners, obedience and discipline were also an important part of a child's education.

Mrs Appleby was appointed Head in 1983 and later purchased the school from Miss Meaby and Miss Robinson. The numbers had expanded and children now occupied the rooms that had once been Miss Meaby's flat. The attic storeroom even contained her bath. One classroom contained an ancient pulley contraption, used as the fire escape before the metal one was built. The thought of the formidable figure of Miss Meaby whizzing down the rope was a source of great amusement to pupils. The top floor classrooms were often very cold and regular warming sessions had to take place in front of the gas fire. Mrs Tosdevin was known to have singed the back of her chair by sitting too close to the fire.

School plays were produced and when the Centenary Hall was built in 1990, plays could be performed on our own stage. Both the vegetable garden, that had provided fresh fruit and vegetables for school lunches, and the netball court had to be sold to help pay for the new hall, but astro-turfing the lower

66

garden gave an all-weather surface for playtime. St Peter's School allowed the use of their netball courts behind CPS and one of their playing fields for football.

With the admission of girls to St Olave's, CPS made a decision to take boys on until 11 years, preparing them for entry to Bootham School, Pocklington and St Olave's. Again CPS had moved with the times and the School's reputation meant that it continued to flourish. Mrs Appleby retired in 1993 and Mrs Anne Jackson took over as Headmistress. Mrs Jackson had hoped to buy the School, but circumstances changed and both Bootham and St Peter's became interested in securing it. Mrs Jean Greenwood was appointed Headmistress in 1994 and in 1995 Clifton Preparatory School ceased to be an independent preparatory school when it was purchased by St Peter's School, opening a new era in the School's history.

For the next two years CPS continued as before, with classes from reception up to year 6. However, the economics of running parallel years 4, 5 and 6 with St Olave's were nonsensical, so it was decided that CPS would expand on the ground floor into Alcuin (the building next door), with two parallel classes from reception to year 3. Under the headship of Mrs Greenwood numbers increased and the School flourished. Teachers took on board the national curriculum and moulded it to deliver an enhanced version to their pupils. Computers began to play an important part and soon an ICT suite was established.

In 1998 Mrs Greenwood was badly injured in a car accident and, despite her heroic efforts to return to the helm, she had to take early retirement. Mrs Arkley took over as Head Teacher in February 2001.

A new uniform was introduced in 2000 to replace the rather drab brown. Brown and blue in the kilts reflect the colours of both St Peter's and St Olave's uniforms and maintain our link with the past. The School was now ready for the biggest change since moving to 13 The Avenue in 1943.

Mrs Arkley oversaw the tremendous upheaval of the move to the Chilman Building and The Denison Building. It was a sad but necessary move as the School was bursting at the seams. Staff, pupils and parents helped us to pack up everything, causing a flurry of tidying and throwing out unwanted items of which had been in the School for a long time.

Autumn Term 2000 saw us in our new buildings, the first time many of us had taught in a purpose-built school. The space in the Chilman Building was wonderful, enabling us to allow the children greater freedom of movement and expression. The nursery was able to expand and spread out in its new premises at the Denison Building, and a wonderful activity playground has been built in the garden at the front of the School. In 2005 the name of the School was modified to Clifton Pre-preparatory School, thus distinguishing it clearly from St Olave's.

All three schools are now on the same campus. This allows much greater movement between them, whilst still allowing Clifton to retain its individuality. After over a hundred years the School maintains excellent progress.

A Brief History of St Olave's 1876–1969

The late John Mitchell

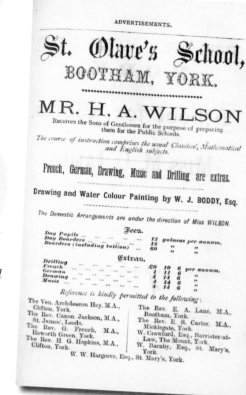

'Mr. H.A. Wilson (late one of the principals of St Martin's School) purposes taking a limited number of pupils, not under 8 years of age, to prepare them for the public schools', The Yorkshire Gazette, *6 May 1876.*

The founder of St Olave's, the Reverend Henry Andrew Wilson MA, was born in 1849. He obtained his degree at Trinity College, Dublin in 1885, becoming MA three years later. He was ordained deacon at York Minster in 1886, and priest in the following year. About 1890 he became Vicar of Rufforth, where he died suddenly on 2 August 1914.

He obviously named his new school after the double-fronted house opposite St Olave's Church in Marygate – St Olave's House can still be seen in the brickwork on the sides of the front door. Some time between January and April 1880 the school moved into Bootham. This house was also occupied by three doctors, so presumably the boys used only the ground floor. The tall redbrick house with steps was no. 38 in those days; now it is no. 50.

White's York Directory of 1895 lists the building as a 'School for Gentlemen's Sons', and also tells us that the Reverend Wilson was living next door at no.52. At that time there were 65 boys in

St Olave's House c1914.

the School, 20 of them being boarders, so presumably they lived in no. 52 with the Head Master. It also shows that he was running the School as well as being Vicar of Rufforth, and there is a suggestion that he was also acting as curate at St Paul's. About 1883 Mr A.B. Norwood joined the staff, and was eventually appointed co-Head Master.

Miss Emily Annie Wilson managed all the domestic arrangements and also taught general subjects to the younger boys, as well as music throughout. Photographs of the time show the boys wearing Eton collars, knickerbockers and sailor suits.

In 1901 Mr Norwood became principal of the Wilberforce Memorial School for the Blind, and the Reverend Wilson, by then living at Rufforth and cycling in daily for his teaching duties, decided to sell the School. The Head Master of St Peter's, the Revd E.C. Owen, entered into correspondence with Messrs Gabbitas, Thring & Co., scholastic agents, regarding the purchase, and also drew up a memorandum, giving details of the School. The goodwill was estimated at £72,000;[1] a lease of the house for £7,230 was available for seven years. In Easter 1901 there were 69 boys, their ages ranging from 4 to 16. It was proposed that in future the age limits should be fixed at a minimum of 5, and that no boys above the age of 12 were to be boarders without the consent of the Governors. Fees were £911 per annum. Eventually it was agreed that 'St Olave's being the property of the Reverend H.C. Owen, now Head Master of St Peter's, the Governors of St Peter's shall, on being empowered by the Board of Education, take over the management of it as their Prep School, purchase the furniture etc. at valuation from the Reverend H.A.Wilson, discharging such part of the cost as has been incurred by the Reverend E.C. Owen, and pay the Reverend E.C. Owen capitation fees on the boys'. (The furniture, valued at £28,900 still had not been paid for in 1903.)

In May 1908 the governors decided to take over a school on The Mount formerly run by Mr Barnes. Alcuin House, as it was known, was to be run in conjunction with St Olave's, for boys in the Tadcaster and Dringhouses area, and an Old Peterite, Mr Procter, was appointed to run it, his salary being paid by the Reverend Owen.

Also in 1908, the owner of the house in Bootham occupied by the School decided to put his premises up for sale, and negotiations began for the School to buy it. In December 1909, however, a bigger and much more suitable building with land was offered for £160,000. This was Clifton Garth, the handsome white building opposite the School, later occupied by Barclay's Bank. The Governors agreed to buy this house, and £34,700 was spent on alterations, including electric bells, fitted at the request of Miss Wilson; quite an early date for such newfangled luxuries.

Perhaps this is why in 1910 the Governors could not afford to asphalt the playground, though an iron fire escape was fitted as being essential. After sports day and a special service, the School's new home was inaugurated by Dean Purey-Cust.

The domestic arrangements were still managed by Miss Wilson. In a tape recording by the Reverend John Mann, who was a pupil there, he remarks on how strict she was. Naughty boys were forbidden to have rice mould for lunch, and if that did not cure them they had to go to a corner tuck shop, in the house now occupied by the Master of St Olave's,[2] to buy a cane to be smacked with!

In 1915 the boys of Alcuin House were moved in to Mr Procter's own house on The Mount. St Peter's bought the equipment at valuation of £1,500. The list still exists which gives an interesting outlook on schoolrooms of the times – glass inkwells, benches, gasoliers, steel fenders and fire irons but only four books! The boys wore green caps with cross keys and each Tuesday and Wednesday walked all the way from The Mount for games with the boys of St Olave's. In 1910 Mr Procter's salary was increased to £800 – a term!

St Olave's continued to flourish, and a York Directory of 1916 lists Miss Wilson as Principal. It was reported to the Governors that extension of boarding accommodation and a new form room was essential. Purchase of a house for £72,300 was agreed, and Captain Badgley was to be housemaster. The name of the

Letter home from W.H. Colley in February 1920.

house was St Helen's. The 1913 York Directory lists it as immediately next door to the Burton Stone Inn, in which case it was later renamed as St Wilfrid's and was bought on October 3rd 1919.[3] (The house next door was also in use as a sanatorium for St Peter's at one time.)

On 3 February 1920 it was announced that Miss Wilson wished to retire, and a Mr and Mrs R.O. Goolden were appointed to take charge of St Olave's. As was customary in those days, the housemaster was responsible for furnishing, cleaning, laundry and food for the boys, the school paying £400 for each boy sent to him, and if fewer than 18 were allocated, £356 compensation was to be paid for each vacancy.

On 8 February 1921, mention was made of the possible sale of St Helen's, now listed as being 16 Clifton (the houses have since been renumbered).

The following year, as 'St Wilfrid's School' was now acknowledged by the Board of Education for grants, it was recommended that it should be added to the senior school. On 27 June 1922, Colonel J.C.R. King was appointed as housemaster in place of Captain Badgley.

A new era for St Olave's began in 1922. The Gooldens had left St Olave's and Mr Goolden had become housemaster of the Manor at St Peter's. On 30 July Mr Andrew Wentworth Ping was appointed.[4] Stories are still told of this forceful character, who was to be in charge of St Olave's and have much influence over the years.

In 1925 St Wilfrid's was discontinued as a boarding house and converted into the sanatorium; the previous one at 2 St Peter's Terrace was sold for £28,500. In 1926, following advertisements for 'St Olave's Preparatory School, Ripon' (started by Reverend Wilson's son) it was agreed that the name of St Peter's Preparatory School should be changed, a suitable name to be decided on later. Fortunately this idea came to nothing.

In 1925 a lucky boy called David Foster was the proud possessor of a wireless set. The Board of Education carried out an inspection of the School, which, in those days, had a Sixth Form, the boys passing straight into St Peter's Middle School. Instead of games in March 1927, the whole school visited Rowntree's Factory and each pupil was presented with a box of chocolates on leaving.

Miss Toyne, daughter of the Head Master, joined the staff to teach French in 1930, and in March 1931 she began the St Olave's Cub Pack, with Mr Chilman beginning the Scout Troop. A proud moment must have come in July 1932 when the school entered

for the American Intelligence Test, and in one section, 'Knowledge', St Olave's was top of all the schools in both America and England. A three days' holiday for the Coronation is noted in 1937, and in 1938 the boys stood on the mound of Clifford's Tower to see the King George VI and Queen.

By that time St Olave's had moved across the road to the familiar white building, now Denison House. As will be remembered, under the old arrangements the housemasters ran the domestic side of the School on a private basis. Mr Ping had obviously been feeding his boys too well, as he was to report to the Governors that he was nearly £14,200 out of pocket each year in 1933 and 1934. The move took place in July 1935, but there was a great deal of repair work to be done. Plans were made for the Duke of York to come and open the restored building, but unfortunately the repairs took so long that eventually the royal visit was cancelled. In that year, because of the recession, the number of boarders had fallen to 15. The recession also explains why, when the previous St Olave's building came up for auction,

St Olave's Boarding House 1920.

The big freeze 1963.

70

the highest bid was £1,140. Eventually it was sold to Mr J.X. Prendergast,[5] who built the present Clifton Bingo Hall on the school yard and gardens. In our centenary year the original school bell, which was still hanging behind the bank, was presented to us, and now hangs by the steps at the end of the White Building.

Wartime conditions caused problems. Four boys who had travelled abroad for the summer holidays of 1939 could not get back, and there was an overflow of boys in the school. The day boys were having their school dinners in the sanatorium. The arctic weather and thoughts of possible invasion must have been disturbing in 1941, but the boys were kept busy, and built igloos in the snow.

In September 1941 there were 125 boys in the School, a new record. St Olave's was then divided into four houses: Trojans, Spartans, Thebans and Etruscans.

The year 1944 saw the very first separate prize-giving for St Olave's. This was held in the gymnasium (now the Alcuin Library) and the prizes were presented by Archdeacon England. In October of that year G.E.K. Reynolds, a former pupil of St Olave's and St Peter's (later a Governor of St Peter's and a Fellow) was welcomed as a member of staff before entering Cambridge. In 1945 the river was frozen, and a 20-yard slide was made. Many food items were still unobtainable, but we are surprised to learn that a grey squirrel was cooked, eaten and enjoyed! Presumably this was the influence of that well-known naturalist Mr Ping, who is also on record as shooting rabbits under the huts, and shooting a weasel in the school playground. Perhaps it was as well for the

wild life that Mr and Mrs Ping retired from St Olave's boarding house in 1955, after 24 years.

In 1946 the former Albany House was altered to become a new junior boarding house, and, in honour of Mr Ping's long service, was re-named Wentworth with Mr Blunt as its first housemaster. The winter of 1947 had been the worst and most difficult period for a quarter of a century. Wintry weather and illness caused the school to close on March 4th and not re-open until March 17th. In 1948 the return of a VIth form for exceptional pupils was instituted, and two rooms in The Rise were taken over as form rooms. By this time there were 188 pupils on the roll. The heaviest rainfall for 100 years caused all the fields to be flooded in November. *The Olavite* appeared as a separate magazine for the first time, and December brought the very first separate carol service. An air- raid shelter on The Rise lawn was converted into a form room. Shortage of room meant that the VIth form had lessons in the Tower Room of Queen's Building.

In 1950 a second boarding house, Alcuin, was opened in The Avenue. In 1952 the school reached 200 for the first time. Coronation year, 1953, saw the first separate school photograph, and each pupil was presented with a Coronation mug. In 1955 Mr and Mrs Ping's retirement ended an era.

In September 1955, Mr J. Scott Cooper, who had been on the staff since 1935 (apart from his war service) was elected to take over the reins as Master-in-Charge of St Olave's. The Houses were reorganised in 1956: Ainsty, Elmet, Alcuin, Wentworth and St Olave's.[6] A Sunday choir was formed, and no. 10, The Avenue was bought, becoming Alcuin Lodge. In 1961 the main building was extended to form ground-floor changing rooms, and new form-rooms and a laboratory were added in 1963.

A change of Master-in-Charge took place in 1964, when Mr Cooper left after nine years in charge, and was succeeded by Mr. A. Tudor Howat, formerly housemaster of School House. In 1967 there were 246 boys in the school, and Alcuin Lodge was converted into a separate boarding house known as Beverley, with John Mitchell as first housemaster. Mr Howat continued as Master-in-Charge until Easter 1969, after a period of consolidation and growth.

1. *All monetary values as of 2005.*

2. *This refers to the house occupied by the Master at the time JVM was writing, not the present Master's house.*

3. *The question of the names of St Helen's vs St Wilfrid's is extremely complicated and has not yet been properly sorted out.*

4. *The school lists of the period still refer to Mr Ping as housemaster, St Olave's (the Junior School) also included Alcuin House, with a separate housemaster and numerous dayboys. The name St Olave's appears on photos both of the House, and of the School as a whole. See also note 5 below.*

5. *Father of John Barry Prendergast, now famous as the composer John Barry.*

6. *'St Olave's' appears as a separate house in 'The Olavite' of 1956. After that date the boys transferred to Alcuin.*

The Memoirs of an Olavite in the 1930s

Guy King-Reynolds

The tumult of that September day in 1931 when I joined other eight-year-old boys entering St Olave's still echoes across the years. A few of us had come from the kindergarten of York College for Girls where, outnumbered by females in an atmosphere of latent feminism, we had been conditioned to believe that 'little boys were made from slugs and snails' whilst little girls were 'all that's nice', at least in the eyes of the mistresses. However, it was a gentle environment devoid of rowdiness and physical assault, other than perhaps the odd pinch from a spiteful little girl classmate.

A. Wentworth Ping, Master, St Olave's 1923–55.

Very different was the reception at St Olave's. After a tremulous farewell to parents, we entered the doors of what we came to know as the 'covered-in', a huge, dank, garage-like area, roofed with corrugated iron, which abutted the Clifton Green side of the main school building (now the site of the Bingo Hall), where an avenue of larger boys greeted the new 'day bugs' by using the hard peaks of their caps to rain blows on heads and shoulders. The onslaught quickly reduced the more nervous ones to whimpers, which provoked the boisterous reception committee to respond with a rhapsody of 'he's a blubber', and the first lesson was learnt: blubbing was regarded with a contempt which roused the mob like sharks in a feeding frenzy.

Rescued at last by a senior boy called Heywood, who looked like a man in short trousers to an eight-year-old, we were escorted in a kindly fashion to a poky, peg-lined cloakroom to deposit cap, coat and satchel, and from there up some steps to a large room divided into two by a heavy cloth curtain, separating the area where JI and JII were taught together, from that occupied by JIII. Almost in line with this division were three or four steps, which gave access to boys called to the Head Master's study through the heavy mahogany door leading to 'private side'. The top step also provided a platform for School assemblies, usually conducted by the Head Master, Mr Ping, who would slowly emerge from his study with a dignified limp as a spring attachment to his boot lifted a war-wounded leg. This mechanical device and his awesome, begowned figure, which commanded 'silence' in a voice which roared like a man-o'-war cannon, reminded his pupils of Captain Hook.

We were seated alphabetically in ancient rickety desks, pock-marked by the carved initials of generations of occupants, to answer a roll-call: 'Anderson, Battrick, Belchamber, Border, Buckler minimus, Calder, Goode minor, Gowland, Harrison, Platts, Powell, Pulleyn, Reynolds, Turton, Wellburn, Wright D., Wright R.A.'. Thus began five years in St Olave's.

By today's standards, it was a harsh environment where bullying was endemic and corporal punishment commonplace. The resultant sense of oppression felt by some juniors was reinforced by an attitude to sneaking, which nowadays would seem equally foreign, in that it was regarded as dishonourable and cowardly, and consequently frowned upon by the whole School, earning on occasions reprimands from the staff (even when bullying was reported) and eventual retribution from the pupils.

The boisterous and hostile greeting of new boys did not end on the first day of the new school year, but was an introduction to a hierarchy which classified them for the next twelve months as 'dirty new kids', who, by this status, merited a clip or worse from any passing older boy with a mind to it, and which was exploited by the known and feared bullies.

This established pecking order was controlled by the boarding Mafia, which influenced a boy's life outside the classroom. Thus, chivvying of some boys was not discouraged, whilst others had protection, sometimes extending to privileges such as making French toast in break-time on the coke-burning stove which provided the heat for the boarders' day-room; a wooden hut, like the dining room, both of which were attached to the rear of the main school building facing on to Clifton.

Behind this building and the neighbouring Burton Stone Inn was the large asphalt playground, bounded by a high wall and fencing running along Burton Stone Lane, where we played during morning and lunch-time breaks, and after school following the seasonal termly cycle of the main school games: soccer in the autumn, hockey in the spring (played with simple, hooked sticks provided by the School and regularly squabbled over), and cricket, French or otherwise, during the summer term.

In the midst of these scratch games, others such as various forms of 'tig', 'pirates', and hide-and-seek added to the confusion and cacophony, until one of the seasonal crazes intervened for several weeks, establishing a uniform activity within which there was keen competition to be amongst the best in execution and/or equipment. The approach of Easter heralded whips and tops, giving way to 'peggy sticks' and hoops, whilst often, the play-ground and paths would echo to shouts of 'no lifts, squares or rebounds' from competitors crouching over a game of marbles when the weather permitted. Late spring witnessed the rearing of Tansey beetles as they fattened on the eponymous leaves, as inevitably as autumn brought conkers and clay ovens to provide competition in conquest and reliability.

There was no such person as a member of staff on duty in those far-off days of the 1930s, or if there was, it was not apparent to the boys. In the distant corners of the playground, partly shrouded in shrubbery, was the 'ring' where fights took place. Fights, as opposed to 'scrapping', which was a daily occurrence and involved no more than wrestling, were more formal affairs to settle grudges or insults using fists. They were supervised by senior boys (though not monitors), to see fair play by imposing the same rules learnt in the gymnasium boxing ring: no hitting below the belt, or punching an opponent on the ground, and no kicking. They were infrequent, and rarely lasted very long; indeed sometimes they never started because the yells of the spectators brought staff speeding on the wings of pacification and retribution, which was swift and salutary for participants and onlookers.

The code of fair play, unfortunately, did not extend to bullying; the sub-culture of the pupils did not see fit to outlaw the painful 'hot toast', when skin on the wrist was twisted in opposite directions, nor the lavatorial torments of urinal shoving and WC-ducking perpetrated by the worst bullies, whose victims lived in a constant state of fear, not daring to sneak either to parents or staff.

St Olave's classroom c1920.

Equally barbaric from the perspective of today was the treatment of those unfortunate enough to forget an oak-leaf buttonhole on 29 May in celebration of King Charles II's birthday and his entry into London in 1660, which recalled his legendary sanctuary in an oak tree after his defeat at Worcester in 1651. It is said that his father, Charles I, visited the School when in York in 1642, and certainly an OP, Sir Thomas Herbert, attended the King at his execution in 1649, so there might seem a fragile cobweb of an excuse for commemorative loyalty. However, one would hope that both Stuart monarchs and Sir Thomas himself would have condemned the nettle-whipping of bare legs, by which the Olavites of the early 1930s punished those who were deemed disloyal in forgetting the anniversary. When did this painful persecution cease?

Slap, slipper and stick,
Slap, slipper and stick.
Cover your bum
With chewing gum
Slap, slipper and stick.

The chant to be heard from time to time in the rough and tumble of the playground echoed the physical approach to general discipline, both in and out of the classroom, which today would land a teacher in court and out of a job.

The Victorian axiom of 'spare the rod and spoil the child' still prevailed in the years between the wars and had yet to be reinterpreted, as the contemporary 'a child responds to spoiling rather than smacking'. Birching and the cat o'nine tails were judicial sanctions open to the courts for certain offences, and corporal punishment was regarded as a legitimate way of imposing discipline in the education of children, acceptable to parents in both state and public schools. St Peter's and St Olave's were no exception, but the writer can recall only two cases in the junior school when a pupil was removed on the grounds of alleged excessive beating.

The ladies of the staff, though zealous in reporting misdemeanours and idleness, which could lead to the slipper or stick, confined their chastisement to the use of a ruler on a held-out hand, if sufficiently provoked. The warning sign of this in Miss Weatherill was a vermilion tide which rose from somewhere

in the depths of her bosom to suffuse her cheeks. The effect was like that of the STOP glow of the new traffic lights, which were replacing the policemen on point duty at major street junctions, to the fascination of York citizens. The use of the ruler was abandoned, however, following a mishap when a miscreant jerked his hand away as the blow fell, resulting in a mishit which shattered a nearby bottle of ink, infecting Miss W, her victim and neighbouring classmates with a uniform outbreak of indigo spots.

There were few inhibitions amongst the Masters in imposing discipline. The stuff of lessons was chalk and talk; the former used, if required, as a guided missile to stem the latter, when it was out of turn or unconnected with the lesson. These two commanded attention and demanded diligence in proportion to the awe and respect in which the teacher was held. Some masters had a very physical approach to their teaching, cuffing the back of the head, tweaking an ear, or, as an ultimate refinement, pulling the short hairs of incipient side-burns while urging a pupil to 'think, boy, think!'. Much of this would be in light-hearted vein, but we were attuned to the menace in a voice which would herald a more forceful punishment, such as the slipper for a serious offence.

The slapping hand most dreaded was that of the Head Master, because, in our eyes, misguided nature had given him a palm the size of a dinner plate, fringed with five hefty pork sausages for fingers, which could span the thigh of the unfortunate miscreant lying across his knees. In this position were Latin declensions imprinted on the mind (and body!) of those idle and foolish enough not to have done their prep. The slap orchestrated a gasp and phonetic response in unison '... Mens ... Ah!'. It was only the Head Master who could cane boys guilty of more serious offences, such as bullying, lying, cheating, wilful insubordination and even bad work, when it was interpreted as the deadly sin, Sloth.

The nature and gravity of the misdeed governed the number of strokes: anything from two to six. 'Six of the best' was regarded by the School in much the same way as capital punishment. If the impending sanction was known about, there was a tension in the air as the time approached for the sentence to be carried out, and a hush descended on the community such as one read about before an execution in Armley gaol. If possible, close friends would escort the guilty one towards the steps leading to the Head Master''s study, until driven out of earshot by staff, where they would hang around waiting for their pal's return.

'How many'? Did it hurt?' were the inevitable questions when the unfortunate lad emerged to join his friends, torn between tears and pride in his short-lived, heroic, martyred status as the victim of 'Hengist' or 'Horsa', the Head Master's favourite canes.

73

The corner of the football pitch c1920.

In the best tradition of schoolmastering, Mr Ping always seemed to be about the place when not in the classroom. Stealth was not in his nature, and when he patrolled the grounds, his thunderous bonhomie as he greeted cap-raising groups of boys warned of his coming by some 50 yards. He would greet them all by name, prefaced with a 'now young ...'. If he spotted a lad who had been recently in his bad books, he would ruefully shake his ample jowls and growl, 'Oh, you wizened boy!'. Young as we were, and much as we feared him, we sensed his sincere interest in our well-being and success.

Morning school began with prayers at 8.45, taken by Mr Ping, which were followed by lessons except on alternate Mondays, when the fortnightly orders, divided into maths and science, and arts and languages, were read out by the Head Master of St Peter's. The pupils realized that it was an important occasion, because the respectfully subdued Staff had been ushered in by Mr Chilman ('Chilly') to flank the steps leading to 'private side'. There they mustered a hypnotic stare, aimed at stifling any incipient giggle or disturbance amongst the whole School, now crowded into the two classroom areas unified by the withdrawal of the separating curtain.

The heavy door opened and all shuffling ceased as the immaculately tailored Mr Toyne emerged on to the top step, followed by an unusually flustered Mr Ping, to intone, rather than to read, the class positions in reverse order. Those at or near the bottom of the forms were treated to a 'forgive-us-our-sins' tone of voice, which gradually took on a lighter and more optimistic quality as the top trio was approached. The latter received appropriate commendation before a return of the sepulchral voice detailed those who should see Mr Ping, and (in a yet deeper voice) those whose effort and work were so poor as to qualify them for an audience with Mr Toyne.

For us in the Junior School, Mr J.S. Cooper had come as a replacement for Miss Betty Toyne, who had left at the end of 1933 to prepare for her marriage. She was a popular, if no-nonsense, teacher who seemed older than her 20 years from the perspective of small boys. We knew her to be the daughter of the Head Master, so there was a certain cachet about her, which was illuminated by her teaching of French, where she would accompany her commands such as 'Ecoutez!' or 'Regardez moi!' with Gallic waving of the arms. She dressed in a revealing, white satin blouse and black skirt, which seemed naughtily foreign.

It was not regarded as any consolation to hear from the Director of Music, Mr P.H. Sykes, that he had represented the choir at the wedding reception, had much enjoyed it and had been asked to convey congratulations to members of the choir on the singing. Generally known as 'Pizzie', he was a good musician, an excellent choral master and teacher of piano and organ to individual pupils, but his success here was inversely proportional to his control of congregational practice and class teaching in school. He was a small man who wore glasses, sported a moustache and affected a pompous kind of drawl. It was rumoured that he had suffered shell-shock in the war, because of his odd lapses into a trance-like state when, with chin cupped in hand, he would lean on the piano for a couple of minutes gazing into space. Meanwhile, the bolder spirits in the class would pull faces and gesture in his direction, apparently unheeded, until he sprang to life with 'What are you doing, boy?'.

With order more or less restored, he would run through a skilful arpeggio before embarking on the vocal exercises which always preceded class singing in JI, II and III. Marching songs, sea-shanties and spirituals were the staple of our repertoire, and most of them in today's susceptibility to political correction could be interpreted as offensive for displaying chauvinistic, racially condescending or anti-feminist features. Thus we sang heartily whilst *Marching Through Georgia*, went nostalgically *Way Down Upon De Swanee Ribber*, lost money at *De Camptown Races*, fell in love with Shenandoah's daughter and worried about *The Minstrel Boy* who had gone of to a war somewhere. Of course, neither teacher nor taught had any ideas of being blood-thirsty or insulting to women and black people, and we thoroughly enjoyed the singing.

The religious and military history of York added to the formality and conservatism of the times which, for Olavites, were reflected in strict school rules, which extended to dress and deportment outside School in term-time. Uniform and caps were to be worn at all times; the latter were to be raised in greeting any known adult and removed on entering any building.

In the early years, we knew little of the world outside, preoccupied as we were with our own lives. Later our horizons expanded, but that was in St Peter's, and that's another story .

St Olave's under John Rayson 1969–90

CLIVE ROBINSON

John Rayson, OP, was appointed at the beginning of the summer term in 1967, during the interregnum of Tudor Howat. He came to St Olave's from Glenhow Prep School in Saltburn. John had always been a keen cricketer and there is a picture of him in The Peterite *being presented with a bat by Norman Yardley, OP, a former Yorkshire and England captain.*

John arrived at a time of growth and expansion. There were 246 boys in the school by 1967 and an increase in demand for boarding and day places. Alcuin Lodge was renamed Beverley House for boarders, while Fairfax was created for day-pupils.

As master-in-charge, John was always firm, fair and friendly with the pupils. He knew them all by name and made a point of teaching each first-year class once a week. John detested poor manners and slovenly dress. Woe betide the unfortunate child who passed idly by his study window, seemingly without a care in the world, tie askew, hands in pockets or socks around his ankles. A shout from a rapidly opened window would alert the transgressor to his doom and a beckoning finger would order him to the study.

It was decided that the uniform should be modernized. Long grey trousers were chosen for JV to replace the short trousers which had always looked so uncomfortable on some of the larger boys. Jackets were replaced by navy blue blazers and caps were discarded after numerous parents complained that they were always being lost. This uniform is still being worn by boy Olavites today.

In the classroom, John felt that teaching methods for the two youngest age groups had not kept abreast of educational thinking. A more thematic approach was therefore introduced. At the same time, however, the teaching of important facts and concepts within individual subjects remained. Streaming of classes was abandoned in favour of teaching the younger children in mixed ability groups. The third-form pupils (Year 6) were setted in mathematics, fifth-formers in mathematics, French and Latin. Tests came half-termly and termly, with a final examination at the end of the year. This was an arrangement that staff approved wholeheartedly and the results were a success. Apart

John Rayson, Master St Olave's 1969–90.

Sweeney Todd 1986.

76

The last of the huts 1989, prior to demolition and construction of the Chilman building.

Drama was an important part of the extracurricular programme. Productions ranged from Lionel Bart's *Oliver!* to *A Midsummer Night's Dream* and *The Thwarting of Baron Bolligrew*. Olavites also joined the senior school in Gilbert and Sullivan productions.

Outdoor activities and educational visits were central to the curriculum. John and Sally, his wife, organized an annual adventure holiday for third-form boys and the equivalent age group of girls from York College to the Cairngorms. Fell walking in the Lake District, holidays to France, ski trips abroad and a Sunday walking group twice a term, all widened horizons. On two occasions the Lyke Wake Walk and the White Rose Walk involved both parents and pupils. Visits included a tour of the Houses of Parliament with Alex Lyon, MP for York; Churchill's War Cabinet Rooms, the Imperial War Museum and even, on one occasion, Buckingham Palace, to sign the visitors' book and present the Queen's private secretary with a specially bound copy of Angelo Raine's *A History of St Peter's School*. A letter was later received saying that the Queen appreciated the gift. Two years later, in 1976, another group of Olavites visited the Palace to present the Queen with a silver sweet dish, with the words 'St Olave's School, York, 1876–1976' engraved on it.

In 1971 St Olave's took part in the celebrations to commemorate the 1900th anniversary of the city's foundation. The Lord Mayor's show included school floats, depicting incidents from the long history of St Peter's, which won the trophy for the best overall entry in the parade.

Music, too, was central to the life of St Olave's. In the late 1970s four pupils were invited to play in the National Youth Orchestra. The chapel choir was admitted as a member of the St Nicholas Guild of the Royal School of Music in 1980. Staff, parents and friends joined the choir on occasions, to give concerts in parish churches or sing Evensong in York Minster.

Attitudes towards boarding had begun to change by the early 1980s, especially at junior level. Some parents, understandably, wanted their children home for weekends, while others were prepared to drive long distances each day rather than pay boarding fees. At St Olave's, it was a priority that boarding houses should be manned by house tutors with families. This was popular with parents and, whilst other schools were shutting down their

from a few minor differences, this resembles the national curriculum today with its key stages, attainment targets and SATS.

Games played a central position in the curriculum. Specialist games staff were employed and pitches were deployed in a more constructive manner: instead of the whole School having games on Tuesdays and Thursdays, juniors and seniors had games timetabled on different days of the week. This made better use of staff and facilities. John's enthusiasm for sport encouraged success in the School cricket and rugby teams. With the arrival of girls the netball, rounders and hockey teams also had several years of successes.

The art room.

boarding accommodation, St Olave's managed to arrest the decline, but not before Alcuin House, which had functioned as a boarding House for thirty years, unfortunately had to close in 1981. This left Beverley and Wentworth as the two surviving boarding houses. Beverley was converted into a girls' boarding house in 1987. It is a great tribute to the way the School was functioning at that time, that the integration of girls into the School posed few, if any, problems. It is difficult to see how we ever did without them.

Eating arrangements came under scrutiny in the late 1980s. The kitchens in the White House were closed and day-pupils joined the cafeteria system in the senior school. For a while longer, boarders continued to eat in the White House, with the food brought across in the electric truck in insulated containers. Eventually, this system was ended too and boarders ate in the senior school dining room.

In 1989 the temporary wooden huts were demolished. They were replaced by the Chilman Building in 1990. Staff were consulted on the requirements for the new building and many of their ideas were adopted by the governing body. The result was a teaching block with large and airy classrooms, a state-of-the-art computer room, a library, vast display areas, a multipurpose room for music, drama and art, now known as the Rayson Room, a new science laboratory and a staff room. It was the envy of many visiting teachers and regarded with admiration by prospective parents. It was opened in July 1990 by Mr Chilman and accommodated the children in the first three year groups.

When John retired in 1990, he left St Olave's with an enviable reputation in York, the north and even abroad. He left a school with willing, enthusiastic pupils and a staff with high morale. St Olave's was a happy, purposeful school under John's leadership. His achievement had been considerable.

St Olave's School 1990–2005

TREVOR MULRYNE

Since 1876 St Olave's has followed a pattern of national preparatory school education, but with its own particular characteristics and qualities. It has gone through the stages of independence, of independent attachment, of total integration with St Peter's until, by 1990, it enjoyed the status of affiliation to the Incorporated Association of Preparatory Schools (IAPS). It has also had remarkably few Masters (also known as Head Masters and Masters-in-Charge). During the period 1990–2005 it has benefited from a boom in independent education as a whole and the increasing standing and regard for St Peter's in the wider community.

The era of co-education at St Olave's had been in existence for only three years by 1990, and it would be true to say that there remained much work to be done to improve the opportunities and provisions for girls. Girls were barely 30 per cent of the school population and some classes had few girls in lessons. Simple things such as a door being labelled 'Masters' Common Room', or notice boards carrying the titles of Games on one side and 'Girls' Games' on the other, showed that there were some entrenched attitudes that only time would alter. By 2005 this ethos had disappeared and St Olave's had become a genuinely co-educational school.

By 1990 there were 300 pupils in the School. Despite many attempts to alter the nomenclature of J1–J5 (Junior 1 to Junior 5) to denote the year groups, it has remained unaltered and the majority of Olavites have continued to transfer to St Peter's. Attempts were made to decide on the ideal size of school. Between 1990 and 2005 this number varied between 275 and 360. The move to the new site enabled the expansion of numbers and this increase led to the creation of a three-form entry at J1 and five classes at times in J4 and J5.

The Chilman Building quickly proved a great asset to the School. York is a popular venue for conferences of all kinds and St Olave's, with its excellent facilities, soon became the host school for several important national conferences and in-service training sessions for prep-school teachers.

The acquisition of more space and increased specialist facilities enabled a greater separation of teaching resources from St Peter's. Within a few years, virtually all subject-specific teaching was done by St Olave's staff alone. This allowed an expansion of subjects. Three sciences were taught in St Olave's labs and German (and later Spanish) joined French. Information Technology was established as a separate department. Personal, Social and Health Education, as well as Design Technology, were also introduced. The appointment of a Director of Studies helped these developments.

This was also a time of great pressure on entry to the School. It was not unusual in the early 1990s to have between three and five applicants for every place available. Ten or more prospective families could be visiting the School in any week in the autumn and summer terms and it was always a great sadness to refuse entry to worthy children, occasionally with important family connections to St Peter's. Nevertheless, physical restraints meant that there was a maximum number of places available, and the need to plan the size of the School was paramount. St Peter's rarely refused entry to an Olavite, so there was a maximum number who could transfer at age 13.

In 2001 the most significant expansion of the School took place since the move of St Peter's to the Clifton site. The City Council closed Queen Anne's Comprehensive School in 2000. It lay empty for a year whilst a decision about its future use was reached. Educational bodies for secondary and higher education, together with a range of commercial and health-

St Olave's School main block – originally Queen Anne Grammar School.

related groups within York, showed interest in acquiring the site. A bid by the Governors of St Peter's was accepted initially, but was rescinded due to a technicality and the offer to acquire was reopened. Once again, detailed bids were called and several public meetings took place involving the wider community in the area. Eventually the St Peter's bid was accepted and it was decided to move St Olave's in its entirety to the new site to open in 2001. Detailed plans for the provision, not only of classrooms, but two halls, a music school, two fully equipped science labs, a drama theatre, two food technology labs, a design technology and art centre, and an information technology room were completed. The refurbishment and decoration were the next priorities. Without doubt this was a major opportunity for the school. There are few prep schools in the country which can match the facilities of St Olave's

The original Queen Anne School had been opened officially by the then Archbishop of York. The Very Reverend Dr David Hope was invited to perform an opening ceremony for the new school. A service of 'beating the bounds' was devised by the St Olave's Chaplain, the Reverend Allan Hughes, and the Archbishop toured the four corners of the site, meeting pupils and staff and praying for the well-being of the school and its future.

During this period other significant additions were made. Despite a steady decline in prep-school-age boarding, the numbers at St Olave's remained at a satisfactory level. Beverley House, the girls' boarding house under Mr and Mrs Kevin

Sargeant (who took over from Mr and Mrs Clive Robinson, the first girls' houseparents), was neither well located nor sufficiently well appointed. The Governors, therefore, took the brave decision to extend Wentworth and bring all boarders, boys and girls, under one roof and one housemaster. Thus John and Jackie Slingsby ran a house of up to 50 pupils, with the girls' wing newly constructed. It was opened by HRH Prince Andrew, the Duke of York, in a memorable ceremony, and has remained a full House.

Sport has always been a major part of both St Olave's and St Peter's. Three victories in ten years at the National Schools' Sevens at Rosslyn Park was remarkable. Under John Slingsby the School had a formidable record in rugby football. In 1995 the team took a tour to Australia and had regular tours in Ireland.

80

The girls' sporting achievements were also worthy of much praise; our girls were regular winners at both regional and national level in hockey, netball, swimming, athletics and tennis. Both boys' and girls' swimming was outstanding, as was cricket and latterly hockey. Judo, fencing, shooting, badminton, skiing and a host of other sporting opportunities were enjoyed by boys and girls.

Music and drama, especially since the move to the new site, have received much high praise for the quality and the volume of work produced. Art, which enjoys such a high profile at St Peter's, has its beginnings at St Olave's, where outstanding work has been evident. Academic work, the backbone of the school, is, of course, hugely important and the quality of teaching and teachers have played a part in public examination successes later achieved at St Peter's. St Olave's has been characterized often as a place of demanding academic standards. Few of its pupils, however, would ever have claimed to be other than stimulated and challenged by its demands.

Grandparents' days, whole-school walks at Castle Howard or in the countryside nearby, two adventure camps where the whole School, children and staff, decamped to the shores of Lake Windermere, skiing holidays, exchange trips to France and Germany, a pupil exchange with two schools in South Africa, visits for groups as far away as France and Pompeii, a staff pantomime, talent shows and a great deal else have given an added dimension to the pupils' lives. A hugely energetic Parents' Association has organized a host of activities for parents and children, including the annual school fête, which raised thousands of pounds for charity. Latterly Mr Andrew Cannons undertook massive fund-and-equipment-raising activities for a province in Bosnia much ravaged by internal strife. The School never seemed to be still and it was rare for a pupil not to be involved in some kind of activity beyond the classroom.

Three Head Masters have kept a benign and generous oversight of St Olave's in this period. Robin Pittman, Andrew Trotman and Richard Smyth have been always greatly supportive of all that has happened in the School. So, too, have the Board of Governors under three chairmen: John Southgate, Teddy Denison and Murray Naylor, who have never failed to recognize the value of the junior school. The success of the School is also a reflection of the hard work and commitment of the staff. St Olave's would not be the school it is today without that dedication.

Academic Perspectives: Change and Continuity

The last 30 years have seen an accelerating pace of change in education. Reform seems to have followed reform at mind-numbing speed. Central to these changes has been a growing accountablity of teachers, heads and governors. Appraisals, inspections, league tables, value-added and base-line testing are all here to stay – until the next set of changes. From the pupil's perception, one exam follows hard on the heels of another.

The improvement in the school's exam results is at the centre of its recent achievements. In 1998, 34.9 per cent of A-level candidates achieved grade A. By 2005 this figure had risen to 62.8 per cent of sixth-formers. In 1998, 57.3 per cent achieved grades A or B at A-level, whereas by 2005 the comparable figure was 84.4 per cent. It is these statistics which have secured the school a place in the first division of the national league tables. The improvement at GCSE is also remarkable. In 1998, 30.5 per cent achieved A*, while 64.5 per cent achieved A* or A. The comparable figures for 2005 were: 42.8 per cent achieved A* and 73.3 per cent gained either A* or A. These results are a tribute to the hard work of Peterites and teachers alike.

Subject disciplines have changed markedly in both content and assessment in recent times and permanent revolution would indeed be an accurate description of recent years.

Exam in the Big Hall c1950.

BUSINESS STUDIES

Business Studies is a relative newcomer to the curriculum and dates back to the late 1970s. As post-16 numbers increased and the failings of some of the alternative subjects became ever more apparent, it was obvious that a subject that could be used in the wider world would rapidly gain ground. The growing importance of marketing, advertising and human resources all provided a rich vein to tap. Pupils could see the relevance of the subject and enjoyed its case-study approach to assessment.

The explosion in higher education business courses at the new universities all provided access to the vast majority of pupils wishing to take the subject beyond A-level. From a school's point of view the subject is ideal: modern, relevant, not reliant upon a mathematical basis nor any set entry requirement. It provides an opportunity for many pupils to make a new start at the age of sixteen and perhaps provide that spark of interest in the education system. In addition, the government's policy of a 50 per cent access rate to higher education has provided a ready market for business studies.

Andrew Severn

THE CLASSICS DEPARTMENT

Changes in this subject have been large, even within the last 30 years. Latin and Greek were once regarded as a necessary staple of British education; the advent of the national curriculum has come closer to killing off the subject than anything else in the last 2000 years. During the 1980s, classics was in real danger of becoming side-streamed at best, or else restricted to those enjoying a university education. Nevertheless, the

Peter Croft, Head of Classics, Housemaster of Temple and latterly Second Master 1980–88.

subject remains reasonably healthy, uptake is increasing (both nationally and within St Peter's), and a large number of pupils continues to leave St Peter's to study some form of classical studies at university.

As regards Latin, a sweeping change in the classroom has been the widespread use of the Cambridge Latin Course. This is a pupil-friendly course book, which teaches something of the civilization alongside the language, and includes a story line which actively encourages pupils to become involved.

Meanwhile, the introduction of classical civilization, an area of study that barely existed in schools 15–20 years ago, has given new life to the discipline. The numbers doing classical civilization both at GCSE and at A level remain very strong. Classical Greek hangs on by its fingertips in those schools that do teach the subject. At St Peter's we reckon to have one or two pupils each year studying, off timetable, for GCSE or AS level. The very real reward is that those who choose the subject are not only bright, but also exceedingly committed. National Greek summer schools help and there are more of them springing up each year.

Matthew Adams

ECONOMICS

Economics, the so-called 'dismal science', exploded onto the curriculum in the late 1960s. The rapid expansion of post 16 education created a huge potential market for subjects that could be offered to prospective A-level students who wanted a change from the traditional academic curriculum that was on offer at the time.

Teaching methods were very traditional. Assessment invariably followed the standard essay approach, emphasizing both knowledge and analysis, but with little in the way of real-life application and certainly no evaluation of policy issues. As exam boards were dominated by university lecturers, the subject increasingly used mathematics as a foundation to many non-essay questions. For those pupils who had both essay and mathematical skills this subject was perfect. For others, however, this approach reduced its appeal.

Fortunately, a new wave of thinking grew out of this malaise. Today the subject is relevant and topical. The result has been an arrest in the decline of the subject and indeed a growth. The role of the media, in highlighting issues such as the oil crisis, global warming and public spending on the NHS, has enabled the economics students to have a huge range of material from which to widen their knowledge. The removal of maths from the subject at A level is a mixed blessing. For those who dislike maths the subject is clearly more accessible, and yet it does fail to recognize that, at university, mathematics is fundamental to the study of the subject. Economics may also be helped by the fact that many of the top universities now cast doubt upon the merits of some of the other newer subjects, while Economics as an A level is highly regarded.

Andrew Severn

ENGLISH

Anyone who tells us that examinations are easier in 2006 than they were in 1976 may not be aware of all of the changes to the curriculum and the examination process during the last few years. Just as a greater number of pupils may appear to be scoring a greater number of higher grades, so are there a greater number of assessment objectives against which a pupil (and teacher's) performance must be measured.

To begin at the beginning, there was, and has always been, a text at the heart of the study of English Literature. Where once, however, all examinations would have been closed-text affairs, recent times have seen the introduction of annotated texts, and more recently un-annotated texts, into the examination hall. Easier to teach, then? I shouldn't say so; the pressures on the pupils are equally intense. Coursework must relax the burden on external markers, we hear? Perhaps, but not on internal markers in the English department, upon whose shoulders the burden of outing the internet plagiarists most squarely falls.

Yet English is a great deal of fun. New forms of media have lent a new edge to a well-established subject, and information technology plays an important part in breathing new life into, say, medieval and renaissance texts. Speaking and listening is presently assessed at GCSE level, and allows pupils to gain confidence in informal and formal oratory forums. Creative writing and practical drama play even more of a part in reading and learning than was the case 30 years ago, and give rise to some magnificent works of inspired imagination from pupils.

The facts that pupils are constantly changing and that poetry, prose and drama are at the heart of our subject are immutable. Any other whim of the examination boards or QCA will be tolerable, so long as the text and child remain central to our concerns.

David Brown

GEOGRAPHY

Within the department the stress on learning detailed material about countries (originally called regional geography) and topics such as farming in New Zealand has, over the last 20 years, seen a significant shift towards the explicit teaching of thinking skills such as the use of mnemonics, classifying and arguing effectively. There has also been a noticeable shift from studying the differences between countries, towns and places to a consideration of the key processes at work at the global, national and local scales. These processes have allowed teaching to focus on the real world and on the daily lives of those we teach.

The most recent focus, originating from the Rio Earth Summit Conference on sustainability, has thrust the Geography course back into the real issues impacting on individuals and on the planet. This has meant examining our individual ecological footprint, which requires an investigation into the way we live in

terms of car use and waste recycling on the local scale. On the global scale, issues such as the increase in temperatures and the rise of the sea level need to be studied.

Within the classroom, using the internet is now possible and it has had a significant impact. Students can now access global satellite images and make use of GIS systems that allow patterns such as local crime and the impact of flooding in York to be seen in real time. These can then be analysed and discussed and practical ways put forward to deal with such problems.

In many ways the subject has gone from description to prediction, from delivering content to exploring and seeking ways to act in the real world on processes and patterns discovered. However at the heart of all teaching lies the need to care for, inspire and motivate those who sit where their parents have sat in years past. The next generation of geographers will, we hope, have a real impact on the way they live their lives and on the life of the planet.

Derek Paterson

GOVERNMENT AND POLITICS

Prior to the purchase of the Queen Anne campus, the history of the politics department had been a nomadic one. Since the conception of the subject, as the constitution, under John Rigby, politics had been taught in various corners of the school. It now resides in what had been School House accommodation until the

The main change for history has been the move away from a content-based to a skills-based approach. The syllabuses on offer from the exam boards (especially at A/S and A2 levels) mean that there is a tendency to study narrow periods of the subject rather than to pursue a broad linear approach. The result has been that the subject has become somewhat fragmented with pupils losing an overall sense of narrative.

The World History course at GCSE, which covers some of the main historical developments of the last century, has been especially popular with pupils. Topics like the First World War, the USA 1918–39, Weimar and Nazi Germany, the Cold War, the Cuban missile crisis and the Vietnam War have all been enjoyed by pupils whose understanding of the century has deepened. However, the problem with the course is that it gives only a partial view of the century. Much has had to be omitted because of time constraints. Another justified criticism of the course is that it does not include enough British history.

Another major change has been the advent of coursework at both GCSE and A-level. This has enabled pupils to carry out research in areas of the subject which especially interest them. The wide range of topics chosen for coursework is testament to the inherent interest in the subject.

There is a constant debate at a national level on the role and importance of history in helping pupils understand their national identity as well as wider international issues. The UK is one of the few countries which allows pupils to discontinue the subject at the age of 14. This must change if pupils are to acquire a better understanding of their own culture and global trends.

Richard Drysdale

ICT

St Peter's began its embrace of computer technology in the mid-1980s, with the purchase of the first BBC Microcomputers. Not long after that, a dedicated computer suite was established in the new science building, with a file server and 16 networked computers. At that time, computer specifications were low and high-end equipment was prohibitively expensive. Since 1994 equipment costs have plummeted and the pace of growth has been unstoppable. Today the school is networked throughout with fibre-optic cable connecting one building to the next. Wiring within each building connects to individual computer access points. Resources and services of the school network are delivered by seven servers housed in the new science building.

There are now more than 400 computers in all three schools. Many are organized into computer suites with clusters of computers throughout the School. Each boarding house a has dedicated room with a number of computers and all day-houses and subject areas enjoy some provision. Computers are, in short, at the centre of the school community.

85

1990s. The four classrooms were named, in the spirit of non-partisanship, after then-serving local MPs: Greenway, Willis, McIntosh and Bayley, the latter officially opening the suite after our own version of Question Time in May 2003.

Over the years, the numbers of pupils studying politics at St Peter's has increased, contra to the national trend. The advent of AS and A2 study and the need for four subjects in the lower sixth caused another explosion. The subject content has remained constant, with UK politics studied in the first year and the ever-popular American politics in the second. The arrival of Robert Mathis in November 2006, a Fulbright Exchange Scholar from Walt Whitman School in Bethesda, Maryland, stimulated that interest further.

In an age when political apathy amongst young adults is well-documented, Peterites remain interested and open-minded, as demonstrated by the surprise win of the Green Party candidate in our 2005 mock election.

Paul Taylor

HISTORY

The department has always believed in giving the broadest possible education. The subject encapsulates economics, politics, sociology, philosophy, ethics, culture and conflict amongst many other strands. There is, in short, something that appeals to everyone in the nature of the subject.

The carpentry room c1920.

Students in the first two years at St Peter's follow a course leading to a qualification which credits their basic competence in computer skills. After that, much of what they learn is either on their own or in the context of their other subjects.

St Peter's is on the verge of moving away from wired to wireless networking. For some time students have brought their own laptops to school and used them in lessons. The trend is towards more mobile, accessible technology. The school will shortly be introducing a laptop scheme, whereby students can equip themselves and make full use of the technology. Soon, streaming media for on-demand delivery of film and audio over the network, virtual learning environments in which teaching materials are delivered via an intranet or over the internet, as well as greater accessibility to information and resources by students from home, will all be available.

St Peter's has never been shy of looking forward, but it maintains a balanced view of the ways in which it should adopt technology. Technological developments are examined and the experiences of other schools are also considered. However, there can be no doubt ICT will remain at the heart of the School's development in the third millennium

Mike Jones

MATHS

Mathematics in the sixth form continues to be one of the most popular choices for St Peter's students. There have been a number of recent changes to the structure and content of the course. Curriculum 2000 created significant difficulties for the government. Nationally, A/S failure rates for mathematics were higher than any of the other 31 subjects and uptake for A-level maths throughout the country reduced dramatically. This resulted in serious implications for employers and some university departments had to be closed. St Peter's bucked this

national trend, with increasing numbers of pupils choosing to study Maths in the sixth form.

There have also been developments at GCSE. The present three-tier entry, consisting of higher, intermediate and foundation level, is being replaced by a two tier system. In 2007 some St Peter's students will be sitting the International GCSE, an exciting new development for the department. Future changes due to take place nationally include a Functional Maths qualification to be taken in addition to GCSE and the introduction of a Further Maths GCSE.

Notable individual pupil successes at various levels have included those by Shuo Shang, Daniel Lightwing, Peter Rowley and Charlie Strickland-Constable; teams from both St Peter's and St Olave's have performed at very high levels in the UK Mathematics Trust Team Challenges In 2004, whilst still at school, Charlie Strickland-Constable had an article published in *The Mathematical Gazette*. He has since had a second article published. The magazine is one of the world's leading journals in its field.

David Spencer

MODERN LANGUAGES

New language, new trips, new rooms, new staff, new technology, new exams – the last few years have been nothing if not 'new'. Spanish was introduced into St Olave's in 1999 and this year's upper sixth group is the first to be taking their A-level exam in the subject. It has proved to be popular and has greatly increased the number of pupils taking two languages to a high level.

More pupils mean more rooms and recent visitors to the school will have seen the Colin Shepherd Language Rooms occupying the former Room M and Harvey Lab. The lowered ceilings and improved lighting create two very pleasant classrooms to join those in the Grove Block, fully kitted out with portable language labs and computer clusters in each room. How did we ever cope without the Internet?

The new A/S exam in the lower sixth is certainly controversial. A system which allows pupils to resit an exam a year later, as far as a modern language is concerned, is odd. Language skills improve the more language one does and so pupils sit their exams in the LVI, knowing they can retake them a year later without penalty and achieve a higher mark towards their A2. I cannot help but hope that there will be changes to come.

Clive Hodsdon

MUSIC

Academic music teaching for GCSE and A level has changed dramatically in the last 20 years. Neither popular music nor jazz were part of the syllabuses then. Today, music covers a wide range

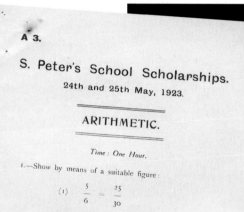

of types from Mozart to Miles Davis and from Fusion to Bhangra. This has widened the appeal of the subject and made it more accessible for pupils. Music computer programmes have made it possible for pupils to listen to their compositions as they write. In this way they can add or subtract parts quickly and easily. The emphasis in the subject now is on playing, composing and listening.

Andrew Wright

PHILOSOPHY AND RELIGIOUS STUDIES

The Department of Philosophy and Religious Studies seeks to encourage the academic study of the phenomenology and ethics of Christianity, as both an historical and a contemporary faith, and of the philosophical traditions which have contributed to Christian theology.

Its organization has changed little over the last decade, with one part-time member of staff sharing with the Chaplain the teaching of the middle school, where RS is a compulsory GCSE, and the teaching of the sixth-form A-level course. Its location, however, has changed dramatically, from two of the oldest rooms in the School, on either side of the Memorial Hall, to a subject

suite of three rooms in the Queen's Building, a move made possible by the relocation of St Olave's into the former Queen Anne School.

The subject content has developed as changes at national level have allowed or demanded. In 2005 the fifth form was the first to be entered for a GCSE assessment that avoided coursework. Coursework had become of no educational benefit to the pupils and an administrative burden to the staff. Instead, a further examination was taken in the image of religion in the media and Christian attitudes to the media, sport and entertainment. This is of some educational value and can be fun to teach. At sixth-form level the national changeover to the A/S and A2 system in 2000 demanded a shift from a heady mix of doctrine, Bible and ethics units to a streamlined course in the philosophy of religion and religious ethics. Echoing the national statistics, which place this kind of course as one of spectacularly increasing popularity, numbers taking the subject at AS level have since doubled in the School. To mark the change, the department began to include the word 'philosophy' in its title from 2000. The course is distinctively different from GCSE, appeals to a wide range of pupils and demands hard thinking. It can be stimulating to teach and gives RS a healthy and contemporary 21st-century face.

Jeffrey Daly

The old Chemistry Lab.

The Sciences

Until the start of last century, science at St Peter's had little resemblance to the science teaching of today. The School had a chemistry laboratory, which was a shed on the site of the old fives court and little else. The science taught could be best be described as natural history.

The School Governors decided that purpose-built science laboratories were required and in 1903, what is now commonly called the 'old science block' was opened by Professor Clifford Allbutt OP. In his address, Professor Allbutt said 'The object is not to make the boys scientific experts, or to start them on careers as such, but the laboratories are to be part of a liberal education'.

In fact the old science block was built in two stages, 50 years apart. In 1903 the building had a physics laboratory, store room, dark room for photography, a workshop and an advanced science classroom on the ground floor, and a chemistry laboratory, lecture theatre and a store on the upper floor. The chemistry laboratory (the Priestley Laboratory) was hardly upgraded until it had a complete refurbishment in the summer of 2006. The extension, completed in 1955, created an additional chemistry and physics laboratory and a biology laboratory.

For many years biology was the poor relation of the three sciences. The boys were required to take O-levels in chemistry and physics, but biology was not even offered as an O-level until the early 1970s. General science was available to those not suited to the O-levels. chemistry and physics to O-level remained the requirement for students and it was not until about 1990 that students were allowed to choose between the three sciences, with the advice that they should choose at least two sciences for GCSE.

In 1995 the School made the significant decision that all students would have a balanced science education, and would therefore study biology, chemistry and physics to GCSE level. After considerable research and discussion it was decided that all

St Peter's Natural History Society 1913 with Sam Toyne in the centre.

students would take the Dual Award examination, in which the three subjects were studied separately and taught by specialists, but that the examination would be worth two GCSE grades. This bold decision, not without criticism, has proved highly successful.

The demand for laboratory space was ever increasing and the acquisition of the old Queen Anne School meant that, in September 2002, the biology department moved to the top floor of C block in a suite of completely re-furbished laboratories, opened by Professor Richard Dawkins FRS. Physics and chemistry then took over the biology laboratories on the St Peter's site, giving each of the sciences at least four large teaching rooms.

As a relatively young science, biology has been subject to dramatic change and this has resulted in an almost permanent state of flux in the nature of the sixth-form course. Much of the traditional material, including botany, classification and dissection work, has been removed from the teaching syllabuses to be replaced with more modern topics, which include genetic modification, DNA technology and human health issues. The department makes much use of practical work, including microscopy (often enhanced by the use of video cameras, which can project a specimen for a whole class using just one microscope), enzyme analysis and some breeding experiments (with fruit flies). Fieldwork is used in GCSE and A-level teaching, with the oldest pupils required to follow a three-day residential course on which they complete individual projects in either woodland or fresh water ecology. Computers are well used by pupils in the completion of these projects, but the technology is also used extensively in teaching, with numerous presentations given at all levels of the school. It is also be used for modelling experiments and abstract pieces of theory.

The physics syllabus has remained fairly traditional, although there has been quite a large fall in content. An exciting development has been the study of atomic and particle physics as the option in the A2 course.

Each year students are entered for national physics competitions: the Physics Challenge at GCSE and the Physics Olympiad at A-level. In 1996 Paul Best came 6th in Britain and in 2004 Charlie Strickland-Constable was the highest scoring student in Britain and represented Britain in the International Physics Olympiad held in Pohang, South Korea. The department was also proud and honoured to receive ten out of the last 18 Certificates of Excellence to be awarded by the Oxford and Cambridge Examination Board to the top three A-level students. In recent years the department has celebrated the Transit of Venus and held an Einstein Week to promote its subject in the community.

The introduction of Nuffield Chemistry had a dramatic effect. Chemistry was no longer a series of facts, but was taught through investigation, with students developing chemical ideas from what was seen. All examination boards took on the

Professor Dawkins opens the new Biology Department 2002.

Nuffield ideas and this is reflected in the amount of practical work that the students now undertake. The use of multi-media techniques mean that students can now see animations at an atomic level; this brings to life the once difficult concepts which permeate chemistry.

The Science Society which flourishes today has its origins in the old Natural History Society, founded in 1903, and renamed the Science Society in 1913. Like many school societies it has met intermittently over the years. In its present form it was re-established in the 1980s, when speakers of note addressed meetings. In 1988 the Society, with support from the CDT department, decided to hold an 'egg race' competition, along the lines of the BBC television programme. This proved to be a great success and an annual competition has been held since. In recent years the Society has held a Christmas lecture demonstration, where members of the three science departments contribute to a lecture on a particular theme. These lectures are hugely popular and reflect the talent that the faculty has in its staff.

Peter Northfield

89

The Egg Race 2000.

Physics creates new hairstyles.

Boarding 1969–2001

Although there are more day-pupils at St Peter's than boarders, the ethos of the school is predominantly that of a boarding school, even if this has moderated over the last few years. The role of housemasters' wives in the successful running of boarding houses has rarely received the recognition it deserves. There is no doubt that a successful boarding house is the result of teamwork between the housemaster and his wife.

GUY SHUTTLEWORTH, HOUSEMASTER OF THE MANOR 1969–81.

Within a fortnight of arriving, we were in the throes of the flu epidemic and within a short time the whole of School House had become the overflow for the Sanatorium. I became involved in serving breakfasts in dormitories as well as teaching. It was in this way that I managed to get to know many of the boys and also Mrs Dronfield. She was a tower of strength and her commitment to the life of the School was remarkable. The flu epidemic gave me an insight into the School's excellent corporate spirit.

In the boarding houses everybody slept in a dormitory with a monitor in charge. Lights were put out between 9.15 and 10pm depending on age. All doors were left open until 10pm. Windows were not locked until lights-out. The doors to the housemaster and the assistant were never locked. There was a common room for each of the juniors and junior middles, two common rooms for the senior middles. The sixth-formers shared studies, except the head of house, who had his own study. Juniors and junior middles did prep in school under a house monitor from 6.30 until 8 pm. This was followed by house prayers and house notices for the whole house. Nobody was allowed out of the house without a master's permission.

By 1981, when I retired from the house, many changes had been made. Fire doors and escapes were in place. Security was tightened. The number in the house had risen to 70 and this included four girls, who lived as day-girls but boarded elsewhere. Fagging had been abolished. The copy system was still in operation and was used for dealing with minor offences by the monitors, which included noise after lights out, hands in pockets, dirty shoes, wrong clothes and bad behaviour in the corridors or dining hall. More serious offences were dealt with by the masters.

Probably one of the most positive sides of life in The Manor was the development of house activities, some of which included the whole school. Some of the activities that took place included saving silver paper to collect £290 for a guide dog for the blind, working for life-saving awards in the evening, a sponsored swim for Shelter, a school dance for the British Diabetic Association, a Christmas house party for MS sufferers where we entertained 90 guests with games, charades, carol-singing and a supper, and house plays, which involved over half the house, directed by the house monitors. The Manor was also always well to the fore in all the School charity events.

Probably some of the best remembered activities were the Christmas parties and pancake evenings, when individuals tossed their own pancakes. The parties included the parents, who produced all the food. Each year-group contributed some act or game around the house. One year the highlight was a beauty contest of the monitors. Another memorable occasion was when about 50 pupils from the School for the Deaf in Boston Spa came to the Christmas party and mixed with members of the house to take part in an 'It's a Knockout' competition. Only sign language was necessary.

KEITH COULTHARD, HOUSEMASTER OF DRONFIELD 1964–81.

When we opened Dronfield House in September 1964, only the first-year members were new entrants to the School, the main body being drawn from the other boarding houses. This meant

View of St Peter's School from the York Wheel.

that we were inheriting an interesting mix of what were loosely called 'traditions'. What we did not realize was the amount of pupil scheming which had gone into the selection of pupils to transfer. Apparently, most of the leading senior games players of the School had offered to transfer and the result was that we seemed to carry all before us in a wide range of sports for the first two years of our existence.

One evening, after the house had been locked for the night, there was a ring at the door-bell. Outside the door was a small group of seniors, led by a strapping member of the School 1st XV. He was very fair-skinned and blushed very easily. Obviously they had found their re-entry into the house barred (I can't think how), and hence the ring at the door. Blushing vividly, the spokesman of the group brought his hand from behind his back and showed a two-fingered pack of Kit-Kat, and said, 'I felt hungry and slipped out to buy this'. One wonders how much of the chocolate each of them would have had.

JOHN BULCOCK, HOUSEMASTER OF TEMPLE, 1980–84, AND THE MANOR, 1984–94.

The day we moved into The Manor the School footbridge was demolished by a load too high; the first evening on duty my study window was shattered by a stone; the second evening 15 boys were caught smoking in the house at 11.45pm. Shortly afterwards I discovered the convenient hole in the front hedge which allowed easy access to the public house and, in the cellar, a vat primed for brewing. Our neighbour was complaining about the number of bottles which had been lobbed over the wall and through his greenhouse during the previous summer term, and he subsequently delivered to the Head Master's study a bin-bag of cigarette ends. Cash was being stolen from the house telephone box, and mail was not safe. Something was clearly amiss in The

Manor, and we understood why the thriving house of 70 boys and girls which Guy and Tan Shuttleworth had handed over in 1981 had slipped, by some 33 per cent, to the 43 which we inherited in 1984. There was a struggle ahead, and I almost lost heart in those early days.

My wife Anne quickly became fully involved; her cheerful presence and her understanding of the needs of a boarding community, of which her own children had once been a part, qualified her uniquely. Memorably, each Shrove Tuesday of our tenure she produced over 100 pancakes; boys queued and ate continuously and every door-handle in the house (it seemed!) became sticky with syrup – and the Hospice received the takings of 10p each. She was always approachable, caring and hospitable. The house could never have been successful without her.

We extended our five years to ten, and there are far too many warm memories to be properly condensed. Amongst the most vivid are the whole house attending an evening in the Theatre Royal for a performance of *A Man For All Seasons*, with Charlton Heston in the leading role, the respect of the upper 6th for the accuracy of the clock in my study(!), watching a member of the house as he progressed though a national TV general knowledge quiz, the rugby team in their first house colours (a caterpillar-like strip), the various 18th birthday celebrations (which I hope we handled in a spirit of reasonable tolerance!), the sartorial elegance and good humour of the Christmas party, and, above all, the support of a succession of fine assistants and Heads of House.

Our aim was to run a caring House where supervision was constant but not intrusive, one which always had an open door to our quarters, and which was only a phone call away from the most distant home. After ten years we were sad to leave a happy House of 54 boys. The bridge had been repaired.

JOHN OWEN-BARNETT, HOUSEMASTER OF DRONFIELD HOUSE, 1986 UNTIL IT BECAME A GIRLS' HOUSE; THEN HOUSEMASTER OF SCHOOL HOUSE (LATER RE-NAMED LINTON) 1988–2001.

It was a sad start to my boarding career when Barry Daniel died in Norway and, as a result, I was offered the housemastership of Dronfield by Robin Pittman. I jumped at the opportunity, even though I knew I could never fill Barry's shoes. Paddy Stephen, David Hughes and I took it in turns to sleep over, every night, in the study for half a term while Cindy and the girls came to terms with their sense of loss and the need to find somewhere to live. My family moved into Dronfield in that late October once Cindy had found accommodation.

The next shock came when Robin Pittman announced that he had decided to make Dronfield a girls' boarding house. The upset for the boys was enormous. The decision seemed so ill-timed and the feeling amongst the boys in the house was that they had been kicked while down. There was a sense of betrayal. A stoic resolve was needed. This came when the house won a place in the senior rugby final against the favourites, School House. We may have lost the match, but house pride was at its zenith.

Peter and Sue Taylor swapped places with us as we both crossed the road and took over each other's house. Virtually all the pupils from Dronfield came with us to School House and with 70 boys we were bursting at the seams. School House looked as though nothing had changed much since it was built in the 1840s. We could not yet do anything about the awful beds, which looked even older than those used in the TV series *Porridge*. It was at this time, however, that more money was beginning to be spent on the boarding accommodation and so improvements were in the pipeline.

In 1994 the School bought Linton Lodge and we packed up every last stick of furniture, even down to the 19th-century brass coat hooks on the back of all the doors, to open up a new boys' boarding house in St Peter's Grove. It was so refreshing to leave the main school buildings. Linton was like a baronial hall by comparison. The garden helped to make the whole experience of boarding more like home. I am so glad to have played a small part, with Ann, in making boarding life a little more tolerable and as close to life at home as I could. I hope the next generation of house staff get as much enjoyment and reward out of their time as we did.

DRONFIELD 1987–1996.

It was the first girls' house, and Peter and Sue were the perfect choice for this new appointment in the School. They were a caring, professional couple of great stature and principle; the girls in the new house were very fortunate to have them as their house parents. Peter died in 2004 and Sue has contributed these memories.

The rumour became a reality in 1987. Dronfield was transformed to make a suitable setting for 40 girls, both boarding and day, who made up the first intake. Out went the plunge baths and in came the shower cubicles. They were not working on the first day of term, but in the excitement of the new era this did not seem to matter.

In fact the plumbing and central heating often caused problems over the years, usually when the weather was at its worst. Pru Bundy recalled recently when, after a mammoth snowball fight between the houses, Dronfield girls returned to house to be told by Peter that there was no central heating. Eventually a solution was found when everyone, wrapped in duvets, crowded into the television room to keep warm.

The house soon developed its own unique character. Christmas cake and carols (accompanied by Peter on the trumpet) became a tradition, as did the strawberry picking in the summer term. A barbecue and an awards ceremony were always held on the last night of the academic year, which was great fun for everyone.

For the first three years Dronfield won the Merit Cup. Numbers increased quickly, and when, in 1991, Dronfield was home to 54 boarders, it was decided that The Rise should become a girls' house too.

Dronfield House 1987.

Crimes and Misdemeanours

RICHARD DRYSDALE

One of the most notable changes in the School over the last few decades is the approach to discipline. There is an incomplete record of disciplinary procedures in the past but, nonetheless, the record that exists is enough for some conclusions to be drawn.

There is no doubt that discipline was more formalized in the past. We have a good record of the regimes spanning the years 1925–71 in both The Rise and The Manor punishment books. Corporal punishment was the norm in most schools until the late 1960s. The Rise punishment book records both the offence and the number of strokes meted out. In later years the offences punished were the more serious ones, but in the 1920s caning was administered for what today would seem minor misdemeanours.

The Rise punishment book gives a detailed insight into the period 1925–30. In 1925, 25 members of the house were caned. Although there is no exact record of the numbers in The Rise at the time, we can deduce from other figures for 1922 and 1929 that the total stood at around 35, and from this, that about two-thirds of the house were caned during the year. One boy suffered the cane ten times in the year, while another had to endure the same punishment on seven separate occasions. The offences so punished vary from the inconsequential to the moderately serious, by present-day standards. Being spotted in town without leave usually meant six strokes, while cutting chapel could carry the standard punishment of four strokes. Failure to tidy up a common room after a warning attracted two strokes. Some of the more notable offences included: seen conversing with two girls on the river bank while boating (six strokes); shining a mirror in the face of complete strangers and damaging the reputation of the school (six strokes); wearing an unentitled blazer (six strokes); smoking up the chimney in the top study (six strokes); seen eating ice creams in town (four strokes); repeatedly late for breakfast (four strokes); persistent grinning while the collection was being taken (four strokes). One can only assume, without further documentary evidence, that these punishments were standard tariffs for the period in other houses.

Wentworth Ping in St Olave's was renowned for having two canes, 'Hengist' and 'Horsa'. Boys about to be punished had the grotesque choice of which cane Ping would use. One OP records how degrading the whole process was for a defenceless child. For some, caning was a traumatic event, which they remember with hurt and anger even today. For others it was simply part of the system and, however reluctantly, they accepted it.

More recent evidence from The Manor punishment book for the period 1959–71 is less detailed, and while the offence is recorded, the punishment meted out is not. We can assume, however, that by this time the punishments were written ones. Offences include: grinning in line (whatever that means); a rose in button-hole; throwing aqueous projectiles (water bombs); uncomplimentary remarks about the monitors; not reporting with clean hands; jumping over the housemaster's wall and having jacket open (which offence was the more serious, one wonders); no cap on cycle ride; making a rude gesture at a monitor; excessive laughing; rioting during roll (which sounds more serious); slovenly posture during house prayers; talking in house prayers and finally, making derogatory comments on the cricketing ability of Dronfield House. In one week in 1971 there were no less than 23 offences recorded, which seems fairly representative of what was going on in the house on a week-to-week basis. Most of these offences come into the category of 'minor nuisance', which, in more recent times, might be rectified by a sharp word from the housemaster.

When Keith Coulthard took over Dronfield House in 1964, he told John Dronfield that he did not want either fagging or corporal punishment in the house. This was accepted. It is difficult to gauge the frequency of caning in John Dronfield's era, because no punishment books survive. We are told that he never had to cane anyone, but caning was carried out by

93

News and Reviews at home and abroad

'I can't help thinking that if I had been caned at school none of this would have happened'

housemasters and monitors. The era of caning by monitors ended at different times in different houses and there seems to have been an ad hoc approach to corporal punishment and its administration. There were certainly two houses in which corporal punishment was continued by monitors in certain tightly prescribed circumstances until Peter Gardiner banned it completely in 1967.

There is no doubt that discipline was more rigid than it is today. The discipline card, with its definition of what constitutes good discipline on one side and the list of historical dates on the other, was at the heart of the system. Miscreants were told to copy out the definition of what constituted good discipline, or learn the dates and recite them to whoever had imposed the punishment. Too many copies in a short period could lead to a caning. As the formality of the School community diminished, so formalized punishments grew less frequent. The power of both house and school monitors over their charges also diminished.

In recent years, discipline has become less formal and more relaxed. Sanctions do exist and are used when necessary. The Children's Act has had an influence on sanctions. It is no longer permissible, for example, to punish pupils by sending them on a run without their consent; running around the Horseshoe is now a thing of the past. Formalized punishment as such is minimal. The Manor's current punishment book, for example, has only 12 registered punishments during the Easter term, 2006. This change is due both to the general ethos and improved corporate and individual discipline of the school. Staff/student

relations maintain a 'formal informality', strange though that phrase may sound. Friendliness between staff and pupils prevails. There is no longer quite the 'them and us' feeling amongst the pupils, but rather a sense of common purpose in what is perceived as a happy place.

SUB-CULTURES

All institutions have their own sub-culture and St Peter's is no exception. Rarely does the adult manage to penetrate this sub-culture, although at times it is partially revealed. Rule-breaking is one example. It is a matter of pride, after all, for adolescents to challenge rules and sabotage them for whatever reason they can. One OP wrote that he smoked at school only because he was breaking a rule, and that he stopped smoking as soon as he left school. The permissiveness of the regime in tolerating disregard of rules varied from regime to regime.

A new Peterite's first priority used to be to learn the pecking order. He was the lowest of the low. Hierarchy was rigidly enforced in a wide range of ways. A third-former, for example, had to have the middle button of his jacket done up and had to keep his hands out of his pockets. A fourth-former was allowed one hand in a side pocket of his jacket. A fifth-former was allowed an unbuttoned jacket and to have both hands in his side jacket pockets. A member of lower sixth was allowed an unbuttoned jacket and one hand in a trouser pocket, while upper sixth-formers had no restrictions at all: the jacket was unbuttoned and hands could be in trouser pockets.

There were, however, variations to these rules, depending on whether or not an individual had been awarded colours. Someone with colours for a minor sport, or for senior colts, could have both hands in pockets regardless of seniority. If an individual had second-team colours, he was allowed to have one hand in his trouser pocket and first-team players were allowed both hands in trouser pockets, regardless of seniority. This system of hierarchy was rigidly enforced by the pupils themselves. It also meant that distinction at sport gave a status which circumvented seniority in the School. The centrality of sport was thus emphasized. These conventions had died out by the late 1960s.

Fagging used to be central to a Peterite's life. Fagging duties included running baths for the monitors, waking them up, cleaning their shoes and tidying their changing rooms. School monitors had a personal fag. Guy King-Reynold's account of life in the school in the late 1930s and early 1940s gives a fuller account of what fagging involved. The practice of fagging seems to have died out between 1964 and 1967.

The school body could make its feelings known if there was a sense of aggrievement. This happened in the late 1980s when a pupil was expelled and the pupils chose not to sing in chapel as a way of expressing their disapproval. This, however, was very much the exception. Normally, channels of communication between the school body and the staff were good.

The other glimpse of this sub-culture could be discerned in the student publication *The Bulletin*, written by sixth-formers on the lines of *Private Eye* in the early years of the Pittman era. The satire and humour were esssentially good-natured and the poking of gentle fun at individual members of staff was tolerated. At break on the day of publication, colleagues would sit in silence in the small dining room with their coffees and scan *The Bulletin* for the latest scandal, or to see if it was their turn to be lampooned. The 'Colemanballs' lifted from *Private Eye* always brought a smile, as colleague after colleague was quoted making some ridiculous statement. One senior colleague was quoted as saying, 'Oh yes, I like to vandalize telephone boxes with bicycle chains', while another was quoted as saying 'Shut up lads – you sound like a herd of bumble bees'. *The Bulletin* sadly survived only for a few issues.

95

St Peter's School, York

IMPOSITION COPY

(Copy out the passage below in your best handwriting, on paper obtained from your housemaster. Only your best writing will be accepted.)

"DISCIPLINE"

Discipline is the means whereby you are trained in orderliness, good conduct and the habit of getting the best out of yourself, all of which are essential to the well-being of the School.

Discipline may take several forms, but the crucial test of its soundness is whether it represents a real sense, on your part, of the rightness of the behaviour that is expected of you. It cannot be considered good unless it is founded upon worthy ideas of conduct that are becoming, or have become, embedded in your character.

An outward show of order can, of course, be maintained by force or fear, but mere repression is effective only while you are immediately under the authority that exercises it. When you are released from this authority, you tend to revert to other modes of behaviour, and, if discipline has not become self-discipline, you may be left at the mercy of any dominant unruly personality or of the whim of the moment.

Discipline implies the teaching of certain rules of behaviour which experience has shown are necessary for the smooth running of our corporate life, and forms an essential part of the tradition of this School.

The basis of good discipline, then, is the willing acceptance by you of the School's standards of behaviour.

ST. PETER' S SCHOOL

DATE CARD - PART VIII

1815 Congress of Vienna. Talleyrand and Metternich **1815**

1818-9 The Zollverein- a commercial union -lays the **1818-9** foundation of Prussian Power

1827 The Battle of Navarino frees Greece from the Sultan. **1827**

1832 The Reform Bill is passed amidst great political excitement. **1832**

1846 The Repeal of the Corn Laws marks the beginning of Free Trade. **1846**

1848 General unrest in European countries. **1848**

1854 The Crimean War revives the Eastern Question: **1854** Alma, Sebastepol, Inkerman.

1857 The Indian Mutiny leads to a new era of British rule in India. **1857**

1859 War of Italian Liberation: Mazzini, the idealist; **1859** Garibaldi, the fighter; Cavour, the diplomatist; Victor Emmanuel, the King.

1861 American Civil War - Abraham Lincoln. **1861**

1869 Opening of the Suez Canal. **1869**

1870-1 The Franco-German War leads to the Prussianisation **1870-1** of Germany, and makes it possible for her to rival Britain.

1878 Treaty of Berlin. Disraeli's Triumph. **1878**

The Alcuin Library

Avril Pedley

Whatever the truth of our claim to be the oldest school in England, we must surely be one of the first to have had what amounts to a Library Catalogue. In Alcuin's famous Latin poem on the history of York in his time, he describes the succession of archbishops, and especially the work of his own teacher, Aelberht, who held the see from 767 to 778. When Aelberht retired to a life of solitary contemplation, he left to Alcuin, one of his favoured pupils, 'his study and collection of books which that famous teacher had collected everywhere, storing these priceless treasures under one roof'.

Alcuin enumerates the specific holdings of the library at great length and explains –

> *There you will find the legacy of the ancient fathers:*
> *all the Roman possessed in the Latin world,*
> *whatever famous Greece has transmitted to the Latins,*
> *draughts of the Hebrew race from Heaven's showers,*
> *and what Africa has spread abroad in streams of light …*
> *There, reader, you will find many others,*
> *teachers outstanding for their learning, art, and style,*
> *who wrote many volumes with clear meaning.*
> *But to include all their names in this poem*
> *would take longer than poetic usage demands.*

As so often in the history of the School, this glimpse into early learning is followed by a long period of silence. While we know or can assume that a library continued, we have no further mention of specific books until the 18th century, and then it is a mention of textbooks; no suggestion of reading for pleasure or wider learning.

In 1735 an advertisement appeared in the *York Courant* newspaper on 3 June. 'This is to give Notice That the Free Grammar School being remov'd from the Bagnio and settled in a large commodious Room in St Andrew-gate Church, all Persons may have their Children admitted, and carefully taught Latin, Greek and Hebrew, according to the Westminster, or Lilly's Grammar, at Reasonable rates, by Z. Blake.' William Lilly's Latin Grammar was a highly popular textbook for many generations (he lived from c1468–1522). Thomas Jefferson's library in the United States included the same work and in George Borrow's *Lavengro* we hear 'Listen to me: there is but one good schoolbook in the world – the one I use in my seminary – Lilly's Latin grammar, in which your son has already made some progress. If you are anxious for the success of your son in life, for the correctness of his conduct and the soundness of his principles, keep him to Lilly's grammar.' So in the mid-18th century our choice of books may be deemed sound if not adventurous.

By the middle of the 19th century and the arrival of St Peter's on its present site, our records are better, though there is still no way of separating books used in teaching from those that might have been in a separate library. Class lists from 1852 to 1864 specify exactly what text pupils are studying in their various subjects. We find Greek and Latin grammar (probably still Lilly), classical authors such as Livy, Horace, Virgil and Xenophon; in mathematics, Euclid features heavily; modern languages used Arnold's first German book, Perrier's *Fables* and Hamel's *Grammar;* English, History, and Geography, which appear in a single column, show Valpy's *Chronology, the History of England*

Left: A debate in the Alcuin Library.

Below: The Toyne Library, c1960.

(unspecified), Cornwallis's *Geography* and *English Poetry for Repetition*. None of these could be considered new and exciting works; Nicholas Hamel's *A New Universal French Grammar* had reached its second edition by 1829.

Numbers of pupils were very variable, and often small (figures of 150 boys in 1864 had dropped again to only 65 in 1898), but none the less efforts were made to maintain a library. John Henry Fowler (1860–1932), a boy who acted as Librarian and who went on to become a distinguished professional in the field, wrote an article in *The Peterite* of July 1929 describing conditions when he first came to St Peter's in 1875. 'The School library was housed in the old sixth-form room (to the right hand of the side entrance, opposite school-house), in cases which were kept locked. Two of the Sixth were librarians, and issued books in the half-hour before lock-up, three times a week.' Fowler believed that a 'creditable' sum of money was spent on the library each year,

> *but the additions were chiefly made by the librarians selecting books from Mudie's second-hand catalogue and presenting this list to the Head Master for his criticism and approval … sometimes we chose novels simply by their titles, knowing nothing of their contents or even of their authors … at least one novel so chosen was found to be unreadable, not because of its license, but because of its excessive goodi-goodiness. I had innocently prescribed it for the consolation of two school-house boys quarantined in the sick-room for chicken-pox, and it was hastily returned by them with a remonstrance couched in language then known as unparliamentary.*

The Peterite of the period occasionally includes library accounts, but these mainly show magazines of various sorts rather than books, and this preponderance of periodicals is mentioned again when the library moved to a different part of the School. Shortly after the opening of the new Science Block in 1903, the attention of the school authorities turned towards other improvements. *The Peterite* records: 'The Old Sixth Form-room has been fitted up into the library, the old site of which is now a dormitory. The museum has also taken up its quarters in the new library. Glass cases for birds and butterflies, and coin cases have been provided, and kind friends have given curiosities and other things, with which to fill them up. There are also about a dozen armchairs. Altogether this is a great improvement on the old library. Now it

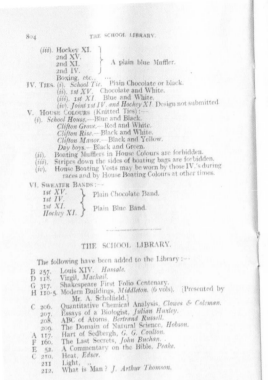

is possible for everyone to see the periodicals and papers, which are placed on a table in the room.' A list of new accessions followed, showing an eclectic mix of fact and fiction. Birds' eggs ('The standard work – for reference only – please take great care'), naval history, the origins of geography, Russia as it really is, Andrew Marvell's poems, and so on. Similar lists appear at irregular intervals in *The Peterite* thereafter.

As School numbers grew and the expectations of pupils and their parents increased, the library facilities, though improved, were soon deemed to be inadequate. In the autumn of 1927, the Governors took the decision to opt for a totally new library building; what is now the right-hand end of Queen's. The main entrance and right wing, comprising the Library and VIth-form room, were to be completed first as the need was urgent, and two large subscriptions had already been received for that purpose (both from A.R. Stephenson, in memory of H.M. Stephenson). Another of the first subscriptions was from the then Head Master, Sam Toyne, and as a result the rooms became the Stephenson Room, with the Toyne Library overhead. The new library was opened with great ceremony in 1929, and there it remained until, once again, changing times, increasing pupil numbers, and greater expectations for library provision resulted in a further move.

In 1989 the old gymnasium (later the drama centre) was converted to become the present Alcuin Library. At the same time the opportunity was taken to begin the conversion of the former in-house cataloguing scheme to the internationally recognized Dewey System, and for the first time the School had the benefit of a librarian, John Mitchell, who was employed for that task alone and was not constrained by the pressures of a teaching role. In 1992 a computerized Library catalogue was begun, and the total stock was counted for the first time: approximately 6,000 items at that time. The library stock has now been fully computerized for many years, and entire classes can be taught in the library with on-line computer terminals (approximately 40 per cent of opening hours are booked for class use). Current stock is nearly 13,000 books of which more than 2,000 are fiction, and the library also holds a substantial collection of CDs and DVDs. This history of the library can end as it began –

There, reader, you will find many others,
teachers outstanding for their learning, art, and style,
who wrote many volumes with clear meaning.
But to include all their names in this poem
would take longer than poetic usage demands.

THE ARCHIVES

That the School has an archives department at all is entirely due to the work begun by the late John Mitchell. His own interest in and deep knowledge of local history inspired him to discover the whereabouts in school (often in various unsuitable locations) of existing records, and to attempt to begin a systematic collection of items for the future. His once well-known bunker at the end of the Alcuin Library has now reverted to proper library use, and the archives have spread into an office and a storeroom, with a computerized system of cataloguing all new accessions to the collection.

The saddest story which has to be recorded here is of 'the one that got away'. In May 1949 the School received a unique relic of its days on the Horsefair in the late 16th century. This was a book of manuscript copies of exercises with the signatures of scholars of the period, effectively a merit book. It was bound in vellum, and was presented to us on permanent loan. The notable

Above: Swimming Blazer

Left: A table top presented by the OP Club made from the salvaged cover of a water butt.

99

John Dixon's hat and scarf made in a POW camp in WWII.

medievalist Professor Christopher Cheney examined the book, and a detailed description was included in *The Peterite* of May 1949. Subsequently it was placed in the museum showcase with a collection of miscellaneous items, mainly coins. There it remained until maintenance staff were asked to clear the case prior to its removal so that decorating could be done. They took the instruction literally and apparently destroyed all the contents.

The loss of the book is particularly unfortunate, as we possess no other manuscript records of the School's early history. Today our collection starts with the admissions register of the school year 1828–29, and its successor, the register that records our arrival on the present site on Clifton. It has to be assumed that with our moves to different locations within the city, caused by the school's varying fortunes and destruction by foreign invaders, fire, and Civil War, earlier records were destroyed or simply abandoned as unimportant.

From 1844 things improved dramatically from an archival point of view. We have comprehensive records of pupils from that date; a very good collection of photographs of day and boarding houses, individuals, buildings and so on; minute books of school societies such as science, debating, and music; sporting fixture cards; records of the Old Peterite Club; accounts; items of uniform; books by and about Old Peterites; a table with signatures of many OPs (made from the top of an old water butt, by the generosity of the Old Peterite Club); a hat with scarf in Old Peterite colours made in a prisoner-of-war Camp by John B. Dixon and friends; the list goes on. Old Peterites and their families, and visiting scholars from varying disciplines, visit the archives regularly. All are most welcome, whether driven by scholarship or nostalgia.

'The Peterite'

RICHARD DRYSDALE

The St Peter's Journal first appeared in March, 1834, and was followed by seven further issues of which there are no extant copies. It was not until 1878 that the magazine that we know today first appeared. It has been published continuously since then. The purpose of The Peterite was to act as a report for the academic year and to enable OPs to keep abreast of what was going on in the School. It was thus a link between OPs and the School.

That link was especially important during both World Wars when the magazine published OP casualties, decorations awarded and accounts of their exploits, including an escape from a prison camp in Germany. Records of why the decorations were awarded make interesting reading. In this way, the School had an intimate account of the impact of both wars on individuals and the community.

If the contents of the magazine are an indication of a school's priorities, then the fact that games reports took up such a high proportion of the space until comparatively recent years, suggests that the School existed for games. Cricket and rugby matches were originally reported on an individual basis at some length. The September 1936 issue, for example, devoted 27 per cent of the magazine to cricket and 7 per cent to boating, while the January 1937 issue devoted 45 per cent of its space to rugby. This was fairly typical for both the decades before and after this period. By 1981 the magazine had started to evolve into its present form, with a different format and more individual contributions of creative writing and art work. The 1981 issue devoted 17 per cent to creative contributions and 15 per cent to games reports. The individual match reports were replaced by a single report from each game. By 2005 the magazine was 142 pages long, with 30 per cent devoted to the reporting of the 13 sports pursued in the school and only 7 per cent on rugby. The wide range of extra-curricular reports reflects the diversity of the school community today.

The idea of political correctness was unknown until comparatively recently. In the past, the cricket and rugby reports could be quite brutal in their comments about individual players.

Criticism laced with humour rather than praise seemed to predominate. Some of these reports were blunt to the point of causing embarrassment. The 1955 edition of *The Peterite* says of one member of the 1st XV, 'He had little love of the game but with physical advantages he was able to cope as well as anybody. He developed an inherent desire always to kick the ball as soon as he gained possession with the result that the sight of 12 stone in full spate with the ball was usually left to the imagination.' It reported of another 1st XV player, 'When in the mood, he got through a lot of useful work'. Or again, 'His passing still lacks rhythm and remains unreliable. His tackling needs to come down two feet at least.' The scrum half of the 1940 1st XV was described as 'Clever but rather slow', while one of the forwards was criticized for being inclined to lethargy in the loose. Another member of the 1st XV in 1943 is reported in the following way, 'At the end of the season he fell a victim into staleness. Something of a plodder, he needs to make more use of his speed.'

The cricketers seemed to have fared somewhat better, with the reports being more positive and relating the strengths and weaknesses of the players. One batsman in the 1st XI in the 1938–39 season had to read the following comment about himself, 'Again a great disappointment with the bat. He should have gone for the bowling with much more determination. He is a good out-fielder but rather slow in starting.' Another member of the team's batting was described as 'agricultural'.

Editorials used to be a feature of the magazine and usually attempted, with success, to encapsulate the main concerns of the past academic term or, later, year. These editorials were a remarkable reflection of the mood of the School at the time.

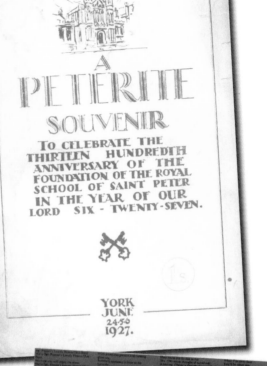

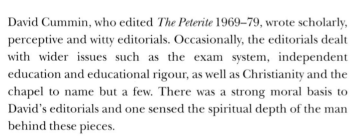

The Peterite 2004 - 2005

David Cummin, who edited *The Peterite* 1969–79, wrote scholarly, perceptive and witty editorials. Occasionally, the editorials dealt with wider issues such as the exam system, independent education and educational rigour, as well as Christianity and the chapel to name but a few. There was a strong moral basis to David's editorials and one sensed the spiritual depth of the man behind these pieces.

The Peterite of today seems to have little in common with its past. Original, creative contributions to the magazine by Peterites, for example, were comparatively infrequent until the early 1980s. The magazine is now almost twice as long as it was in the 1970s. While photographs and illustrations were in short supply until the early 1980s, the magazine is now well-illustrated and visually inviting, with colour photos predominating. From being a magazine that essentially covered the School's sporting achievements, it now covers all the School's activities in some depth. It is a vibrant magazine in both content and illustration. Readers are presented with an image of a lively school achieving success in a whole range of areas from the academic to the cultural and sporting. The School is accurately portrayed as an exciting, friendly place to be, for both staff and pupil. The magazine certainly more than fulfils the aims of its creators.

The Careers Department

PENNY BOLLANDS

John Dronfield asked Keith Coulthard to set up the department in 1953. It was one of the first careers departments in an independent school in the country. Before that Dronfield had regarded advice on careers and higher education as part of his individual responsibilty as Head Master.

The first careers convention was organized by Keith in 1962 and lasted two days. It filled several rooms with displays mounted by a wide range of employers. The conventions usually included lectures and demonstrations. On one occasion, the Young Farmers' Club together with their parents and agricultural suppliers brought agricultural machinery, including a combine harvester. The wide range of contacts from the early careers conventions led to the setting up of the annual careers forums, which have proved to be so successful. At this time the Public Schools Appointments Board, later to be re-named the Independent School Careers Organisation, was a useful resource.

In these early days the careers information was held in two small rooms at the back of the music department. Fifth-form pupils sat the Birkbeck psychometric test (a forerunner to the Morrisby test, which is currently used) after which they were interviewed by a member of the careers staff and a report was compiled to help with decisions for A-level choices, higher education and possible careers. It is worth noting that between 1954 and 1959, just over 50 per cent of all leavers went to university, which contrasts sharply with the 98 per cent who go today.

With Keith's retirement in 1990, Dick Hubbard became head of careers. Initially the department was run from the physics laboratory, but it was soon moved to its present location in what had been Temple House. This gave it a central location in the School.

At first, Dick's role was predominantly concerned with university applications as well as fifth-form subject choices. The careers forum was expanded to include a wider range of professions. The preparation of applications for Oxford and Cambridge took up an increasing amount of time and mock interviews were integral to this process.

Later Dick introduced a number of new initiatives. As part of the general studies programme an external training organization came into school to run sessions for sixth-formers on a range of topics, including management and presentation skills. With the demise of general studies, the 'management day' was introduced. In the first year the Industrial Society organized the day.

University applications remain a key focus of the department. Outside speakers from universities are now invited on a regular

Dick Hubbard presiding over a lower sixth management day.

Above: The careers convention February 2006.

Right: Fourth form skills day.

basis, to give talks on topics such as writing the UCAS personal statement, interview skills and university choices. Preparing pupils for independent learning is also important, so study-skills training has been organized. Pupils in the fifth-form still undertake the Morrisby psychometric tests and have one-to-one interviews, to help clarify future options and choices.

In addition, there is a recognition that the central part of careers today is about making sure that pupils understand their own strengths and weaknesses and realize the opportunities that are open to them.

The Early Days of the CCF 1860–1948

On 24 October 1860, St Peter's Company (No. 4 Company, 1st Volunteer Rifle Corps, York) was sworn in at School. There had been a threat of a French invasion in 1859, which had evoked the idea of a cadet movement, and a young master, Mr F.M. Scargill (himself a Major-General's son), received a commission as Captain and was instrumental in setting up the corps. St Peter's was one of very few schools to have such a group at the time. A rifle range was also set up alongside the existing boundary wall (where the new part of the science block now stands). The uniform adopted was dark grey with blue braid, buff belts and silver ornaments. A cadet corps of 15 younger boys wore the same uniform, with short swords, and both groups lasted about a year. An upstairs classroom, near the Head Master's study, was used as an armoury, which later appears to have been transferred to what is now the main school office. Age was not regarded as important, but the boys had to be of a certain size to qualify. They drilled with the other three York companies at a rifle range in Bootham.

Sketch by Dorothy Cooper (née Turner).

The CCF Band c1959, marching past Queen's House.

In the Spring of 1903 a miniature rifle range was opened at the School. It was hoped this would lead to the formation of a cadet corps (officers' training corps or OTC), and this was eventually founded by the Head Master, Sam Toyne, in 1913, shortly before the beginning of the First World War.

In 1941 the OTC was superseded by the Junior Training Corps (JTC) which was in turn reborn as the CCF (Combined Cadet Force) in 1948. Its existence in School has not been continuous from that day, but gaps have been short-lived. Today both the army and air force sections flourish (and are, of course, co-educational), but the Royal Naval section, which was formerly popular under John Bulcock's vigorous leadership, has been discontinued.

Avril Pedley

THE CCF 1966–93

I joined the CCF at St Peter's in September 1966 as a Second Lieutenant proudly wearing a pair of parachute wings, my somewhat presumptuous contribution to Cold War warrior

Mackenzie, who toured Canada in 1966 with The Athelings, the Great Britain School Cadet Team.

Lt John Maw, RNR, was a conscientious man who excelled as Freddie's successor, to the extent that I did not hesitate to accept a change of service from Army to RNR lieutenant in order to lead the section when he left the School, assisted by his successor, Mike Dawson. It was a thriving section which I was fortunate to inherit. In the meantime, Philip Harris and John Gaastra were also fully involved in the RAF and Army sections respectively, and the contingent as a whole continued to benefit from the experience of these men. Richard Drysdale took over the RAF section when Philip retired and its continued success was therefore guaranteed. I became Commanding Officer when David Cummin retired in 1980.

Weekly visits by professional instructors, the wide choice of annual camps (from Loch Ewe to the Rhine), sailing and sea experience for RN cadets, flying for the RAF section (additionally from nearby airfields), the presence of the girls – all have contributed to the thriving CCF which we now have. The School too has done its part. Sadly no officer was available from the staff to run the RN section when I became CO, so it had to close, but the School wisely continued to provide for a permanent instructor. Al Tooms' appointment was particularly significant - an experienced man from whose expertise many cadets benefited, to the extent of several taking up service careers. Three members of this era have commanded Gurkha battalions : Craig Lawrence, David Wombell and Tim Warrington MBE. The parachute wings have faded but the tradition of those officers and gentlemen from the 1960s remains strong.

John Bulcock

CCF parade c1973.

status. The medals of my fellow officers, however, did not appear until the biennial inspections: David Cummin (Commanding Officer), Leslie Le Tocq, Philip Harris, Freddie Waine and John Gaastra were men who had seen real war service, one at sea and two in far distant theatres, and Peter Croft had been the youngest officer in the Education Corps. The SSI was Paddy Power, a former serving NCO, loyal and very humorous. There was therefore some depth of character in the contingent, but the revolution of the 1960s tested us all. Long hair was creating problems with the school uniform, let alone the military one, and Paddy's solution at parade one Tuesday afternoon was unique: he set up a barber's chair outside the contingent offices, took a large pair of scissors and personally sheared every cadet whose hair would not fit under the beret. No complaints.

Leslie Le Tocq (a gentleman in every sense of the word) was an inspirational shooting coach: small-bore in the miniature range, full-bore at Strensall, Bisley and Altcar. Events were often won at Bisley, particularly in The Marling. Outstanding shots from Leslie's era include David Harding, runner-up Queen's Medallist Regular Army (1977) and later Queen's Medallist Territorial Army (1978), Simon Dench (winner of *The Daily Telegraph* Prize at Bisley and member of the Great Britain under-25 team), Neil Moxon (Great Britain Touring Team) and John

CCF Field Day.

105

The CCF in 1990 commanded by Lt Cdr R.J. Bulcock.

THE CCF TODAY

The aims of the Combined Cadet Force are to develop qualities of self-reliance, responsibility, resourcefulness and leadership within a military framework. About one-fifth of the pupils join this voluntary organization. The experience for pupils is different from their other school activities in several important ways. They wear a different uniform and are trained by staff members of an outside agency, as well as their normal subject teachers. The skills that they learn are immediately transferable to practical tasks in the field and are subject to an inspection every two years. A few cadets eventually join the Armed Services, some having won prestigious Army or RAF scholarships.

For most cadets, however, the CCF is a positive diversion from their school activities. Those serving for four years find promotion, based on merit, allows them to take on increasing responsibility and to develop leadership skills. After two or three years of instruction, the senior cadets are responsible for conducting the training of the juniors. They are, of course, supervised, but the junior cadets appreciate the knowledge of the NCOs and aspire to the same role, which offers a rare pedagogic opportunity for Peterites.

In most recent times, Al Tooms and Stewart Howman have been at the frontline of the CCF as School Staff Instructors (SSIs). Their first-hand military knowledge and understanding are vital to the success of the organization and training programme. The SSI relies for a large part on the support of staff at the School and other military sources. St Peter's School CCF has also been helped by some dedicated and loyal officers among its teaching and support staff.

The cadets' training syllabus sets out to challenge, enthuse and exercise them, both physically and mentally. It is particularly rewarding for staff to see the sense of satisfaction and pleasure of the cadets, whether it is from hitting the target on the rifle range or taking control of an aircraft in an aerobatic routine.

Every year there is a field day at Strensall Military Training Area, and every other year this doubles as the biennial inspection. The real highlight of the year is summer camp, which is so popular that it is over-subscribed. The cadets' training culminates in a week-long series of exercises on an army training camp or RAF station. The days at camp are long and tiring, but the satisfaction is palpable. The glint in the tired eye and the question, 'Can we do it again next year?' says it all.

Matthew Grant

The Debating Society 1937–90

RICHARD DRYSDALE

The Debating Society and the Science Society are the oldest School societies still in existence today. The Debating Society had originally been set up in 1878, but, like many societies, failed to survive on a continuous basis. It was re-established in 1937 by John Dronfield, who became its President, and although meetings have not been continuous since then, it has nonetheless met frequently over the years.

There were fewer debates on political issues in the late 1930s than one might expect, given the growing international tensions that were to lead to war. The motion 'International sport promotes international ill-feeling' was defeated 16–4. The only other debate which considered the political tensions of the time was on Chamberlain's policy towards Mussolini's Italy, after the invasion of Abyssinia. The vote went in favour of the Prime Minister, 20–4. On the other hand, Peterites thought, rightly as it turned out, that British government proposals for the carving up of the Czech state in late 1938 were disgraceful, by a 40–7 margin. In April 1939 there was support for conscription, but only by the narrow margin of 13–8. The execution of the war was debated in the motion 'This house would approve a policy of purely reprisal raids over Germany'. It was carried 19–11.

Many of the issues debated have relevance today, even though they need to be seen in the context of the times: the Cold War, the retreat from empire and Britain's role in the world. The debate on America's influence in the world, held in 1957, was one such example. The motion was 'This house regrets the influence of the USA in the modern world'. The motion was carried 42–18. In 1959 a similar topic produced a different result. 'This house believes that the Atlantic is not wide enough' was defeated 60–14.

While Peterites may have been politically independent during these years, their views on racial segregation were more ambivalent. The motion 'This house believes there is a place for racial segregation' was narrowly defeated 35–39. One of the staff who took part in the debate is quoted as arguing, 'Political segregation was necessary as the blacks have no sentiments for politics'. The response to apartheid and the growing momentum of the American Civil Rights movement had clearly been missed in his case. Green issues were discussed in the motion that argued for industrial expansion, regardless of dangers to the environment, debated in 1989. Peterites proved themselves to be in the vanguard of the green movement by defeating the motion 35–15. The morality of nuclear weapons as an effective deterrent was defeated 30–9 in 1985.

At time of the Suez Crisis in 1956, the motion 'This house deplores British policy in the Middle East' was carried 79–16. Wider British public opinion was also split on the issue, but the Peterite view was more vehemently opposed to it. There was, on the other hand, support for British colonialism. The motion 'This house deplores colonialism' was defeated 11–29. The issue of apartheid was addressed again in 1960, with the motion 'This house would support a boycott of South African goods'. The motion was carried 41–13. The troubles in Ireland were clearly in mind when, in 1987, the motion to 'never negotiate with terrorists' was discussed. The motion was only narrowly defeated 20–18. Contrary to what one might have expected, Peterites had their reservations about Mrs Thatcher when the motion 'This house looks forward to the next ten years of Mrs Thatcher' was defeated 23–14. Relations with the US were at the heart of the debate in 1986, 'The British bulldog has become Reagan's poodle', but the motion was defeated 21–7. The EU found surprising favour when withdrawal from it was rejected 24–10 in 1986, at the height of Thatcherism.

On social issues a certain conservatism is apparent, except in matters of sex. In 1958 the motion 'This house believes class distinction is both inevitable and desirable' was carried 31–19.

36

The fourth meeting of the term was held in the Lecture Theatre at 6.30 p.m. on Saturday 30th Nov.

There being no business after the minutes had been read and signed, the Chairman called upon Mr L.H. Crowther to propose the motion "This House considers that Advertising has deteriorated to such an extent that it ought to be abolished."

Mr Crowther said that modern advertising was based on a study of human psychology. He said that there were two methods of advertising the first could be represented by Coca-cola, the second by a seaside advertisement dominated by female charms. He said that advertising aimed at controlling human behaviour and those who wished to be free should vote for the proposition.

Mr R.L. Evans then rose to defend advertising. Advertising, he said, was both an art and a necessity. Without it we should have no information about what we could buy. In several swift strokes he completely ruined our commercial system, by abolishing advertising. In conclusion he showed how in actual fact advertising had advanced not deteriorated.

Mr D.N.L. Beresford then rose to second the proposition. He desired to emphasise the word

An extract from the Debating Society's minutes.

Views towards women were more robust. The motion 'This house believes that women are the weaker sex' was defeated 32–9. The same motion was debated in 1990, when the School was co-educational, and the result was an overwhelming defeat 90–14. The motion 'Women can no longer be regarded as the weaker sex', debated in 1945, had been defeated 23–12. One of the speakers, later to be a governor of the School, contended that women's *possible* equality in intellect was nullified by practical application. In stark contrast to this, the motion 'A woman's place is in the home' was defeated 41–17 in 1987, suggesting that the co-educational character of the school was making itself felt.

Sex before marriage was debated in 1969. The motion, 'This house believes that sex before marriage is bad for sex and marriage' was defeated 20–10. Could it ever have been otherwise? Marriage was again debated in 1990. The motion that marriage was an outdated concept was defeated 45–4. Peterites showed themselves to be against a hedonistic way of life when they rejected such a lifestyle by 49–12. Abortion was debated in 1987 and led to a heated debate, with a defeat for the motion that abortion was murder by 49–11. Some 44 people abstained. There was an acceptance of the role of religion in the modern world when the issue was debated in 1989, and the house rejected by 27–9 the argument that it had no place in the modern world. The issue of drug-taking was debated in 1987 in the motion 'The taking of drugs is a person's own affair'. The house thought otherwise and the motion was narrowly defeated 31–29.

On issues directly concerning the School an apparent ambivalence against the pre-eminence of the 1st XV in school life is evident in the 1958 motion 'This house looks forward to the day when a place in the school orchestra is as coveted as a place in the 1st XV'. The motion was carried 45–15. There was a certain anti-scientific bias evident in the carrying of the motion 'Science plays too large a part in education' by 78–41. The issue of co-education was discussed in 1942. The motion 'This house is in favour of the introduction of co-education for all' was carried by only 27–24 votes. It was again debated in 1970 and was somewhat oddly rejected by 26–0. When one speaker pointed out that going co-ed would mean replacing some housemasters with housemistresses, there were apparently loud cheers. A similar debate about going co-educational in 1986 was carried by the convincing margin of 30–13, although one opponent of the motion argued that if the school did go co-ed, it would become a 'bed of vice'.

The School's feeling towards Christmas was amply shown one year, when the motion 'This house is itching to return to its studies after the pagan orgies of Christmas' was carried 69–30.

The monarchy, the House of Lords and the Church of England were all the subjects of debates over the years. The resulting votes suggested that Peterites were unsurprisingly traditionalist in outlook. Issues surrounding the welfare state were discussed. This received short shrift in 1959 when the motion 'This house believes that decadence begins with the welfare state' was carried conclusively by 37–13.

The fortunes of the Society waxed and waned over time. This was the case in the early 1970s. Fittingly, one of the debates the society held in 1972 discussed the motion 'The end is nigh'. It was a tight vote and the motion was lost 30–28. After a few years' inactivity, the Society was resurrected and continues to this day.

109

Community Service

JULIE BAINBRIDGE

There is a strong feeling of responsibility at St Peter's towards the local, national and international communities. We like to think that it is beneficial for the whole campus, pupils and staff alike, to be aware of the needs of the community in which we live. This is particularly significant locally, where our participation as good neighbours is vital.

All pupils and staff are given the opportunity to volunteer. There are fund-raising events throughout the year when members of the community are invited to give their time, enthusiasm, expertise and financial support to everything from fun runs to sponsored walks. New ideas are always encouraged. In recent years we have seen pupils organise a wide range of events from talent shows to Valentine's Day and Comic Relief celebrations, each one in aid of excellent causes nominated by members of the School.

An increasing number of local groups have been invited into St Peter's in recent years. Pupils host a popular annual party for the local elderly at Christmas and also help to organize and run events throughout the year for groups of special-needs children. We hold a computer club on Saturdays offering one-to-one tuition for local senior citizens, who are proud to call themselves the St Peter's Silver Surfers. In the summer term our Open Day for Community Action is always well attended, and our volunteers enjoy taking their guests around the campus to show them what goes on in the School.

The Beverley Fun Run.

Going out into the community as volunteers is an important part of the sixth-form extracurricular programme, and pupils do regular placements in York. There are successful links with local primary schools where pupils work as classroom assistants, and a number of charity shops welcome our pupils every week. The School enjoys an excellent relationship with the Wilberforce Trust, which provides training opportunities as well as valuable experience for many of our sixth-formers. Pupils can also join a local group which works to bring able-bodied and physically handicapped young people together.

St Peter's has been delighted with the support and encouragement offered to our volunteers by local organisations. The Minster Lions in particular have worked closely with the community service group and have also donated a generous annual prize in recognition of community action. After the summer examinations, seniors are invited to give up their free time for a week to take part in a project working with local groups. The School is indebted to The Glen Respite Care Unit and the Arclight Shelter for Homeless, amongst others, who have enabled these initiatives to function.

A recent gift of a considerable sum of money from an extremely generous anonymous donor has meant that plans for even more projects have been developed, and, as a result, the future looks promising. Any venture which gives pupils the skills and confidence to work with others in the community is hugely beneficial to all concerned. St Peter's looks forward to seeing the School's role in the community continue to grow.

110

The Community Service Christmas Party.

The Spiritual Life of the School

The School Chapel Today

JEFFREY DALY

I am suspicious of schools which claim that the chapel is at the heart of their community. Despite current pressures in the Church of England to include 'fresh expressions of church' in worship in schools, it is surely the case that schools are principally learning communities. And yet any school community will need to address all that is required in moral and spiritual education, as well as what is demanded academically. It will also need to address its own dynamic and values if it is to flourish. Chapel life is crucial to this process and while, to be authentic, it must keep worship of God at its centre, it must also allow the ways of the school and the ways of the world to find articulation and assessment in the light of the Christian gospel. St Peter's School, committed to the wisdom of 'the ancient ways', is a school where certainly the heart of the community can be found in chapel.

In 2005 Professor John Cottingham published a book on the philosophy of religion with the title *The Spiritual Dimension. Religion, Philosophy and Human Value.* That title could be used as a summary of what a present day Peterite finds in chapel. He or she will find religion three times a week, when the whole school is together for 15 minutes. On each occasion it will sing two hymns, soon to be taken from the School's own hymn book. These will bring the best of old and new words to life as the poetry and music of the church are made our own. Peterites will also find philosophy and human value. They will hear prayers and be invited implicitly to say a personal 'Amen' to the belief as well as to the wishes expressed. Once each term the whole School will celebrate a sung eucharist, the chief sacrament of the church, setting forth the core faith of Christians in Christ crucified and risen. Typically some 80 to 90 will receive communion and a further dozen or so will ask for a personal blessing. Each year an average of 15 Olavites and Peterites will commit themselves more firmly to the Christian faith in the confirmation service.

The addresses, given by the Chaplain, a colleague or a guest from among the Minster and other clergy, or by a representative of a charity which the School is supporting in various ways, encourage listeners to reflect upon what people do and what people believe they should do. And listen the School does well. Many a guest, in Chapel for the first time, will comment afterwards on how concentrated the listening has been and how palpable, too, the sense of community. At the very least, the buzz of conversation before the School falls silent at the beginning, and the buzz as the School leaves at the end, is evidence of friendships strengthened and of commitment to the good of the whole. Once a year each house plans and takes a chapel service, and the fun that is generated by the exercise, often after some agonizing on matters of theme and rehearsal, spreads well beyond the house which is taking the lead. Such regularity in the rhythm of chapel life enables chapels after a tsunami or a 9/11 to be secure times, when some of the horrors of the modern world can be acknowledged and reflected upon, in a way that enables the community to live through the human mix of joys and sorrows. Such regularity also means that the annual Remembrance Service, now held on the 11th day of the 11th month (unless a

Commemoration, 2006, in the Minster.

Chapel, Spring 2006.

The Leavers' Eucharist, before study leave begins for the Upper Sixth, always draws virtually the whole of that year, a witness to the belief of those young men and women that the chapel is a place of support at testing moments. Voluntary services on days such as Ash Wednesday and All Souls' Day see much smaller numbers, but are moving and meaningful to those who come. Memorial services and funerals for recent and not-so-recent Peterites comfort people in grief, awaken memories and renew friendships. On average, two or three babies are baptized each year from staff families, and increasingly OPs celebrate their marriage in the chapel.

The grandest religious occasions in the year take place in York Minster. Although the formal ties between the School and the Minster, at governor level, have become thinner over the hundred or so years that now separate us from the time when the Dean and Chapter ran the School alone, the School feels at home in its cathedral church, and never fails to be uplifted at the carol service in December and at the Commemoration service in July. Upwards of 1,600 people come to these services and they are fitting ends to the Christmas and Summer Terms. As Chaplain, it is a delight to spot faces of OPs on both occasions, and to ponder how the work and life of the chapel has formed something of lasting value in all who have experienced it.

Sunday), is but a more intense expression of the School's concern to engage with the moral and spiritual challenges of life that each generation has to meet.

Chapel life also includes the meeting of smaller communities within the larger structures of the present school and of the OPs.

Three Chaplains Remember

CHAPEL 1977–82
John Roden

The replacement for Noel Kemp-Welch's 30 year reign as Chaplain failed to turn up at the start of the 1977 Spring Term, forcing the Head Master to appeal to the Bishop of Whitby (OP) to find someone suitable for the post. By chance, I was looking for new work after a four-year curacy in Saltburn. Peter Gardiner, at interview, stated that he would like considerable change in chapel, with the pupils being challenged. He felt that the time was right for someone with my radical views and concerns for Third World issues to be appointed. Dean Jasper wondered whether I could cope with such a highly educated and powerful group of senior staff. Certainly, to follow a deeply spiritual, and musical, traditionalist priest would be no easy task.

After the sheer terror of leading worship for the whole School on that first day of term, I determined to introduce as many different forms of worship as possible; to get away from normal Anglican public school fare, and to make the ten-minute start to the day as exciting and challenging as possible. The ever-wise Philip Harris took me to one side after a few days and said, 'Whatever you do, you'll be up against the housemasters and the Dronfield tradition!' Peter Gardiner had hinted at this in my interview. As time went on, the housemasters and I came to respect our differing views and most came round to the changes, rightly curbing my occasional over-the-top enthusiasms. Not all the boys were necessarily eager for change, and I remember one – perhaps slightly eccentric – pupil, who would dive into the nearest classroom doorway if he saw the 'chaplain-devil' (as he termed me) approaching down the corridor. One year on, as he left, he did thank me for 'an interesting view of Christianity'.

It seemed right to implement various changes in the encironment of the chapel and its surroundings. The ante-chapel was unwelcoming. After its repainting, I had display boards mounted and spotlights fitted. The boards frequently featured Third World posters and projects. The chapel itself was dull and dingy, and a programme of repainting was agreed. The hanging Cross was an outstanding addition to a much brighter building. The installation of a hi-fi system enabled me to play a variety yof tapes during the services.

The major changes under Peter Gardiner and Peter Hughes were the variety, frequency and conduct of the chapel services. The monthly Sunday evening community services for all pupils were quickly abolished. This happened despite the comments of one housemaster that 'these Services should stay, as they are the only chance the boys get to wear their suits'. Sunday evening Compline was similarly phased out. Dr Sheila Dronfield, widow of the previous Head, said to me, 'I hear you've stopped chapel services'. I was not quite that ruthless.

Houses and individual staff and pupils were encouraged to take some of the morning chapel services, which resulted in some very brave and exciting worship. We broke from the Milner-White nine-lessons-and-carols straitjacket at the annual December service in the Minster. Secular readings, coupled with a break from the usual hierarchy of readers, helped to make the service more acceptable and exciting to the majority. David Hughes' reading of Old English in one such service was a memorable moment. The introduction of whole-school communion services, rather than the 1.30pm communion for a dozen, was a risk and certainly an exhilarating experiment and experience. Objections reached the ears of Dean Jasper, Chairman of Governors, who summoned me to appear before him during one summer holiday. At his intimation that 'outrageous things' were happening in chapel, I had to point out that I was not dancing naked on the altar. Alas, he possessed no humour and was not amused. It transpired that his main reason for interrupting my holiday was to censure me for prayers and words used in the Commemoration service in the Minster. Those school governors who were also on the board of Rowntrees were incensed that I had included prayers for any involved in the sanctions against South Africa. Rowntrees was active in South Africa throughout the apartheid era. Peter Hughes did, however, support me on this occasion.

The automatic conferring of confirmation on the majority of public school pupils never seemed right to me and I strenuously resisted it. In my view, it made much more pastoral sense for a person to be confirmed in his or her own parish. However, it was clearly appropriate for some boys and, after suitable preparation and stimulating weekends away at Marrick Priory, a Residential Centre in Swaledale, there were some memorable and moving confirmation services held during my time.

Apart from the termly special services, occasions such as the sudden deaths of Pope John Paul I, John Lennon and Steve Biko resulted in changes from the normal morning format. These services were appreciated by many of the pupils.

The Chaplain has always also taught RE/RS. When I started, only a very few pupils took O-level / GCSE Religious Studies. I persuaded Peter Gardiner to allow the whole School to take the examination. This was introduced to take place at the end of Year 4, 'so as not to interfere with the other exams'. I accepted this and it worked. Even pupils who stated that they were 'anti-chapel' and 'anti-religion' grudgingly enjoyed doing well in the RE external exam.

After six years I felt that I had run out of new ideas. There was a danger of a cycle of repetition. The major changes regarding chapel and worship had been established, and on account of my increasing battles with both the Head Master and Dean Jasper, it was clearly time for me to move on. All that was needed on my last day in chapel was to 'show what the best-dressed Chaplains wear under their cassocks'. The sight of Peter Croft's face as I exited in a bright, canary-yellow 'Superman' jumper, given to me by the pupils, was a memory to cherish. I would not have missed those six years for anything. It was a privilege to work with great colleagues and pupils.

Chapel 1983–87
Stephen Griffith

I was appointed as Chaplain on the understanding that after four years I would return to parish life. The Chaplain was then primarily in a pastoral role and so I began my work in a new world at the beginning of 1983.

My predecessor's radicalism made innovations in Chapel life easy, and we continued with a wide variety in Chapel. One day Keith Pemberton played 'Do they know it's Christmas' as the opening music, and helped launch a Live Aid campaign which involved many pupils and staff, with my Rice Krispie cakes selling in the Memorial Hall and a team bagging vast amounts of flour for Ethiopia. House weeks continued, with some Houses managing to put on three or four stimulating services, and others none. The Rise and School House were always the best singers.

My office tended to attract a wide variety of pupils, sometimes tearful, often gossipy and frequently bursting with laughter. When *The Bulletin* was launched by Dan Conaghan I managed to supply him with plenty of titbits to make sure I had some editorial control: his taste in gossip prepared him for his later position as the gossip columnist on the *Daily Telegraph*.

Singing was key in making compulsory Chapel palatable in those days, and so I introduced some Taizé chants. One, *Jubilate Deo*, was sung in canon, and was taken up by some of the rowers who were heard singing and rowing in canon on the Ouse. I introduced the tune of *Land of Hope and Glory* for *At the name of Jesus* and the rafters shivered with the sound.

It was an unstable time in the life of the school, but many of the staff were passionate about education and the pupils, and I was inspired by teachers in many departments to encourage pupils to think beyond the curriculum and not just about passing exams.

In my final summer we had the tragic death of Barry Daniel. The memorial service was unlike any I had ever arranged, with Barry's own collection of quotations read out, and a Chopinesque piece by Paul Thompson with a falling motif which still remains in my mind.

York City was a significant part of life in those days, winning the Division Four Championship, and I was charged with organizing a sixth-form visit to Bootham Crescent as guests of the club to watch York v Chester. I had a major row with Peter Croft in the small dining room about the safety aspect of going to the match. This was the only time I won.

Ian Lowe, agnostic as he was, made a very positive contribution to Chapel, and was a real support to me. He made a famous entrance as a workman coming to fix the organ and ended up in a clever dialogue; but his production of *Zigger Zagger* gave me an opportunity for acting not only as the Head Master (Robin Pittman backed out) but as myself as 'The Football Fan Vicar.' And I was.

Chapel 1987–96
Steven Harvey

I became Chaplain of St Peter's in March 1987. I vividly remember my first experience of Chapel – because of the hearty and enthusiastic hymn-singing of *Immortal, invisible* and *Be thou my vision*, if I recall correctly.

115

Hymnody has always been important in my spiritual life, and, for such a priest, ministering at St Peter's was a great joy. I well remember the Risites (boys in those days, of course) coming into chapel and eagerly looking to see whether the word 'rise' was to appear in either of that morning's hymns. And also the occasion when, as a protest about the suspension of a boy, almost the whole school refused to sing.

It was a great privilege to work with such talented and supportive musicians as Andrew Wright, Keith Pemberton and Joanna Marsh – each of whom had a profound understanding of music's role in the liturgy (a great blessing for any priest). I recall with great pleasure the 'state occasions' in the Minster twice each year – and not least the hauntingly beautiful introits which made such effective use of that great building, and the privilege of welcoming such figures as Cardinal Basil Hume and Bishop David Jenkins to preach.

The issue of compulsory chapel is one with which most Chaplains have to engage. I actually enjoyed the often heated discussions I had with pupils throughout my time at St Peter's. This issue arose in a particularly pronounced way in the discussions surrounding the introduction of a termly whole-school Eucharist. I felt it was important that, as part of their introduction to, and experience of, Christian faith and worship, the school should experience what is, for most Christian traditions, the central act of worship. I remember with gratitude the goodwill of staff and pupils towards an innovation which was not universally welcomed. We also experimented with a voluntary Eucharist on Sunday evenings, and, towards the end of my time, with Eucharists in the boarding houses.

The annual round included the Confirmation Service. Confirmation preparation usually included a visit to the Community of the Resurrection, an Anglican monastic community at Mirfield. For several years, Fr Barry Orford, then a monk at Mirfield, came to spend a week at the School. He gave addresses in Chapel, spoke to several classes and, in the evenings, held discussions with groups of senior pupils in my flat in Alcuin. One particular year, the issue of science and religion came up every evening. I followed this up with an invitation to Archbishop John Habgood, who came and spoke to the Science Society. His title was 'The interface of science and theology'. The lecture was very well attended and gave rise to an excellent question and answer session afterwards. It was, I felt, a significant evening for several pupils.

In addition to welcoming Confirmation candidates to Mirfield, Fr Barry also invited groups to visit the Community – usually on a special day in the liturgical calendar. Several visits were made – during which we joined the Community for the Sung Eucharist in their fine church, and were then entertained to dinner by the students at the theological college which the Community runs.

Among my memories of staff contributions to Chapel are Dick Hubbard's week, at Remembrance-tide, about some family letters from the First World War, and David Hughes' week on the poetry of that conflict. In my first year we established a Leavers' Service, held on the day before Commem and attended by the whole School. The idea was that the address should not be given by the Chaplain but by another member of staff (usually a leaver). Guy Shuttleworth started us off memorably in 1987.

We had a Chapel Committee, the main task of which was to select the charities we would support during a given year (one local, one national and one international). While I always sought to guide the deliberations, I was somewhat hurt on one occasion when one member of the Committee declared that the only qualification necessary for serving on the Chapel Committee was the 'ability to say "Yes" in fifty different languages'.

It is a priest's privilege to preside at the Occasional Offices, and my memories of St Peter's include many baptisms, weddings and funerals. In addition to conducting the weddings of several OPs, I was privileged to conduct the weddings (or blessings) of several members of staff. Sadly, there were also funerals, or memorial services too.

Material changes during my years at St Peter's included new eucharistic vestments, a new lectern made by Stephen Whalley, new choir gowns, and new candle-holders which did much to enhance the annual Advent Carol Service.

A later ministry involved me in responsibility for appointing school Chaplains. At interview, I always asked candidates which words and images they would use to describe the role of a school Chaplain. For me, the key words are 'priest', 'pastor', 'teacher', 'prophet' and 'sign'. It is an enormous privilege to be given the opportunity to exercise such a ministry, and I look back on my nine and a half years at St Peter's with huge affection and with a deep sense of gratitude to the pupils and staff who made those years such happy, fulfilling and rewarding ones for me.

Music 1986–2006

ANDREW WRIGHT

The strength of a music department, I believe, depends on the strength of its singing. Its ability to reach out and touch the lives of as many pupils as possible is also crucially important. Many pupils have musical ability that can pass unnoticed and I hope that we are efficient talent-spotters at St Peter's.

In 1986 the St Peter's and St Olave's music departments operated from the music school. The whole operation was smaller then, of course. Adding the annexe was beneficial in providing extra teaching space and later, when St Olave's moved to the Queen Anne site, it led to further development of this area, first in providing a computer room and a recording studio to cater for the tremendous growth in composition work. Secondly, the Recital Room named after Francis Jackson, one of the most notable organist-composers at York Minster in the 20th century, was opened by him in 1996. It has given us a tremendously useful rehearsal area and room for exams and performing.

We also gained a room equipped with computers, all with Sibelius software, which enables pupils to compose easily and efficiently. The stock of pianos has improved greatly through the years. The Friends of St Peter's have helped, especially with percussion. We now have three timpani, a xylophone and vibraphone, which add great colour to large-scale performances.

When St Peter's Lutheran Chorale from Brisbane visited us on their European tour, the logical next step was for us to tour. The first St Peter's Music Tour in 1991 went to Germany, to Bremen and Münster. It set a trend and inspired an enthusiasm which still lasts. Most of the major tours have included the choir and wind band and have contributed greatly to the musical standard of the department.

The first tour to the US was remarkable for its scale: 80 pupils and ten staff touring for two weeks. One of the concerts was in the Rose Bowl near Philadelphia, to an audience of 3,500 people. In 2005 we went to the US for the second time, with almost 100 pupils. A service and concert in St Bartholemew's in New York, with a huge congregation, and evensong in Washington Cathedral were highlights to be remembered.

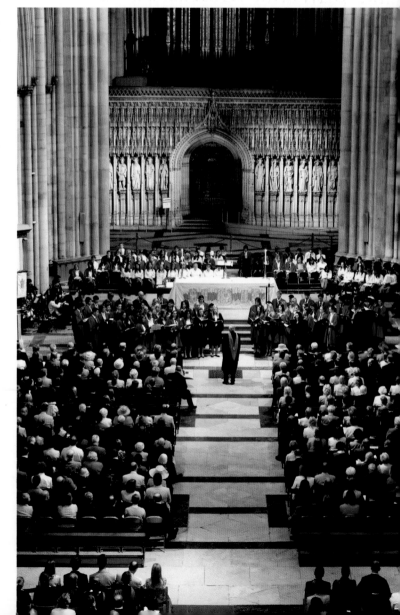

Right: The Choir in the Minster.

a recital, with video screens all around the Chapel to give a view of his nimble footwork on the organ. We now have an efficient instrument which is also good for teaching. Alex Woodrow's organ scholarship to Magdalene College, Cambridge, in 2004 bears testimony to the value of the new organ.

Participating in a musical is all-absorbing. The degree of focus needed is such that it takes over one's whole life, as any pupil or member of staff will know. It is this degree of intensity which is so valuable. Those who were involved with *My Fair Lady*, *Kiss Me Kate*, *Grease*, *The Threepenny Opera*, *Close the Coalhouse Door* or *Guys and Dolls* will understand this, whatever their part in the team.

It would be impossible to mention all the teachers who have given such devoted service to the department over the last 20 years. Nonetheless, I must single out Keith Pemberton, my predecessor as Director of Music, whose help was invaluable. I was especially grateful for his support. Jeffrey Gray, Head of Music in St Olave's 1987–94, did a huge amount to establish the firm base of music within the junior school. He also worked in St Peter's, where he established the barbershop group, which still continues as a lasting legacy.

Irene Stanley's piano teaching reached the highest standard that I have witnessed; Jo Marsh's appearance as School organist and her lively approach was a tonic in the 1990s; Maggie Lamb made a major contribution in developing the structure of the string department and ensuring that its teaching improved. This has led to a vibrant area of the music at school, which Penny Stirling has taken to new heights. Chris Blood's arrival in 1993 has seen the reorganization of the wind and brass into a strong force. His work with the brass group for our major services in the Minster has been outstanding.

Tours closer to home have continued to play an important part in the life of the music department. The 1998 tour to Barcelona was another large affair. Chapel choir tours with strings have gone twice to St Malo, where singing in the Abbey at Mont St Michel is a special memory. We have also visited Austria, Prague, San Remo and Venice.

By the 1980s the chapel organ was in a perilous condition and it had to be rebuilt in 1992. Once it was rebuilt, Carlo Curley gave

Left and below: The Brass Group.

The strength of the music department lies in its groups, of which we have a large number. They were referred to as the 'jewel in the crown' in the 2005 Inspection report. As the standard of music has improved, so these groups have developed. The chamber choir, swing band, brass group and string quartet are but four of the many groups currently in operation.

The School choir has grown remarkably over the years and now numbers some 160. In 1995 we sang at a special service in York Minster to remember the author James Herriot, whose grandchildren had all been involved in music at School. Since 1997 a chapel choir has been selected from the School choir and we reinstated the tradition of singing choral evensong at York Minster at least once a year. We have also gone further afield, to Durham and Lincoln cathedrals. Choral scholarships to various Oxford and Cambridge colleges have been a regular achievement by our pupils.

In 1996 we combined with Durham School and produced two major performances of *The Dream of Gerontius*, in York Minster and Durham Cathedral. These proved to be particularly memorable occasions. Large-scale choral concerts have taken place in school each year, including Mozart's *Requiem*, Haydn's *Nelson Mass* and Britten's *Rejoice in the Lamb*. When we sang Britten's *St Nicolas* we also took it to St Peter's Church in Norton, as we did with Bernstein's *Chichester Psalms* and Rutter's *Gloria*. Bach's *Magnificat* in 2006 was a particular achievement and it was rewarding to see pupils getting so much from this music.

Our symphony orchestra has tackled a number of demanding scores including Sibelius' *Karelia Suite*, Tchaikovsky's *Fifth Symphony* and Dvorak's *Eighth Symphony*. In 1990, when the Duchess of Kent visited the school, we produced a special concert in the chapel. It was a superb occasion, culminating in Elgar's *Grand Imperial March*. The orchestra benefited at this time from Tiffany Richards, violist, who was a member of the National Youth Orchestra.

In 1993 we instituted the first of our cabaret concerts, which have been among the most popular evenings in the musical calendar. Selections from *Les Miserables, West Side Story,* 1960s medleys and Beach Boys' songs have all featured in the programmes.

We have always tried hard to encompass all types of music within the department. One can write much about the major events, but often it is in the small-scale, informal concerts where individual pupils make the greatest progress. The act of standing up to play in public is a great character-builder and so much a part of our work as educators. Lunchtime concerts on Saturdays fulfil an essential role in this respect.

Our musical development has been enormously aided by the music scholars within each year group. They set high standards and form the nucleus of the many chamber music groups, as well as larger groups in the department. Their concert every November is a very special musical event.

There is little doubt that the music department now enjoys a high profile in both the School and wider community. I hope it continues to touch the lives of as many pupils as possible.

The Barbershop Quartet.

Art

JOHN DARMODY

Every Head Master recognizes the importance of art, if not for its status in the curriculum, then at least for its value as the shop-window of the school. St Peter's has certainly gained from the kudos that art has brought. The School has, for many years, been recognized for the high level of its pupils' achievements in art and has been fortunate in having some very fine teachers, who have driven the subject on through various times and changes. Some fine artists have taught at the school. These include William Boddy, John Gaastra and John Brown.

Since the School moved to its present site, art has been taught in some unlikely places. These include the first floor of the main building, a small attic-like space still known as The Sculpture Room, and the upper level of the cricket pavilion. All of these spaces were considered to be cramped and the problem was finally rectified when the art school moved to its present location in 2001. It is now housed over two floors in what was once the science block of Queen Anne's School. The accommodation, which incorporates the impressive Whitestone Gallery which was established through the generosity of donors, is sufficient to house a wide range of disciplines including drawing and painting, printmaking, ceramics, sculpture and photography. A busy and vibrant atmosphere is apparent throughout the department, with work filling every available space and spilling out to the exterior walls and immediate vicinity. The gallery exhibits not only our pupils' work, but also that of practising artists. This provides inspiration for our pupils as well as bringing a service to the community.

Our ethos is that all pupils can and should be visually literate. We aim to equip all those who study art with a visual vocabulary with which they can express their feelings and opinions, and through which they can enhance the quality of their lives.

Above: 'Portrait of father' by Alex England.

Right: Albert Moore, St Peter's 1854–55, 'A Garden' (1869).

'Buildings' by Wai Hong Lang.

123

Drawing is regarded as fundamental and is the foundation stone for everything we do in the art school. It underpins our painting, printmaking, sculpture and ceramics. Our students are encouraged to look and record, translate and create.

Whilst St Peter's does not have a long list of famous artists who attended the school, it includes Albert Moore (1841–93), one of the most remarkable artists of the Victorian era, whose quest for true beauty was a fundamental aspect of his paintings. In an age when drawing from the antique was all important in the development of a young artist, Moore would have undoubtedly have had some grounding in this respect in his early days at St Peter's and then at The York School of Design, before moving on to Kensington Grammar School at the age of 14. Moore's work reflects the fashion of the time for Greco-Roman artefacts, but with a fresh approach to aesthetics. His work is akin to the late flowering of the pre-Raphaelites, especially Edward Burne-Jones and Frederic Leighton.

One of the great design icons of the 20th century, the London Underground map, was the creation of another Peterite, Frank Pick. A memorial plaque to him stands in the school grounds. Much has been written and said about this work, which has become the blueprint for public service travel worldwide.

124

Top right: Bethany Smith self-portrait 2006.

Top left: 'Abstract' by Meghan Sinclair 2006.

Above: 'Street scene' by Emily Outhwaite.

Left: 'Church exterior' by Sophie Crossley.

Design and Technology

MIKE DAWSON

The subject of design and technology in St Peter's School has its roots in carpentry classes, which were organized in the evenings to occupy boarders. It has come a long way since then. The design and technology department is a creative environment, which demands a variety of skills, based on problem-solving, to produce functional and aesthetically pleasing projects. The whole ethos of the subject is to design and make products which fulfil the needs and requirements of the user. Innovation and evidence of quality are central to this process.

When the subject was exclusively woodwork or metalwork, there was little freedom of choice. Nonetheless, both subjects required a high level of skill in cabinet-making or engineering. Now we use a whole range of materials and processes and choice is limited only by imagination. CAD (computer-aided-design) and CAM (computer- aided manufacture) are used in many of our projects. These processes are more akin to those used in the wider world and they demonstrate what happens in an industrial environment.

The subject has changed markedly in recent years and, if anything, become even more demanding. The quality of the work in the department is testament to the ability and skills of pupils.

Left: Lamp project by Ian Macalister.

Top Right: Land yacht by Simon Bell.

Right: Clock project by Ceri Bowring.

125

'The play's the thing ...'

AVRIL PEDLEY

Drama at St Peter's has a long and notable history. References in medieval records indicate that the boys took part in a variety of dramatic performances and by the 1570s evidence is strong. John Pulleyn (Guy Fawkes' Head Master) formed a company of players among the boys, and there is clear evidence that their efforts were not confined to school premises. The Chamberlain's book of York Minster in 1575 records payments to troupes of players attached to Lord Stafford, the Earl of Essex, a Lancashire group, and 'xx shillings to the Scollers of the Horsefair [i.e. St Peter's] players'. Ten years later the York City Chamberlain's records showed 'To John Pullen skollers which played in the Common Hall 40 shillings'; The same ledger showed payments of only ten shillings to the Earl of Worcester's players and 20 to Lord Oxford's men, so perhaps the boys from the Horsefair were particularly popular.

As so often in the story of St Peter's, a gap in the records then ensues and it is not until the 19th century, when the School was firmly fixed in its present premises, that plays began to be produced in earnest on a regular basis. It may well be that the fluctuating, mainly small numbers in the School in the intervening years, and the unsuitable premises in which those numbers were housed, made attempts at drama virtually impossible.

It was in December 1864 that amateur theatricals began with a charade and *Box and Cox*. The following year two plays were put on in the hall and costumes were hired from Covent Garden in London. There was music between the acts: 'Mr Athorne gave a comic song'. (Tom Beverley Athorne was a pupil of the School 1855–65.) The full house greatly appreciated the show, though the local critics thought the first play (*The Sleeping Draught*) was not happily chosen. Christmas activities of this type went on for only another two years, their place being taken by musical diversions thereafter, but in 1876 plays were resumed, under the banner of the 'Royal School of St Peter, York, Amateur Dramatic Club', and apparently at a much higher level of competence.

The Critic in that year was followed by *The Merchant of Venice* in 1877 and *Twelfth Night* (with another play, *Chrononhotonthologos*) the year after. The two items together lasted over four hours. In 1878 George Yeld, our longest-serving-ever member of staff, took over responsibility for the event, and from 1880 he began the custom of writing an Epilogue, in which past and present members of the School who had distinguished themselves were mentioned in verse. Shakespeare was most frequently chosen, and *The Peterite* reported all productions. Plays continued all through the headmasterships of Messrs Stephenson (1872–87) and Handford (1887–1900), when the title of 'The School Play' is first used, but under Canon Owen the newly-formed School Musical Society proved so popular that the Christmas theatricals temporarily gave way to a breaking-up concert. In 1909 the School participated with enthusiasm in the great York Pageant, and we are lucky enough still to have photographs of the event, a marked-up script and a full printed programme.

Later, the new Head Master, Mr Toyne, was a very keen actor. He initiated the rebirth of the St Peter's Amateur Dramatic Society in the year of his appointment, 1913; masters as well as

Above: School group for York Pageant, 1909.

Right: The Pirates of Penzance, *1963.*

boys appeared in the cast. Shakespeare was replaced by lighter fare: *She Stoops to Conquer* in 1917, *The Speckled Band* in 1920, *The Admirable Crichton* in 1924 and so on. For the Toynes, drama was a family affair and not confined to the Christmas Term. *The Peterite* recorded Mrs Toyne's 'constant readiness to denude her house to furnish the stage' and her foundation of 'The Curtain', a society for reading plays during the year.

Even the war years did nothing to stop the popularity of drama and it is clear that 'the show must go on' was a precept valued at St Peter's. In the 1940s and 50s, Leslie Burgess was both Senior Classics Master and Second Master under John Dronfield. 'Bung', as he was widely known, produced most of the school plays during his time with us and also wrote several plays which were professionally produced. The best known was *Sounding Brass*, based on the life of the Railway King, George Hudson, which was premiered at the Theatre Royal in York as part of the Festival of Britain celebrations in 1951.

Then along came the 1960s. Mr P. H. Bolton was the producer of a range of shows of widely varying type. There was *The Strong are Lonely*, or *The Holy Experiment* by Fritz Hochwaelder in 1963 and *Pirates of Penzance* the same year; *Henry IV Part One* in 1965; *Penny for a Song* by John Whiting in 1967 and so on, followed by a few years when a variety of producers and directors took up the challenge.

Step up a new Head of Drama in 1972: an institution had arrived. Ian Lowe took over the reins in that year and finally relinquished them 30 years later. An unbroken run of 30 productions by one staff member must surely be a record for any school, and from the first moment everything looked very different. *The Peterite* of May 1974 said of Ian's production of *The Fire Raiser*s by Max Frisch, 'As soon as we entered the Memorial Hall we knew that this was to be no ordinary play'. It was to be no ordinary 30 years. In that period there were also notable ventures not produced by Ian at all. Among others, a pageant, *Poorlinus was here*, was presented by David Cummin to mark the School's 1350th anniversary; under Dick Hubbard's guidance, *Oh What a Lovely War!* took to the stage in 1984 and Arbel Lowther and Andrew Wright superintended a wonderful production of *Pirates of Penzance* in the Joseph Rowntree Theatre in 1999.

On Ian's retirement from his role as Head of Drama, the school welcomed Kat Edgar-Hunt, and drama took on a new dimension: examinations. Drama and Theatre Studies are now taught at both GCSE, A/S and A2 levels. Pupils are taught practical skills and enhance their appreciation of drama by studying a range of texts, in both their historical and social contexts and through investigation of different dramatic styles. In addition to the traditional school play at Christmas, there are a variety of productions such as the middle-school play, large-scale musical productions and various drama clubs and events throughout the year. Recent productions have included *Macbeth*, *The Threepenny Opera*, *Two*, *Bed*, and *Blue Remembered Hills*. As ever, 'The play's the thing…'

Above: The Pirates of Penzance, *1999.*

Left: Guys and Dolls, *November 2002.*

Right: Harlequin and Guy Fawkes, 2005.

Below: Dave Hughes as Kent in King Lear.

Below right: Ian Lowe as King Lear in November 2001.

129

My Sister's Sixth-form Boyfriend Fancied Me

GREG WISE

I was, it has to be said, quite lovely: bottle-green tights, body-hugging dress, flowing locks … I was playing the part of Phoebe, the love interest (in love with my geography teacher, if memory serves) in Gilbert and Sullivan's *Yeoman of the Guard*. To add interest to the piece, my treble voice decided to break over the performances, so the chaste Phoebe ended up decidedly baritone.

Over the years at St Olave's and St Peter's I played the parts of two girls, a scarecrow, a pirate and a bored Shakespearian. I had my first smell of grease-paint and learned that you could take off makeup with Brylcream (haven't tried that one since). I made props, helped hang the theatre lights, had my first stage kiss (with my bearded geography teacher) and fell in love with drama.

Like so many, my choice of profession was motivated by a teacher and I am eternally indebted to Ian Lowe. Ian was my English teacher. He introduced me to Shakespeare, poetry, prose and to Bob Dylan, arguing with the Examination Board that Dylan should be granted the status of an important 20th-century poet. Ian's lessons were drama. His infectious love of his subject would make him jump about and bash into desks. We would all be allocated parts and create the Roman Senate or a Dorset farmhouse in the classroom.

Ian directed plays in the Drama Centre. At 16 I tackled Tom Stoppard's *Rosencrantz and Guildenstern are Dead*; quite a difficult, existential role for one who'd only just started shaving. We did alternate performances over a week with Samuel Becket's *Waiting for Godot*, the two tramps played by my sister and my girlfriend. Previously the School's approach to drama casting had been very Shakespearian, with boys playing the girls' roles as we had no girls at school. So now that girls were present, why should they not play male roles? This is what drama was at St Peter's; giving the students an opportunity for exploration, insight, taking up a challenge, learning and performing. A wonderful extracurricular activity, but I would go a step further and say an essential element in the

education of a pupil. As academic learning expands the brain and sport expands the lungs, so drama expands the mind, showing us other worlds and lives that we can briefly inhabit and understand. A York shopkeeper's son can be Hamlet, Prince of Denmark's girlfriend, and we in the audience suspend our disbelief and go along with the idea. He was, by the way, very convincing.

Very few students may end up, as I did, pursuing a career in drama, but all who participated in acting at St Peter's will have had their perceptions changed, their adrenalin stimulated and hopefully found a part of themselves that surprised, pleased and gave them confidence; a confidence that they will carry with them into their adult lives.

World Challenge Expeditions 2001–05

MIKE AND SAM HALL

In the summer of 1999 we approached World Challenge Expeditions, who offer exciting destinations combined with comprehensive support and safety systems. Their programme involved an 18-month run-in before the expedition, where pupils (mainly sixth-formers) fund-raise for the trip and design their own itinerary. Each expedition included four phases: an acclimatization trek, a demanding trek, which stretched even the strongest pupil, a community service phase and a much deserved rest and relaxation phase.

ECUADOR EXPEDITION, JULY 2001

Thirty-three pupils went on this five-week trip. The popularity of the first expedition was such that we had a waiting list. Once in Ecuador, we split into two teams for the entire time in the country.

World Challenge Venezuela, 2005.

Cotopaxi Team

This team had set their sights on climbing the famous Cotopaxi Volcano, part of the Pacific 'Ring of Fire'. At a colossal 5,897m it is one of the highest volcanoes in the world. In the UK the team had undergone winter training in the Cairngorms, getting used to using crampons, an ice axe and the cold. Once in Ecuador the whole group climbed the volcano Illiniza Norte (height 5,126m) as a warm-up, and apart from a few members of the team having to pull out of the summit attempt, 15 Peterites reached the top of Cotopaxi.

Riminahui Team

This team's community project was based in Quito, where they spent a week in a homeless shelter, cleaning and painting the inside of the central hall of the main building, as well as interacting with the children. The main focus for this group was to climb volcano Riminahui (4,712m) in the Cotopaxi National Park. Two pupils succumbed to illness prior to the ascent. The remainder of the team, however, climbed the peak and enjoyed the spectacular views along the Andes.

ECUADOR EXPEDITION, JULY 2003

The second expedition to Ecuador was made up of 15 pupils and lasted five weeks. The entire group climbed the volcano Illiniza Norte (height 5,126m), which was a considerable achievement given the wintry conditions on top and the thin air at this altitude. They also spent a week in a rural primary school, helping to repair and paint the entire school, much to the delight of

World Challenge Morocco, 2004.

teachers and parents. After a day spent white-water rafting, they trekked with a local indigenous Indian guide through jungle terrain and lived with his extended family.

MOROCCO EXPEDITION, JULY 2004

Some 17 third- and fourth-form pupils went on this two-week trip to build enthusiasm for future expeditions. Based in Marrakech, the team completed two separate treks. The first began from the famous Todra Gorge and passed through valleys and foothills on the edge of the Sahara Desert. The weather remained fiercely hot, but the pupils coped well. The second trip was in and around the Atlas Mountain chain. On both occasions a team of guides and mules was hired to carry the camping equipment and food. On both treks the team made the most of the opportunity to interact with the local guides and village inhabitants. One student learned the secrets of the tea ceremony, whilst others were soundly beaten in a football match.

VENEZUELA EXPEDITION, JULY 2005

Seventeen pupils went on this five-week expedition. The main focus of this trip was a community project in a remote village (found only by travelling up river in boats) in the Amazon jungle. Here the team spent a week sleeping in hammocks and teaching English to the local children and adults. There was also an improvised cricket match. This time the choice of a sport unknown to the indigenous tribes of the Amazon resulted in an English victory!

Two week-long treks formed the main physical challenge of the expedition. In order to acclimatize, the team trekked through dense jungle, passing over the range of coastal mountains that form the backbone of the Henri Pittier National Park. After five days in the bush, the team emerged triumphant at a small beach-side village on the Caribbean Sea. Following this they travelled to Santa Elena, close to the Brazilian border, to begin their attempt to climb the famous tepui, Roraima. The tepui are table-top mountains rising sheer above the flat, savannah plains of Southern Venezuela. Roraima was the inspiration for the book *The Lost World* by Sir Arthur Conan Doyle. Following the long climb, the Peterites enjoyed spectacular views, as well as admiring diverse flora and fauna, much of it unique to this mountain.

The First World War Battlefield Trips 1987–2006

RICHARD DRYSDALE

In 1987 the history department took the first group of pupils to the Ypres and Somme areas of France and Belgium, where the fighting had been intense and so many from both sides had perished, including many Peterites. Some 19 school trips have now visited these battlefields. The extent of the cemeteries and the scale of the losses is overwhelming. There are, for example, 12,000 buried at Tyne Cot near Ypres. Just under 56,000 names of British and Empire soldiers who have no known burial site are recorded on the Menin Gate in Ypres. One treads lightly, with a sense of humility and sorrow in the cemeteries. With adult groups who have gone from the School it is common for individuals to be reduced to tears at the sight of the graves of so many young men.

In 1998 Bill Hudson and Mike Bainbridge, representing the Governors, joined a school party at the Thiepval Memorial on the Somme and laid a wreath, after Simon Austin, a fourth former, had sounded the Last Post. This was followed by a minute's silence. All that could be heard was birdsong. The occasion was extremely moving for all who were there. School parties on the battlefields trips have since laid wreaths in remembrance at the Menin Gate ceremony held each evening in Ypres at 8 pm when the Last Post is sounded. It is one of the duties of the history department never to allow such terrible events as the First World War to be forgotten.

134

First World War Battlefields Trip 2005.

The Duke of Edinburgh Award Scheme

ANDREW SEVERN

St Peter's has been actively involved with the Award for many years, and it is not surprising that pupils have gained much from the scheme. For many, the highlight is the expedition element. Until the end of the 1990s, groups would participate at all levels in expeditions on the Moors and in the Lake District. The increased role of Health and Safety legislation and the requirement that staff have mountain leaders' qualifications has, for the past years, confined pupils to working for the Bronze Award. This, however, has not detracted from the experience. Invariably, expeditions are characterized by weather conditions which range from poor to appalling. The determination of Peterites to complete the task, no matter what the conditions on the North Yorkshire Moors is remarkable. Record numbers on the Moors at any one time were 56 tired and rather wet fourth-formers.

The service element provides our pupils with a wide range of opportunities, many originating from the hard work done by staff running the community services option. Work in charity shops, visiting the elderly and recycling projects represent a few examples of what can be done for the Award.

St Peter's is able to offer many opportunities to complete the skill and physical activity sections, although a significant number of pupils have, over the years, embarked upon their own ideas.

Over the next few years we expect to offer the Gold Award as part of the scheme and we confidently expect the Award to flourish at St Peter's.

135

Above: Duke of Edinburgh Award Expedition 2003.
Left: Duke of Edinburgh Award Expedition 2002 .

Yr Hafod: Winter Hill Walking and Mountaineering 1986–2002

DAVE HUGHES

It is difficult to frame this narrative: it feels like trying to take freeze-frames of a kaleidoscope: the outline and the pieces and the colours are always the same, but the pattern never is. There have been, and continue to be, many years of hill-walking trips from St Peter's, but if I try to deal with them all, the stories will spill beyond all containment. So I shall largely confine myself to the successive years of our trips to yr Hafod in the Ogwen Valley of Snowdonia. We went for three days on the hills between the end of term and Christmas itself, with a day's travelling either side.

Barry Daniel had run the trips previously, before his tragic death in July 1986 on Svartisen glacier in Arctic Norway. There was a brief feeling that this accident meant the end of such trips; then a sudden upsurge of emotion that it should not. Those who had enjoyed earlier times wanted to revisit in a kind of pilgrimage; and I was willingly dragooned into going with them, a nominal leader who did not necessarily think he had much say in things. Many pupils wanted to come as well, and I have to say how much I admired their parents' courage in allowing them to do so. As usual, we had two groups out on the first day, in very strong winds on Snowdon itself, and it did feel right to be back.

Yr Hafod, 'the hut', mutated into an almost luxurious hostel over time. The only way of keeping less than damp in the early days was to hope that one of the more naïve beginners would bring a down-filled sleeping bag and so mop up the moisture. Books immediately went crinkle-cut. One year the needle of my hygrometer bent at 120 degrees humidity: if it had been anything above freezing, we should have been living in a rain-forest. It was, of course, colder and wetter outside. Now there are radiators and de-humidifiers, showers and a well-equipped kitchen.

What pleases me is the mixture of people who took part, and the way in which so many of them kept coming back to help. For life in the hut there were three or four superb cooks of evening meals, and no shortage of volunteers for lesser tasks. (I take no account of my more workmanlike bacon and eggs each morning.)

On the hills themselves, while the trip was designed for the pupils, it would not have been possible without fantastic loyalty from ex-Peterites. There were a number who came on every trip for all those years; there was never less than one experienced 'returner' to guide every pupil and there were often more. All were experienced in the area, having been with us four or five years in succession, even as pupils. Many were – and are – excellent, safe, general mountaineers; and a lot of them became so hooked that they took up the sport seriously in their own lives. There are qualified mountain instructors, both civilian and military; there are sometime members of mountain rescue teams, including the one in the Ogwen Valley. What we became was a mountaineering club, not a school trip. The evenings were invariably hilarious, with the kinds of conversations and jokes which reduce you to tears of laughter, but which are either unrepeatable or unfunny out of context.

The sense of expertise on the hills can be gauged from a bad-weather story on Moel Siabod. We were effectively in a white-out, where almost all the world disappears in a blur of wind and snow, and I could see that some of the youngsters were beginning to wonder if we could ever get out of it. We did. Years later, at his wedding, one of those pupils said to his stepfather, 'They looked at a clump of grass, and they knew which way to go. We couldn't believe it'. I certainly was not the only one capable of such a trick. We occasionally tried to add up the combined number of days that the leaders had spent on those hills we were using, not

Snowdonia in Winter.

137

counting experience elsewhere; we always had to give up when the total reached 300.

And the weather could be bad. Occasionally we resorted to visiting famous shipwrecks of Anglesey. We once saw one of the leaders doing finger-tip press-ups in lower Cwm Idwal while wearing a 50lb rucksack – with the wind under him. Funnily enough, this was the same person who, as a pupil, saw me stick my head round a protective rock on the summit of Glyder Fawr, take one more step, and then blow back above him. I landed on my feet. One year, it took a group the best part of nine hours to ascend and descend Tryfan, a mountain whose summit is only half a mile from the starting point on the road – and they were proud to have done it.

There were also fabulously beautiful days: one whole group on the Glyders tuned themselves into choruses of *Walking in a Winter Wonderland.* Some people came for years and never saw a view from Snowdon. Others came up on days of such clarity that you could see all the kingdoms and principalities: the Pennines, the Peak District, Ireland north and south, Man, the Lake

Snowdonia Expedition.

District, the Brecon Beacons. Such times were rare, but all the more precious for that. On the Carneddau range, on the last trip of all, we were paced by a magical 'Brocken spectre', where you are above the cloud, looking down on your own shadow and seeing it surrounded by a halo of rainbows: I have only ever seen that twice in 40 years on the hills.

These days, these events, are a privilege reserved for very few teachers. I am grateful for them all, and grateful to all those who shared them with me.

The Sahara Expeditions 1978–93

JOHN BULCOCK

During the Easter holiday in 1978, the first of 13 lower-sixth expeditions to the northern regions of the Sahara took place, each lasting between three and four weeks. The Easter vacation in a lower-sixth year which was then free from public examinations was considered the ideal time to fulfil the aims of these journeys: travel, companionship, self-reliance and the experience of a small part of the third world. In this context, the students carried garments and gifts for distributing to the remote village community of Meski.

Al Tooms was co-driver for nine journeys, with Barry Daniel and Peter Bell each contributing twice. On the first expedition the students flew to Malaga, where I met them with the bus and equipment; on future journeys we travelled from York by road and the Plymouth–Santander ferry. Two buses were used over the years, both Mercedes: a 207D for the first four journeys, and subsequently a more powerful and larger 507D, towing a capacious trailer, which also served as a galley where we could shelter when preparing meals during wind-swept desert conditions.

After initially visiting the far south of Morocco and the great dunes at Targhit in Algeria, the later expeditions followed a fairly regular itinerary: Plymouth – Santander – Madrid – Algeciras – Straits of Gibraltar – Ceuta – Tangier – Asilah – Marrakech – High Atlas – Ouarzazarte – Errachidia – the Blue Springs at Meski (camping for one week in the desert, swimming and collecting drinking water at this oasis, which was five miles away) – returning to the Straits and Spain via Meknes and Ceuta.

Accommodation was varied: ferry cabins, sleeping under the stars or in tents, and occasionally hotels. Memorable meals were those taken round our table out in the desert, framed by the sun and the snow on the distant Atlas peaks, before the evening chill. The most popular excursions were the markets of Marrakech, where prizes were awarded to the most and the least successful hagglers, and the sunrise over the dunes at Merzouga, which needed a 2.30am start for the journey south from the desert site, at times driving by compass bearings when crossing the wilderness in the crepuscular glimmer.

The expeditions were mainly free from crises, the worst being in 1981 when an appendix, which had first grumbled in Algeria, eventually needed surgery in Santander, and in 1993 when a leaking Mercedes water pump was brilliantly repaired by a local mechanic on the edge of the same desert region where we had once rescued a stranded nomad. The 13 expeditions covered nearly 70,000 miles; 39 girls and 145 boys travelled on them; the first cost £225 and the last £585.

They were great journeys: self-reliant, companionable, entertaining, and the experience of a lifetime.

Sahara Expedition, 1985.

A Morrocan meal.

138

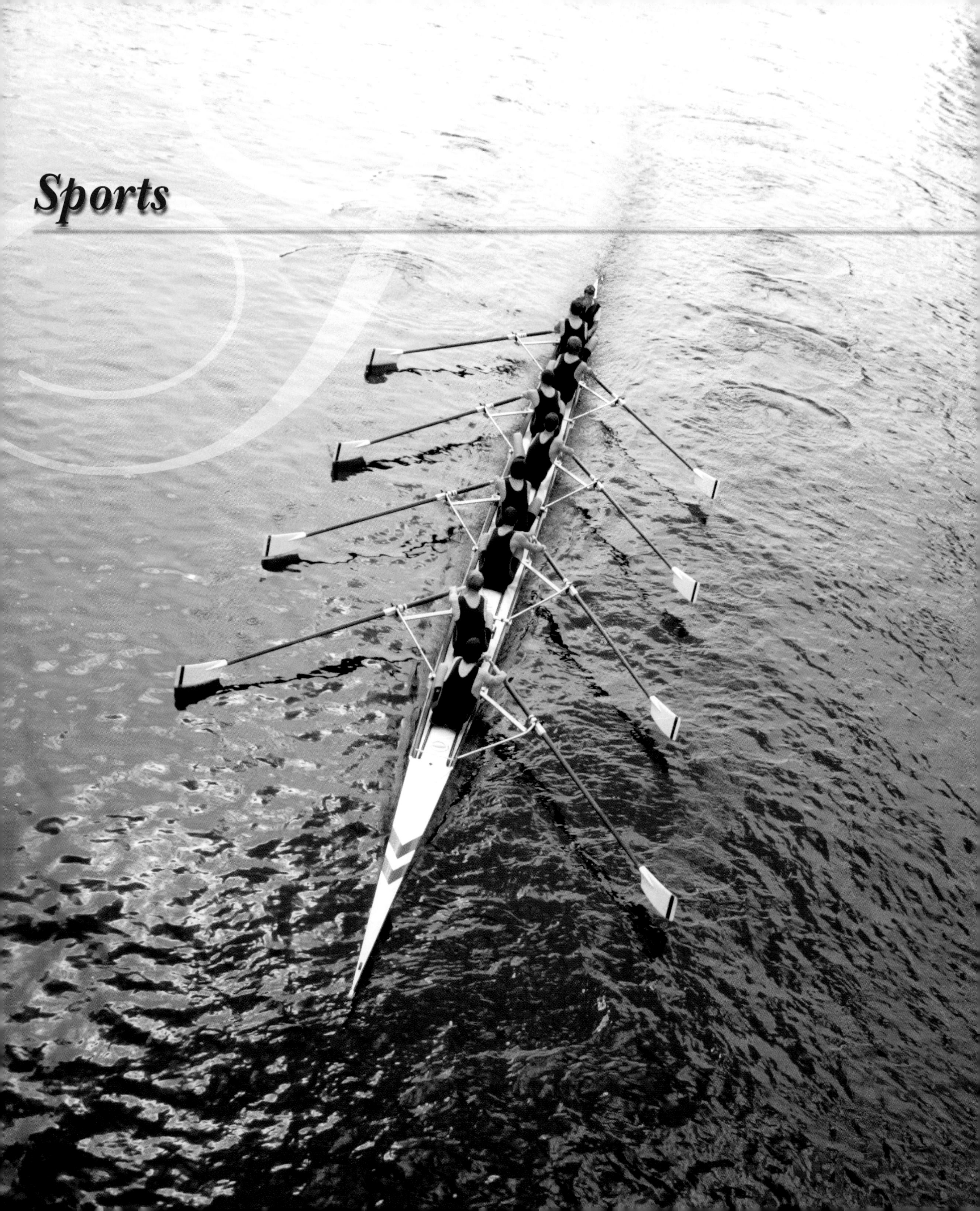
Sports

Girls' Games 1976–2005

Wendy Shepherd and Pat Fletcher

Five girls joined St Peter's in 1976 and the School games programme changed forever. Three of the girls joined Queen's and the other two joined Grove. Initially, there were no girls' changing rooms and there seemed to be a rather haphazard approach to the issue of girls' games. A budget was set up only after Wendy Shepherd saw Robin Pittman and argued forcefully that the girls' games programme had to be financially supported.

Tennis and badminton were the first games played. Swimming was available but only once the boys had vacated their changing rooms. Netball and tennis are now played by most girls throughout their school career. There have been some impressive inter-school results in both sports, especially at senior level. Girls have been selected at county level in both netball and tennis. The fact that the girls' games programme is staffed primarily by fully-qualified staff has been instrumental to the girls' successes at local, regional and national levels.

HOCKEY

Hockey was soon added to the girls' games programme and Derek Paterson was put in charge in 1979, a task he continued until 1990, when Pat Fletcher took over. In the early years girls had to be converted from lacrosse to hockey, but somehow we never managed to inherit goalkeepers. The build-up to fielding School teams at each level was inevitably a gradual one. In 1987 the under-15 hockey team took to the field. By the 1988–89 season hockey teams represented the School at under-14, under-15, 2nd and 1st XI levels. By 1981/82 the girls' 1st XI represented York and District in the Yorkshire Final of the under-18 National Championship. Their success was a tribute to their enthusiasm, commitment, hard work and talent. Hockey teams have won more than their share of tournaments and rallies over the years.

Above: Girls' Hockey 1986–87.

It has often been remarked how well we have done, given the comparatively small number of girls there were in the school in the early years of co-education. Individual players like Jo Sargeant, who represented the North of England under-19s, and Amelia Smalley who played for the under-16 England team, have excelled.

Tours to places as diverse as Edinburgh, East Anglia and Barbados became an integral part of the sports programme. In 1998 the School reached the north of England finals of the British Aerospace National Hockey competition in Blackpool.

SWIMMING

Swimming has been especially strong in the School. The first few swimming matches were held in 1988. By 1991, with Esther Williams as captain, these became far more regular events. Debbie Newman's coaching achieved early successes at the John Parry North of England Relay Championships. In 1996 the team

Girls' Swimming Team 2000–01.

of Jo Sargeant, Erica Smith, Sarah Metcalfe, Sophie Lloyd and Lizzie Sargeant won the Championships. In 1998 the team was invited to the National Relay Championships at Crystal Palace and came 15th overall. Since then the girls' team has competed annually at Crystal Palace and there have been outstanding successes. In 2002 we won a silver and a bronze with a team comprising of Jenny Hoggard, Sally Henderson, Sarah Woods and Sarah and Pamela Kinnell. In 2004 we won two bronze medals, while our best performance came in 2005 when we won two silver medals for both freestyle and the Medley Relay Competitions against the best teams from the UK. The team on this occasion was made up of Sally Henderson, Katherine Wackett, Pamela Kinnell and Alice Sunderland. The School has rarely lost an inter-school match between 2000 and 2005.

The Hoggard family deserve special mention as Lynsay, Karly and Jenny have all been outstanding swimmers and team captains for the School. Other memorable past captains included Sarah Metcalfe and Sally Henderson, and one of the most charismatic captains was Antonia Hazelrigg in 2000. No one from her year will forget her pacing the poolside, almost swimming everyone's race for them.

CROSS COUNTRY AND ATHLETICS

Cross country and athletics have always been minority attractions, yet the few who have participated have achieved notable success. After reaching the National Cross Country Finals in 1992, Rachael Ogden went on to win the 800m in the English Schools' Athletics Championships in 1994. She was then chosen to represent the Great Britain under-20s team in the 800m, an outstanding achievement. Karly Hoggard and Claire Taylor reached the National Cross Country Finals in 1993, while more recently, Lara Gibbs achieved great success in national cross country races. Success in cross country has often transferred on to the track and we have had several strong middle-distance runners: Katie Mellor and Emma McAllister Hall ran in county championships, although both have been plagued by injury. Other athletes to achieve county success were Erica Smith in the 200m in 1999, Sophie Cuthbertson in the long jump in 2005 and Jo Sargeant, an all-rounder, who reached the National Schools Athletics Championships in 1999 throwing the javelin.

The inter-house cross country remains compulsory for the middle-school girls, but most sixth-formers enter too in a spirit of good humour. In the 1988/89 season, the senior girls won the York and District Cross Country Competition for the fifth year running. The teams of 2003/04 competed as the North of England winners at the National Schools Championship in Chester, but unfortunately the team had been decimated by illness that day.

142

York and District Schools Tennis Champions 1995–96.

Girls' First Tennis Team 2003.

TENNIS

The success of girls' tennis since 1989 has been quite remarkable. There has been strength and depth. The available results show that, over a 15-year period, the 1st VI have won 84 per cent of their matches. The 1st VI teams of 1997, 1999 and 2005 won all their matches.

More recently, street-dance, body toning and trampolining have been added to the games programme to give greater variety. The occasional mixed matches, with boys playing, have always been popular. Those who miss games still face a compulsory swim at 4pm on a Saturday. Many OPs will be glad to know this session still functions.

143

Cricket 1945–2005

DAVID KIRBY

St Peter's earned its reputation as a fine cricket school well before the Second World War. The first big name in the school's cricket history was Frank Mitchell (1884–90). After leaving school he played for Cambridge University, Yorkshire, then England, and later returned to this country as Captain of South Africa. He was followed in the 1920s by Brian Sellers, who captained Yorkshire, and in the 1930s by Norman Yardley, who went on to captain both Yorkshire and England. It did no harm to have Sam Toyne as Head Master 1913–36, as he had played county cricket for Hampshire and did an immense amount for cricket at St Peter's.

Since 1945 the standard of cricket has remained consistently high and St Peter's has been a leading school in the north of England. It has helped that in 60 years there have only been two Masters-in-charge of the 1st XI, Robert Harding and me. In the early years after the war, the School had several good seasons and were three times unbeaten in school matches, with teams captained by John Rayson, Peter Baker and Murray Hodd. After a few lean years, 1957 saw the start of another excellent run. In the next 16 years, only 11 inter-school matches were lost and in eight of those seasons the team was unbeaten. The 1966 and 1972 teams, captained by Bill Pickersgill and Stephen Coverdale, were undefeated in all matches.

The 1st XI field situated behind the School has always been excellent, though its shape is somewhat eccentric. The straight boundaries are short and in one corner a squash court used to jut out into the field. Sadly for cricketers, when the new science block was built in 1984 the unusual corner was retained. The pitches are ideal for batting, especially since 1976, when covers were bought for the School. They were the first gift from the Cricket Social Committee, which was formed in 1975. This group of parents and members of staff has done a lot to support cricket and to provide extra facilities. The stock of blazers which the players borrow and the electronic scoreboard were particularly valuable gifts.

The 1970s saw some significant and beneficial changes. The opening of the sports centre in 1973 meant the availability of indoor nets throughout the year. The acquisition of covers not only allowed

Norman Yardley presents an autographed bat to John Rayson, Captain of Cricket, 1946.

Above: Brian Sellers and David Kirby 1958.

Right: First XI c.1888; Frank Mitchell standing on the left with his bat.

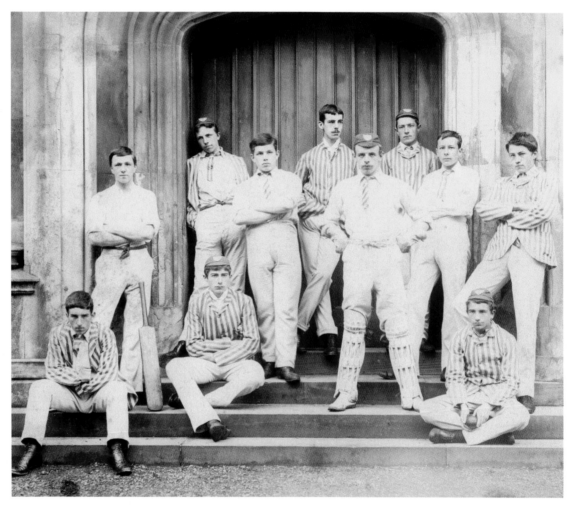

145

us to play when previously the pitches would have been too wet, but they were helpful for pitch preparation. In 1977, to celebrate the School's 1350th Anniversary, the 1st XI did a short southern tour. Our opponents included Sutton Valence School and for the next five years we were invited to their festival.

In 1985 we became part of a five-schools' festival. Cranleigh hosted the first of these, which also included Merchant Taylors Northwood, Bryanston, Rossall and ourselves. The five became six in 1986 when Loretto joined. Five of the six schools remained members of the festival until 2005. We were hosts in 1988, 1994, 2000 and 2006, when only Cranleigh, Merchant Taylors and St Peter's out of the original six took part. It is to be hoped that the festival will continue. It is rare for six schools to be involved in a festival, but the value of five matches in a week after the end of term has been enormous.

The bowling and batting records are recorded in the addenda. It is not easy to evaluate fielders and wicket-keepers, the judgement being inevitably subjective. Malcolm Woodruff (1958–61), Ian Hindhaugh (1978–80) and James Taylor (1999–2002) won the Fielding Cup three times, and Tom Mitchell, Joe Richardson and Stephen Coverdale were wicket-keepers who played representative cricket. Certainly St Peter's has never lacked talent at wicket-keeping and there have been many other fine keepers. Anyone who has watched York CC in recent years will testify to the brilliance of Nigel Durham (1986–88). Who knows what level he could have reached had he been able to play full-time cricket?

Certainly one of the highlights of St Peter's cricket was the 1992 tour of South Africa. A party of 15 players and four staff spent over three weeks touring the country and playing ten

matches. It was a particular pleasure to play against two development teams. The whole trip was a great experience; the hospitality was superb and the cricket very competitive. We even had the privilege of having a century scored against us by Jacques Kallis, the future test star.

We should pay tribute to the many members of staff who have coached the school teams, and to the professional coaches: Benny Wilson, the former Yorkshire player who coached for 13 years after the war; another former Yorkshire player, Ron Aspinall, and George Curry. In 1977 Keith Mohan, a former Derbyshire player, became coach until 2001.

The new century brought a number of excellent seasons, in which four all-rounders, Tom Bartram, Ben Hough, James Wackett and Tom Woolsey, played major roles. Tom Bartram's two years as captain (2003 and 2004) were unbeaten in school matches, the second in all matches. In 2004 they were joined in the 1st XI by Jonathan Bairstow, son of the former Yorkshire and England player David Bairstow. Jonathan went straight into the 1st XI as a third-former and soon showed his outstanding ability. In 2005 he scored 167, not out, against Ampleforth, an astonishing innings for an under-15 player. By the end of 2006 he was already playing regularly for the Yorkshire Academy and had played for Yorkshire 2nd XI and England under-17s. With him and several other talented young players in the School, a bright future for St Peter's cricket seems assured.

Rugby 1846–2005

PADDY STEPHEN

Rugby football is a relative newcomer in a School with such a long history. The earliest drawings nationally of the game date back to 1846, when younger boys were introduced to the sport by taking part in 'massed assaults', where they could show their mettle without too much fear of injury. Rules for the game first appeared in 1856 and were revised in 1873. Both prohibited the throttling or strangulation of opponents, but positively encouraged hacking over. This was often brutal, with boys attaching metal toecaps to their boots. Injured players were treated with little sympathy, the then School House butler famously turning away a limping and bleeding boy from another house, with the comment 'Let them bury their own dead'.

By 1874 the School had finally chosen its famous chocolate and white jerseys that remain to this day. No accurate records exist of fixtures played before *The Peterite* was first published in 1878. However, teams played included York, Hull, Richmond Grammar School, Thorpe Arch School, Leeds Medical College, Durham School and University. The first documented School game was played against Leeds Grammar School in 1874. During the 1981 or 1978 season (depending upon the differences between the school records) the centenary of fixtures between St Peter's and Durham School was celebrated with a fine win for St Peter's on both occasions. The earliest fixture card still in the school archives dates back to 1904 and shows many of the schools we still play today.

During the 1300th anniversary of the school in 1927, the 1st XV embarked on a London tour, the highlight of which was the defeat of Kings School Canterbury, 13–9, at the Rectory Field, Blackheath. This victory finally decided the thorny issue of which was the oldest school in the country. Representative honours came in different forms. Two Peterites, for example, played for the Yorkshire Public School XV in 1928 against the Welsh Public School Boys. The captain on that day was Douglas Bader.

No history of rugby at St Peter's would be complete without mentioning the huge contribution made by Robert Harding, who was 1st XV coach 1946–69. His 1949 side, captained by Douglas Walter, was unbeaten and in recognition of this rare achievement a special dinner was held in their honour at the Royal Station Hotel. Maurice Kershaw, a member of this side and

later a Cambridge Blue, wrote of this recently in these splendidly understated terms, 'We didn't realize what we were achieving until the end of the last game. Then the congratulations came and we were given a Dinner! It finally dawned on us that perhaps we were quite good.'

The next unbeaten side, in all normal school matches, did not come again until 1978, under the captaincy of John Ellison, who went on to play for England schools in 1979. John and his back-row partner of the previous season, Martin Gargan (who gained three Blues), were to feature together again in the 1983 Varsity match at Twickenham. On this occasion they were opposing number 8s. John was also a Universities Athletic Union winner, at Twickenham in 1980 with Durham University, a feat that was to be repeated by Richard Pike, who, as captain of Durham, lifted the British Universities Sports Association trophy in 2004. Alex Drysdale, Nick Rusling, Indraneil Basu were all members of the victorious Cambridge Rugby League team which beat Oxford in 2005. In 2006 there were again three OPs in the Varsity Rugby League match: Alistair Robertson, Alex Drysdale and Indraneil Basu; again, Cambridge won.

The idea of touring abroad became more popular as travel improved. 1st XVs toured Holland, Portugal, Yugoslavia, France, Spain, Scotland, Wales and Ireland. These tours provided tremendous experiences and cemented friendships that have gone on to survive the test of time. This is really what rugby is all about, and all who have ever worn the chocolate and white have done so with pride and passion. More recently the tours have

148

Below: Daily Mail Cup U15 Winners 2002.

taken on a more serious purpose, coming before the new season rather than at the end of the old. These tours have been longer and have gone farther afield: Argentina and Uruguay in 1999 was followed by Canada in 2002 and Australia in 2004.

Teamwork, dedication to training and pride in the shirt have taken rugby at St Peter's through 160 years of varying periods of success, from the outstanding seasons of 1889, 1904, 1913, 1918, 1925, 1933, 1949 and 1978 to Twickenham in 2002 and 2005. When the School went fully co-educational, there were dire predictions of the demise of rugby. However, this was to prove unfounded and rugby has gone from strength to strength. Success in the Daily Mail Cup, which the School won at under-15 level in 2002, showed just how strong the sport is throughout the School. The same group of players, under the captaincy of Alistair MacLeod, went on to be pipped on the final whistle in the under-18 competition in 2005. In this same year the under-15 team reached the semi-finals for the third time in eight years, under the watchful eye of their coach, Maurice Monteith.

Much of this success has been due to the excellent stream of players who have come through St Olave`s under the coaching

Peter Wackett U18 and U19 England player in action.

James Ramsden U18 England 2005.

skills of John Slingsby. Triumph in the National Prep School Sevens in 1996, 2000 and 2004 has been followed by outstanding years at St Peter's. The school has been represented in all three major age groups at Rosslyn Park, where it has demonstrated the value in promoting a more fluent running style of rugby.

It is not, however, only the boys and OPs who have stepped on to Twickenham's turf. In May 1995 Connelee Morris helped Loughborough win the Universities Women's Final. Success is not easily gained on a tough circuit.

However important these successes are, rugby still remains a huge part of the lives of hundreds of pupils on a weekly basis. There is still a thrill in representing the School at any age group and in any team. Records are just as jealously guarded away from the 1st XV and 'A' teams. None more so than the 2005/6 under-16 'B' XV, who managed to complete their eighth successive unbeaten season, quite some achievement. Strength in rugby undoubtedly lies in the history and the tradition that underpins it at St Peter's. It also lies in the dedication of the pupils, parents and coaches, who enjoy the camaraderie and passion that this unique team sport offers to all those who play, coach or watch it.

Alex Drysdale U15 Scotland 1997.

Tom Denton U18 England 2006.

Tom Woolsey U16 England 2002.

Andrew Springgay U18 England 1999.

The Boat Club 1990–2006

CHRIS HALL

The sight of Arthur Ellis-Davies in his red Goretex jacket, clutching a lit cigarette in one hand and a can of petrol in the other, is an image that will stay with many St Peter's rowers of the last 15 years. Because of his significant contribution alongside that of many other coaches, the Boat Club has gone from strength to strength. Not only has the number of rowers increased, but with them the level of success locally, nationally and internationally.

In the early 1980s, Mike Dawson and David Hughes were key figures in sustaining rowing at St Peter's. Their work in turn provided a base for Ann Hodgson to drive rowing forward, for both boys and girls. Indeed, under her leadership, rowing became a truly co-educational activity, a significant achievement at a time when St Peter's was still regarded by many as a boys' school with girls in it. Ann's gentle persuasion brought many coaches on board, including Arthur Ellis-Davies, Jacqueline Finney, Nick Jones, John Ward, Ian Doyle and myself. With funding, foresight and a great river location, the Boat Club blossomed and in 1991 St Peter's raced at Henley Royal Regatta for the first time in a considerable number of years. The crew of James Butler, Joby Taylor, Charlie Barlow, Alistair Birch, Stuart Clarke, Chris Rowland, James Hague, Chris Lloyd and cox Lindsey Daniel was recognised as being instrumental in laying the foundation for future success. Although the boys lost to Emanuel School on the first day, the event was rightly commemorated by the then head of art, John Brown, who painted up a blade that now hangs in the Rhodes Room. Since then, boys' and girls' boats have raced almost annually at Henley and in the National Schools' Regatta, with spectacular and record-breaking success.

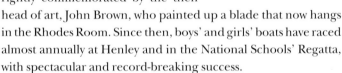

St Peter's Scratch Fours tankard 1865.

The presence of St Peter's at major rowing events over the last ten years has put the Boat Club firmly on the rowing map. The significant amount of work put in by Arthur Ellis-Davies, John Ward, Ken Shanks and, more recently, Jamie MacLeod and Richard Smalman-Smith, has seen School boy and girl rowers compete at the highest level. Since 1998, St Peter's has had individuals representing their country at world and European championships, as well as home internationals, national championships and inter-regional events. Rowing has become an activity not confined to term-time afternoons, but also for holidays and the highly successful and effective early morning sessions. 6.30 am is a magical time to row on the Ouse, particularly in high summer and with a low river. The benefits have been vast.

Several names must be mentioned: Gemma Bentham and Andrew Dangerfield competed in the Coupe de la Jeunesse (Junior European Championships) in Italy in 1998. Gemma came home with bronze and silver medals, Andrew with a bronze. In the same year Helen Austin came fifth in the World Championships in Austria. In order to reach such lofty heights,

Hannah Thomas.

Alastair MacLeod and Rory Robertson.

Helen Austin and Gemma Bentham.

151

Kristina Stiller.

all three had been subjected to a rigorous Great Britain Junior Squad training programme and trials schedule. The following year Helen and Gemma competed at the National Schools' Regatta in Nottingham, in the coxless pairs event; they took gold with a time of 74.5.73, a record that still stands. In the following year in Cork, Helen won a gold medal in the Home Internationals and Gemma won a gold medal in the Coupe de la Jeunesse. All three had impressive rowing careers at St Peter's; they set the tone and we have since seen magnificent performances from, amongst others: Victoria Johnston, Natalie Baldry, Daniel Janes, Rosie Gaunt and William Eastwood. More recently Tina Stiller, Hannah Thomas, Rory Robertson and Alistair and Rory MacLeod have taken centre stage, by competing and winning at the highest level.

To many, however, St Peter's rowing is about community spirit, comradeship and generating a real sense of fun with purpose. Life-long friendships have been made ploughing up and down the River Ouse and at smaller, less prestigious events than those by which we would usually measure success. Amongst others, Tees, Newark and Ancholme in Lincolnshire are attended annually, the latter being the first whole-School fixture of the year. Here, rowing blunders have been plenty, but sights, however modest, have been set for the year ahead. Like Ancholme, other regional events have over the years become engraved in the Boat Club fixtures list. The Bradford Regatta's 600m course was a significant event in the summer calendar of the 1980s and 90s. At the Head of the Float, a head race held in Liverpool just before Christmas, rowers would race two lengths of the dock. This proved to be an almost surreal experience, to race past the United Molasses Refinery and on one occasion an enormous Nigerian oil tanker moored half-way down the course.

Today these events have been left behind, as the Boat Club sets its sights on greater things. However, the Easter term fixtures list remains more or less the same: Trent Head, The Yorkshire Head, The North of England Head, The Schools' Head and The Tideway. Often falling on consecutive weeks, these events test the worth of winter training.

When Ann Hodgson moved to St Edward's in Oxford in 1995, I took over as master-in-charge of rowing, until 2000, when the post was handed over to Mike Hall. During this time the number

of rowers has increased and now includes over a fifth of the school. The decision to develop sculling as well as sweep-oar rowing has served a dual purpose: firstly, it allows younger rowers to take to the water, and secondly, it enables the School's top athletes to trial effectively for the top Great Britain racing boats. It does, of course, also provide twice the fun during games and at competitions.

The Boat Club has been fortunate to have a supportive and enthusiastic band of fund-raisers, who have provided time and cash to purchase rowing boats worthy of a boat club that has seen success on such a wide and varied scale. The Guy Fawkes Boat Club was set up in the early 1990s by Ben Gill, Edward Alton and Mike and Liz Porte. In return for use of the School's boats it has provided cash donations that have been invaluable over the years. Gill Ward and her team have also been generous. The highly successful dinner held in 2006, at which Olympian Ed Coode was guest speaker, raised enough capital to purchase a new girls' racing eight, and whilst our racing boats are still far behind our major school competitors, St Peter's is at last beginning to accrue a fleet capable of securing success in the future.

After a very successful period in office, Mike Hall retired as master-in-charge in 2006 and he was succeeded by Jamie MacLeod, as the newly titled Director of Rowing. Jamie is a very experienced oarsman and has all the criteria necessary to continue developing rowing at St Peter's. The status of rowing continues to grow, not only at St Peter's but, as a consequence of Olympic success, nationally.

Hockey 1897–2005

MIKE JOHNSTON

The first recorded mention of Hockey at the School came from a letter to the editor of The Peterite *in 1897. In it, 'Sloper' suggested the introduction of hockey to the School sporting calendar. The plea was successful and in the following year the magazine reported that the school boasted a number of hockey enthusiasts, who disported themselves on the football field armed with murderous-looking clubs.*

In 1899, a certain Mr Wilkes is mentioned in the context of the game, so he may be the first master-in-charge. There were no inter-school matches, nor even proper goalposts, but this did not prevent unofficial house matches being played. The first recorded house match in 1901 resulted in a 4–0 win to the day-boys.

Inter-school matches began a year later in March 1902. This was also the start of a close relationship with York Hockey Club,

which continues to the present day. In common with the other sports, Mr Wilkinson, a member of staff, played for the School. In the early 1900s the matches played were against men's teams. Inter-school fixtures began in 1906, with matches against Pocklington and Ripon Grammar. In 1912 Ampleforth College was added to the list and a 2nd XI was fielded.

The debut of Kenneth Chilman took place in 1913 when the 2nd XI played away to Ripon Grammar. 'Chilli' went on to

Hockey XI 1923, with (back row) Sam Toyne, far left, and Kenneth Chilman, far right

represent England 1923–30. He also coached the school side 1914–48, a task he shared with the Head Master, Sam Toyne. School results improved as a result of their coaching as well as their participation in many of the games. The fixture list increased

and included many of the local regimental teams and clubs. The strength of School hockey can be judged by the fact that in 1922 a School past-and-present team beat a Yorkshire select XI 7–4, and the following year the School had an undefeated season. In 1931 Norman Yardley played for the School for the first time. The School hockey colours were formalized as royal blue and white in 1935.

The Second World War caused an interval in hockey, and in 1947 only house matches were played. Inevitably the name Chilman is mentioned in re-establishing the game. Canon Patteson, the new master-in-charge, helped him.

Alan Dodds, an accomplished player and Yorkshire captain, became master-in-charge of hockey in 1949. The result was that the excellent tradition of hockey at St Peter's continued. His son, Richard, went on to captain Great Britain to Olympic Gold. During the 15 years Alan Dodds was in charge, the emphasis in matches changed from club to school. Hockey was played in the Easter term, so inevitably the weather took its toll on fixtures and hockey reports in *The Peterite* reflect this problem. In 1958 Mike Ranson made his debut and went on to play for Zambia. It is a testament that so many players went on to play club and representative hockey.

In 1962 Gordon Gildener, the School goalkeeper, cajoled Alan Dodds into taking the School to the Bridlington Hockey Festival. It was so popular, that in the following year the team went again as St Peter's Old Boys. The team needed a name and, as some of the players won a panda at bingo, this became both the mascot and team name. The Pandas have been to every subsequent festival and 'Billy' Hudson has attended no less than 40 times.

In 1965 it appeared that the game was about to go into decline as it was proposed that players should not play until their third year in the school. This would have stifled any chance of creating a competitive 1st XI. A compromise, however, was reached. Hockey continued under the new master-in-charge, Gordon Craine. In 1970 a change of policy was pioneered which allowed a hockey option in the Christmas term. This proved successful. It meant those not playing team rugby could play hockey on hard, dry pitches in September and October and this change proved invaluable in giving players experience. Dick Hubbard succeeded Gordon Craine in 1970 and held the post until 1998. Paddy Stephen also played a vital role in coaching in the 1980s and 1990s.

As part of the 1350th anniversary, the School past-and-present played a strong Hockey Association XI and lost 3–0. Bill Pickersgill and Bill Cloughton, both OPs, played for the Hockey Association. Three years later in 1980 a side captained by Andrew Precious had the distinction of beating Scarborough College 7–0. Andrew was especially pleased as his brother, John, was the Scarborough coach. Nigel Chapman, centre forward, also particularly enjoyed the game as he scored five goals. In 1981 Andrew Jackson made his debut for the School and later represented England Schools.

In 2001 a decision was taken to make hockey the major sport during the Easter term. Matches were played at all age groups and full-time training was instituted. All junior boys would play hockey for at least one year. The success of this policy can be seen by the fact that, in January 2006, the School fielded 14 teams against Worksop College.

The School is now one of the premier hockey schools in the north and we look forward to the acquisition of synthetic pitches in the near future.

Governance

Governors' Tales

*T*eddy Denison served as a Governor from 1977 to 1981, when he was made Vice Chairman. In 1995, under the new constitution, he became Chairman. He stepped down from that role to become the first Foundation Chairman in 2000.

The period 1977–2000 was not an easy time for the independent sector as a whole or St Peter's as an individual school. The School itself was well known for its historical foundation, but outside Yorkshire was probably not highlighted for its academic, cultural or sporting activities. It used to be said that boards of governors fell into three categories: hands-off, hands-up or hands-on. Luckily, and in spite of our antiquated constitution, we did have some individual governors who were willing to take a hands-on approach and accept responsibility. The prime responsibility of any board of governors is to secure and back the best possible Head for the School. During my time we appointed four Heads of St Peter's, one Master of St Olave's, one Head of Clifton Preparatory School and one Bursar.

There were six major developments during my period as a Governor. The first of these concerned the constitution for the governing body which was recognized as being flawed by the then Dean of York, John Southgate. There was no influence over who was to be appointed by the nominating authorities and the automatic appointment of the Dean as ex-officio Chairman was no longer appropriate in the climate of the times. With the assistance of the Charity Commissioners the structure was altered, so that co-opted members were in the majority and the Chairman was to be elected. John Southgate was a much respected person in his own right and was elected first Chairman; following his retirement I was deeply honoured to become the first non-cleric to be elected to that office, and with the effective support of selected Governors, Head Master and Bursar we were able to move towards a modern management structure, and transform our financial position from overdraft to surplus.

The second major issue concerned co-education. This was a fundamental shift in the ethos and direction of the School, but in my view a correct recognition of the wants and needs of an independent school in a city environment, where more and more parents are rightly involved with the school activities. We believed it was a proper recognition of the wants of parents of today and it certainly seemed to have an impact on the behaviour and reputation of a fairly robust boys' school.

The acquisition of Clifton Prep School was another extremely significant development. I remember being horrified, on my return from holiday, to be told that Bootham School was in active discussions for the acquisition of CPS, which had been a feeder school for St Olave's. It would have been devastating to see CPS go elsewhere. Luckily our decision procedures enabled us to take immediate action and secure it. Another acquisition of great significance was the purchase of Linton Lodge. This proved to be another roller-coaster. When it came to market we were out-bid by one of our own parents. However, we kept in close touch and when those parents decided against proceeding, we were given first choice to acquire and thus bring it into our network of properties.

On a wider educational front, the arrival of league tables, whether they are good or bad for the independent sector, could not be ignored. It has been a source of satisfaction that, under the guidance of Robin Pittman and Andrew Trotman, with the Governors' backing for quality of staff and facilities, we are firmly ensconced in Division One and recognized as the leading co-educational school in the North East.

It was a personal pleasure to host the Duchess of Kent when she came to open the Chilman Building and to be able to present her to Kenneth Chilman, after whom the building was named. 'Chilly' taught me when I first entered St Olave's in 1936 and I remained in touch with both him and his family until he died.

I have merely added one or two milestones in a journey of nearly 14 centuries and to oversee the creation of the Foundation which, had it taken place a few centuries before, would have given the School a background of legacies and donations currently enjoyed by some of the great livery companies and the Oxbridge Colleges. However, one must not wander into the field of regrets. I have been enriched by a school connection of over 70 years and immensely honoured by the naming of Denison House.

*M*urray Naylor was appointed to the Governing Body in 1991 and served as Chairman from 2000-2005.

The governing body of a school has many important responsibilities, not least that of monitoring the direction which the school should take to secure provision of the best possible education for its pupils at fees which are affordable. In achieving such an aim while ensuring that the school's finances are soundly based is clearly one vital responsibility, as is the need to maintain the recruitment and retention of the best possible people to lead the school, both academically and administratively.

During my time as Chairman both these considerations were constantly to the forefront of governors' minds. In particular they were faced with a requirement to negotiate a considerable expansion of the School campus while later undertaking a series of selections to replace senior staff whose tenures happened coincidentally to be ending and without in either instance unduly disrupting the life and smooth running of the School.

The task of governing a school is no sinecure. Commitment, time and the ability to pick up issues and deal with them quickly and fairly are all demanded of governors, who are themselves invariably busy people. As well as being sympathetic to independent sector education governors must be prepared to contribute their own experience to further a school's aims. A mix of professional and human skills can contribute enormously to the effectiveness of the governing body; in my time St Peter's was fortunate to have as governors people with experience gained in academia, education, property, finance, the law, military service, the church, business, the medical profession and as old boys of the School. Such a combination of skills made for an extremely competent board.

I joined the board in 1991 and served my last five years as Chairman, stepping down in 2005. It was a period of enormous interest and considerable satisfaction upon which I shall always look back with pride and pleasure.

A governor's relationship with the Head Master and other senior officers must self-evidently be right if they are to be able to co-operate to give the school the joint leadership it requires. That involves each respecting the other's position and being able to speak openly and without ambiguity when needed. I was fortunate to work with Andrew Trotman and Richard Smyth during my chairmanship and before that with Robin Pittman when I was first appointed as a governor. All were different, each was the man for the moment when he was appointed and each contributed a very great deal in his time.

Subsidiary appointments are no less important and the fact that within the space of two years between 2003 and 2005 it was possible to replace the Head Master, the Master at St Olave's, the bursar and the clerk, all of whose allotted tenures had been completed, says volumes for the trust and friendship engendered by the close personal relationships which existed between non-executive governor and executive school officer.

In 1999 the School undertook a review of its campus which by then had become a confused panorama of shared buildings and sports facilities serving three schools but without clear delineation between them. However, while the results of this review were still being considered it became known that the

adjoining City of York 'Queen Anne School' had been declared surplus to requirements and would in all probability close. The latter's boundaries were partly contiguous with those of the St Peter's campus which it naturally complemented. Successful acquisition would permit the rationalization of internal boundaries, while at the same time increasing the size of the campus to accommodate new facilities and provide much-needed extra space for each of the constituent schools.

It was anticipated that competition to acquire the Queen Anne site would be intense and so it proved. An initial bid was submitted in January 2000 and after many twists and turns, the City of York Council finally decided to sell the site to St Peter's the following November for the sum of £4.8m. By the end of 2003 the whole St Peter's campus was contained between the Avenue to the north and Queen Anne Road to the south, with only three St Peter's boarding houses located outside the perimeter on the east side of Clifton. However none of this was achieved without rigorous scrutiny of the affordability of such a development; St Peter's is not a well-endowed school and careful calculation and negotiation with the school's bankers was essential to reach financial decisions which were sustainable. A good example of when governors really do work for the privilege of their position!

Expansion of the St Peter's campus to almost twice its physical size and the consequent reconfiguration of internal boundaries was probably the most significant development in the School's history. The decision was not taken lightly nor was it at any stage assumed that St Peter's would be successful in its bid. It was the governors' confidence in the future of independent education and their trust in the School's continuing ability to be a leader in that field that persuaded them that every effort must be made to achieve success.

Towards the end of my time as Chairman it became clear that, like all schools living in close proximity with neighbours, St Peter's faced a major challenge to sell itself, its activities, its aspirations and its future plans to the community within which it lived. Proposed solutions to problems generated by traffic, the development of new facilities or the need to provide the highest standards of security to safeguard pupils can have unintended consequences for neighbours. Schools must be ever more sensitive to their local communities. This equation is often complicated by ignorance and resentment of a school's culture and status and great efforts will be needed to overcome such attitudes. This will be a continuing challenge to be met by future generations.

157

The Foundation

BUFF REID

Despite being one of the oldest schools in England, St Peter's has never been a well-endowed institution. For centuries it sheltered under the wing of York Minster, gaining full financial independence only at the end of the 19th century. Unlike many ancient schools, it does not enjoy the sponsorship of the City Liveries or other charitable institutions. As a result it has lived a fairly hand-to-mouth existence, raising funds as necessary for development, bursaries and scholarships through land and property sales, legacies from past pupils and staff, fees and occasional appeals. For a time there was a scheme for 'City Scholars', through which the most successful boys at 11-plus could attend St Peter's, supported by, among others, York City Council and the North and East Riding County Councils, a scheme which lasted until local government reorganization in 1972. Under the last Conservative administration, St Peter's also benefited from the government's Assisted Places Scheme.

Buff Reid.

Following the example of American schools and colleges, which have created a culture of long-term giving through charitable foundations, many British schools began to investigate the possibility of following the same path. In 1999, Teddy Denison, the recently retired Chairman of Governors, set up a working party to look at the possibility of starting such a body to support St Peter's. The idea was that the St Peter's School Foundation would be an institution established for the purpose of creating a permanent, sustained source of income to assist the attainment of the long-term vision of the School. This sustained 'culture of giving' would allow St Peter's, over the years, to satisfy the different aspirations of donors and would benefit the School by providing and maintaining the highest standard of facilities and teaching. The Foundation would assist less well-off but able children, thus preserving a cultural and social balance. It would build relationships by identifying possible donors and renewing their enthusiasm for the School by informing them about events in their particular field of interest, thus encouraging their participation. Finally, the Foundation would have a permanence and continuity difficult to achieve by individuals.

Once the idea had finally been accepted by the Board of Governors, the Archbishop of York formally launched the

Foundation in York Minster at Commemoration 2000. It was, of necessity, a low-key start, with much to be done to appoint trustees and a director for the fledgling organization. An office had to be set up and a database of alumni, past parents and friends of the School had to be produced. Tory Gillingham, the first Foundation Director, worked hard on all fronts to further the aims and objectives, working closely with the Old Peterite Club. The database was a particular challenge as the Club's records of past pupils were far from complete. In addition, the School had kept no reliable records of past parents or friends of the school. At the same time Tory also set about planning and running experimental events and reunions for past pupils with particular sporting or cultural interests in common. As a result, some generous donations were received and several new sixth-form science and languages scholarships were set up, some being funded through the generosity of the well-known Shepherd family of York. A Merchant Adventurers' and an Ogden Trust Scholarship were also founded. Patrick Shepherd and his sister Jane Robertson also set up an 11-plus, means-tested scholarship for a York child from a state school, starting at St Olave's, in memory of their father, Donald Shepherd. In addition, St Peter's has always been most fortunate in the loyalty of its own staff and

Some of the girls who left in 1999 at the 30th reunion in 2006.

on several occasions this has been reflected in generous gifts to the school and the Foundation.

As the new body began to practise its skills, it hosted several enjoyable reunions, including a rowing reunion for crews now in their seventies – a particularly jolly party, with some of the participants meeting for the first time since their school days. With the help of the Old Peterite Club, successful reunions were also held to mark special anniversaries at Queen's and Dronfield Houses, and in 2004 many OPs from the south of England enjoyed a wonderful reception at the House of Lords. As a direct result of this event, Howard Gatiss, himself a City Scholar, helped us to set up another 11-plus scholarship for a York child from a state school.

The Foundation has also been able to undertake a variety of capital projects. Two magnificent donations from past parents resulted in the creation of the Whitestone Gallery, to display the work of both School and outside artists; the Foundation also helped with renovation of the Clifton Pre-preparatory School playground and the purchase of a new boat.

The year 2005 gave us a chance to launch our most spectacular event to date: the 'Plotters' Ball', marking the 400th anniversary of the Gunpowder Plot. In a huge marquee on the 1st XV pitch, with fireworks, magnificent dinner, big band, charity auction and Jacobean-themed 'fayre', 860 people raised the amazing sum of £38,000 which was shared between the Foundation, Martin House Children's Hospice and York City Fire Brigade for their work with disadvantaged youngsters. The 30th anniversary of the admission of girls to St Peter's was celebrated in 2006, and the Foundation was able to welcome well over 100 female former pupils (including some of the brave first five from 1976) to a reception with lunch, entertainment by current pupils, and tours of the School. Many past and present staff also attended.

With the current uncertainty of political attitudes towards independent schools, it is even more important that the Foundation should succeed. The main focus now is to secure endowed bursaries to fund pupils' education between the ages of 11 and 18. The School has had a long and distinguished history of opening its doors to pupils who have lacked the funds to pay, in part or in full, for their education. In recent years we have witnessed the opportunities that the City Scholars and Assisted Places financial aid has brought to children. These schemes no longer exist, so it is now the responsibilty of the School and its wider community to do all it can to ensure that St Peter's remains an institution which welcomes children who will thrive here, regardless of their background. Funds raised will be invested and the income generated used to cover the cost of school fees in perpetuity, meaning that bursaries will be available on an ongoing basis. The long-term goal is to have bursary assistance available for up to 10 per cent of the School. This is an ambitious target, but the breadth and depth of benefit received by bursary pupils makes it an objective worth pursuing, whatever the hurdles.

The Non-teaching Staff

PETER SIMPSON

The Administration Staff 2006.

St Peter's never sleeps! The teaching staff and pupils are supported by an army of administrative, clerical, maintenance, laundry, catering, cleaning and ground staff, who work throughout the year to ensure that everything runs smoothly. A typical St Peter's day will start with laundry and catering staff arriving at 5.30 am. The School does all its own laundry and with over 200 boarders that is a large amount of clothes-washing to be done.

The catering department has expanded over recent years to accommodate the varying needs of the three schools. A total of seven chefs, under the supervision of the catering manager and her deputy, work with 38 catering assistants to produce over 1,200 meals a day. The work does not stop at weekends and boarders enjoy a cooked-to-order brunch on Sundays with a full roast meal in the evenings. As well as catering for the needs of the pupils and staff, the department also has to provide meals for visiting teams, conferences and special occasions.

The Kitchen Staff 2006.

The School occupies over 40 acres of land and the maintenance of so much ground is a task that never ends. St Peter's takes great pride in maintaining its grounds to the highest level. Working on the buildings is rather like painting the Forth Road Bridge; the jobs to be done are continuous. The School is fortunate to have a dedicated team of maintenance staff, working under the direction of the Estates Manager. School holidays are a particularly busy time for the team, when much rebuilding work and upgrading of facilities is carried out.

Cleanliness is important in every work situation, but it is vitally important in a boarding school. Over 40 cleaners help to keep all the buildings bright and fresh. Staff are assigned to boarding houses and help to make study-bedrooms and dormitories home from home. With so much sport played on a daily basis there is always plenty of work for the staff responsible for the changing areas.

Each of our three schools has a dedicated set of clerical staff supporting the teaching staff and, in addition, the bursarial staff look after the normal office routines of salaries, wages, purchasing. The School has its own Sanatorium, which is staffed 24 hours a day throughout term-time, to see to the needs of boarders and day pupils who fall ill. Security is a vital part of any school and St Peter's employs seven staff to assist visitors and to maintain a secure site.

The Maintenance Staff 2006.

All the support staff at St Peter's are employed by the School. The present policy of not contracting out catering or cleaning services reflects the importance the School places on looking after its support staff, who in turn do so much for the teaching staff and pupils.

160

The History of the Old Peterite Club

Richard Harding

'A book like this is not just written for Peterites and Old Peterites of today, but also for those of the future; though perhaps the chief responsibility lies in the endeavour faithfully to do justice to the long and noble line of those who during the past 1300 years have been educated at this school …' The History of St Peter's School *by Angelo Raine, the author of the first history of the School published under the auspices of the OP Club in 1926.*

The Old Peterite Club was founded on 25 September 1866 by the then Head Master, the Revd H.M. Stephenson. A provisional committee was appointed, with the Head Master as President ex-officio. The first annual meeting was held at the end of the Christmas term and 61 gentlemen were proposed, seconded and elected as members of the Club.

It is a matter for speculation as to how and when OPs gathered for social or sporting occasions prior to the formation of a club, but it can be assumed that informal gatherings took place in the taverns and inns of York. However, the first recorded Old Boys' dinner took place at the Black Swan in Peasholme Green in 1868.

The first London dinner was inaugurated at the Holborn Restaurant on 28 June 1888 (the eve of St Peter's Day), but was soon moved to the beginning of July to coincide with the first day of the University cricket match at Lord's.

Records are scarce from the early years in Clifton, as the school magazine did not feature on a regular basis until December 1878. We do know that the first known OP sporting contact with the school was on the cricket field in 1861, when the team was named Old St Peter's. In the Old Boys' match of 1863 the school scored 44 and 47 and the OPs 39 and 36, a reflection, perhaps, of either the pitches or the game. The 1860s also saw a further development in rowing when Thomas Badger, an Old Peterite, presented five silver cups for four-oared races.

OP rugby against the School was played with a past-and-present team. *The Peterite* report of a match in 1881 is very much to the point: 'A match was arranged for 10th December against the Old Boys, but only six appeared. The deficiency was supplied from the remainder of the School and junior members of the team. The match was a complete failure, and resulted in an extremely easy win for the School.' The 1st XV captain on this occasion was Louis Stevenson, who later played for Cambridge University and won Blues in 1883, 1884 and 1885.

In 1894, the School received a substantial gift from an OP, the Reverend Herbert Bloomfield, in the form of the Gymnasium, which greatly improved sporting facilities. The old panelling containing the honours boards in the gymnasium (which now houses the Alcuin Library) was a gift to the School from the OP Club in 1897. The panels have become a source of much interest over the years and the 'old gym' still brings back many nostalgic memories for the older generation of OPs.

One of the major tasks at the beginning of the 20th century was to build and finance a science block. Canon E.C. Owen (Head Master 1900–13) appealed to OPs, who were at first slow to respond. 'May we not trust to the loyalty of our Old Boys?' he asked in *The Peterite*. The new building was finally completed in the summer term of 1903 and formally opened by the eminent scientist and OP, Professor Clifford Allbutt FRS, of Gonville and Caius College, Cambridge. Subsequently, the OPs helped fund the building of the swimming pool (1922) and the library block (1927).

The School's celebration of the 13th Centenary, in June 1927, made the Commemoration weekend a unique occasion for OPs and former members of staff. The chief guest at the speeches and prize-giving was the Archbishop of York, Dr Cosmo Lang, and the OP Dinner was held at the Royal Station Hotel. On the following day the Bishop of Ripon, Dr Edward Burroughs, preached in the chapel at the Commemoration Service.

The minutes of the OP Club in September, 1866.   *Old Peterite London Dinner 1952.*

The anniversary building, incorporating the Toyne Library and the Stephenson Room, was opened on 20 July 1929 by the Vice-Chancellor of Leeds University, Dr James Baillie. Once again OPs and many other well-wishers had responded to the building appeal. In the words of the Head Master, Sam Toyne, 'When we remember what the Old St Peter's owed in the 9th century to its library, we may well ask ourselves whether there could be a more fitting memorial of its foundation'. Further projects continued through the difficult 1930s, in particular the completion of the new buildings which were attached to the library block of 1929. The official opening took place on 11 October 1935 when Lord Halifax formally opened the new accommodation for the day-boys (later Queen's House) and for the junior school (St Olave's).

It is only possible to mention a few of the sporting activities which have come under the umbrella of the OP Club. In 1936, the year that Mr Toyne retired, the OP squash players reached the semi-finals of the Public Schools Old Boys' competition for the Londonderry Cup. This was a considerable achievement for the team.

The first OP gathering after the Second World War was in London and once again the Holborn Restaurant was the chosen venue for 14 November 1945, at which the Chairman of the Governors, Dean Milner-White, was present. The year 1946 saw the return of Commemoration at the School and nearly 100 OPs attended the dinner at the City Arms Hotel on Friday, 26 July.

The generosity of OPs, both individually through school appeals or through the Club, was evident in the many projects undertaken during the 30 years of John Dronfield's headmastership (1937–67). One of the major tasks in the late 1950s was the raising of enough money for the extension of the Big Hall. Tom Lewis, (Honorary Secretary 1955–64) and Dr Marcus Clegg (President 1958–61) were both prime movers behind the project, which was financed solely by the OPs. Their energy, drive and strenuous efforts, coupled with their personal loyalty to Dronfield, were instrumental in its successful conclusion. Dedicated to the Old Peterites who fell in both world wars, the Memorial Hall was officially opened by the Bishop of Durham, Maurice Harland OP, on 23 July 1960. On this occasion, Dr Clegg delivered the following words to begin the Service of Dedication, 'Mr Dean: on behalf of The Old Peterite Club we ask you and the Governors to accept this Memorial Hall as a gift to the School and, we trust, a fitting completion of the School's memorial to those past members who gave their lives in two world wars'. No sooner was this done than the OP Committee decided to issue a further appeal, to add to a grant from the War Damage Commission, for the refurbishment of the front of the school.

Dronfield's last Commemoration as Head Master took place over the weekend of 21 July 1967. He was unanimously elected as Vice-president of the Club in his own right. The annual dinner was held in the School dining room, where tributes to 'J.D.' were heard by a record number of 207 OPs. The time-honoured toast of 'The School' was proposed by John Harding, to which Robert Harding replied. The main toast of the evening, 'The Head Master', was proposed by James Brockbank. The Head Master responded and received a standing ovation.

163

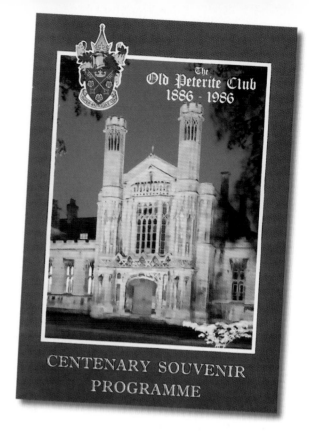

Many OPs have given much time to the welfare of the Club. From the list of officers, mention must be made of Hugh Creer and Colonel Henry Scott, who served both the Club and the School in a remarkable variety of senior posts between 1919 and 1967, including, in each case, the secretaryship of the Club for 30 years and more. The devotion and commitment of these two men ensured the furtherance of the Club's objectives in maintaining a close connection between St Peter's and the OPs. At the same time the Club had the interest, support and assistance of successive Head Masters as well as the staff of the School.

In March 1962 the first St Peter's Careers Convention was organized for sixth-formers, at which members of the Old Peterite Club gave willingly of their time and expertise. Subsequent conventions and forums have been greatly supported by OPs from a wide range of business and professional backgrounds and their advice has been greatly appreciated by Peterites.

The Club has been particularly fortunate in having three long-serving OP masters, whose connection with St Peter's at different stages spanned most of the last century and totalled 125 years. They richly encouraged good fellowship between the School and Old Peterites and their contribution was immense. Kenneth Rhodes served as OP Secretary and President. The second is Kenneth Chilman, who was Vice-president of the Club. David Kirby is the third member of staff who has given unstintingly to the Club as Secretary and President.

Sport has always been a catalyst for OP reunions. OP golfers gather each year to play for the Founder's and Burnett Trophies on the Sunday of Commemoration. In 2002 in the Grafton Morrish Old Boys' competition (following a scratch foursomes format), St Peter's reached the third round, beating Westminster and Bradfield before losing to Epsom College. On the hockey front, the Pandas' Hockey Club has continued to thrive since 1962.

In 1978 the first group of girls joined the OP Club, and in celebration of the Commemoration dinner that year, the front of the School was floodlit for the first time; the floodlights were a gift from the Club. Almost 30 years' later, the number of girls in the senior school has reached 217.

The OP Club centenary was celebrated at the School on Saturday, 27 September 1986. The board commemorating the Old Peterite Club presidents, secretaries and treasurers was presented and unveiled by Tom Lewis, President 1964–67. An evening reception was held in the Memorial Hall, following a thanksgiving service in the chapel. A special prayer of thanksgiving was read by the President, John Harding. The Venerable Norman McDermid, Archdeacon of Cleveland, preached the sermon, taking the text from St Mark's Gospel,

Chapter 9, Verse 5: 'And Peter answered and said to Jesus, "Master, it is good for us to be here".' As a result of the generous response by Old Peterites to the centenary appeal, the gift of communion silver to the school was presented and dedicated at the service. The whole day was a happy and convivial occasion and it was a particular pleasure to have Mrs Betty Sewell (née Toyne) and Mrs Sheila Dronfield as guests for this special anniversary in the history of the Club.

Many OPs have continued to enjoy not only the regional dinners, of which there are now five held each year around the country, but also the gatherings in early September, where they unite to take part in matches with the School. The friendly rivalry and the camaraderie of the social gatherings which follow have been a hallmark of these sporting fixtures in recent years and are particularly enjoyed by the younger OPs. The President and Secretary of the Old Peterite Club attend each dinner along with a representative of the School, usually the Head Master. Recent reunions, and the annual dinner at Commemoration, have focused on gathering together different OP year groups. The 50th anniversary of Queen's House was celebrated in September 2003 with a luncheon at the School, followed a year later by a reunion at Dronfield House to celebrate a span of 40 years. These very enjoyable and successful events will no doubt set a pattern for the future.

The current OP Club of over 4,500 members has grown far beyond the dreams of its founders. It is hoped that all OPs will consider membership of the Club, not only as a pleasure, but also a privilege, and thus help it to achieve success through active support. There can be few whose thoughts do not sometimes go back to the days they spent at St Peter's. By strengthening old ties and renewing old loyalties, the Club stands as an expression of real unity.

Famous Old Peterites

JOHN AISLABIE (1670–1744)

Aislabie was elected as MP for Ripon in 1685. By 1710 he was Lord of the Admiralty and by 1718 he had been made Chancellor of the Exchequer. He was closely associated with promoting the South Sea Company, which went spectacularly bankrupt. Aislabie was found guilty of accepting a £20,000 bribe for promoting the company and was imprisoned in the Tower of London for 'the most notorious, dangerous and infamous corruption'. Aislabie is renowned in gardening circles for being the first person to introduce natural landscaping and creating the water garden at Studley Royal.

SIR CLIFFORD T. ALLBUTT (1836–1925)

Clifford Allbutt was educated at Cambridge before returning to Leeds to work in the General Infirmary. He invented the three-inch clinical thermometer which we use today. (The previous thermometer was 12 inches long.) In 1892 he was made Regius Professor of Physic at Cambridge, where he edited his 'System of Medicine', which for many years was the doctors' bible. He was made a Privy Councillor and a Fellow of the Royal Society, as well as receiving nine honorary degrees for his contribution to medicine.

JOHN BARRY (1933–)

John Barry's musical achievement has led to the award of five Academy Awards and four Grammies for his film music. He is best known for the 007 theme, but he has also written the music for 11 of the 14 James Bond films, including *Goldfinger*, in which he perfected the Bond sound, and the scores for *Midnight Cowboy*, *Out of Africa* and *Dances with Wolves*. No other contemporary English composer has received so many accolades.

John Aislabie

165

Sir Clifford T. Allbutt (By permission of the Master and Fellows of Genville and Caius College, Cambridge).

John Barry, in the Alcuim Library with Andrew Trotman and Charlotte Black, Head of School.

Sir William Vernon Harcourt by Sir Francis Carruthers Gould ('F.C.G.'), early 1900s (National Portrait Gallery, London).

166

Sir Thomas Herbert

LAURENCE EUSDEN (1688–1730)

Laurence Eusden was a Fellow of Trinity College, Cambridge, when he was made Poet Laureate in 1718. Eusden had no family wealth or social connections which would have bettered him, so he took to writing. His flattering commemoration of the Duke of Newcastle's marriage secured him the position of Poet Laureate at the age of 30, the youngest person to hold the position. His poetry invoked derision from his social and literary peers. He ended his days as Rector of Coningsby in Lincolnshire.

> *Eusden a laurel'd bard, by fortune rais'd*
> *By very few was read, by fewer prais'd*
>
> *Alexander Pope*

SIR WILLIAM VERNON HARCOURT (1827–1904)

Sir William Harcourt is the most distinguished politician St Peter's has produced. He gained a First Class Honours Degree in Classics at Trinity College, Cambridge. In 1868 he was elected as a Liberal MP for Oxford. His rise in politics was swift. By 1873 he was Solicitor General and by 1880 he was made Home Secretary. Between 1880 and 1892 he was Gladstone's deputy in the Liberal Party. Between 1892 and 1895 he was Chancellor of the Exchequer and responsible for introducing graduated death duties. Ironically, he later inherited an estate in financial crisis because of the graduated duties he introduced. He was one of the most prominent politicians of the late 19th century.

SIR THOMAS HERBERT 1606–82

Sir Thomas Herbert is best known as the courtier who accompanied King Charles I to the scaffold in Whitehall in 1649. Herbert was born in York and studied at both Oxford and Cambridge before going on an embassy to Persia 1626–29. He visited Madagascar, Goa, Ceylon and Mauritius on this journey, and was later to write an account of his travels. At first in the English Civil War he sided with Parliament, but later served in the King's household for two years. During this time he became deeply devoted to the King. Before Charles was beheaded he gave Herbert his cloak. Herbert wrote a lamentation, *Threnodia Carolina*, in 1678, about the last two years of King Charles' life.

David Hill

Sir Charles Medhurst

Christopher Hill (by permission of The Oxford Mail).

CHRISTOPHER HILL (1912–2003)

Christopher Hill was one of the outstanding historians of the 20th century. He has been described as 'the dean and paragon of English historians'. Hill specialized in the 17th century and is regarded as the point of reference for historians studying the period. His particular interest was the English Revolution and the Civil War. Hill's approach was the embodiment of secularized disssent – something he attributed to his Methodist background. He enjoyed a glittering academic career at Oxford University where he was Master of Balliol College 1965–78.

DAVID HILL (1840–96)

Hill was trained as a Wesleyan Methodist Minister. He went to China in 1864 and spent virtually all of his life there. His famine-relief work in Shansi province led to an expansion of his ministry. He was responsible for establishing hospitals as well as homes for the blind, the aged and orphans. Hill became one of the central figures working for Christianity in China in the 19th century. He died there in 1896 from typhus.

AIR CHIEF MARSHAL SIR CHARLES MEDHURST KCB, CB, OBE, MC (1896–1954)

Charles Medhurst was commissioned into the army, but joined the fledgling Royal Flying Corps in 1915 and fought on the Western Front. He had a distinguished military career. By 1941 he was Assistant Chief of the Air Staff with responsibility for intelligence and later, policy. He was the Commander-in-Chief of the Middle East and Mediterranean Command, 1945–48, then Head of the Joint Services Mission to Washington 1948–50.

ROBERT MIDDLETON (1571–1601)

Robert Middleton was the nephew of the Catholic martyr, Margaret Clitherow, who was brutally put to her death for her faith in York in 1586. Middleton trained in Reims and Rome for the Catholic priesthood. He was arrested in Lancashire in 1600 and treated with inhumanity and brutality. At his execution, his sister pleaded with him to renounce Catholicism and spare his life. He refused and was put to death.

Albert Moore

ALBERT MOORE 1841–93

Albert Moore is regarded as one of the most original of British painters. His rise to fame was swift. He attended the Royal Academy schools and by the 1860s was designing tiles, wallpaper and stained glass for William Morris. His paintings have a neo-classical character. He was influenced by the Elgin Marbles and Greek sculptures. Moore is best known for paintings of females in classical settings. His works can be found in the Tate, the Victoria and Albert Museum, the Courtauld Institute and galleries in Manchester, Liverpool and Birmingham. He became part of the late 19th century Aesthetic Movement and believed firmly in 'art for art's sake'; that the purpose of art should be its beauty in form, composition and colour.

168

C. Northcote Parkinson

C. NORTHCOTE PARKINSON (1909–93)

Northcote Parkinson was a distinguished naval historian and author of 60 books. He taught in Malaya and at Harvard, Illinois and Dartmouth Naval College. He is probably best known for Parkinson's Law, a satire on bureaucracy. His dictum that work expanded to fill the time available made him world famous. He explained the inevitablity of bureaucratic expansion and correctly predicted that the Royal Navy would eventually have more admirals than ships.

FRANK PICK (1878–1941)

Nikolaus Pevsner, the noted architectural historian, called Frank Pick the greatest patron of the arts the 20th century has produced in England. Pick was the Director of the London Underground in the 1910s and 1920s, which later merged with the bus network to become London Transport. He was instrumental in establishing the world's most progressive public transport system. Pick commisssioned artists and designers to promote London Underground in their work. He is responsible for the design of the Underground map and for the modern, designs of several of the underground stations. In 1932 the USSR asked him to help with the design of the Moscow Underground, a task for which he was awarded a badge of honour. He was the founding Chairman of the Council for Art and Design, the forerunner of the Design Council. Frank Pick was characterized by modesty, drive and intelligence. In 1940 he was made Director of the Ministry of Information, but sadly died in 1941. He refused both a knighthood and a peerage.

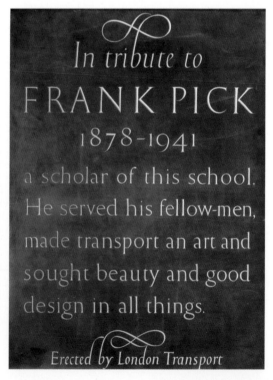

In tribute to
FRANK PICK
1878-1941
a scholar of this school.
He served his fellow-men,
made transport an art and
sought beauty and good
design in all things.
Erected by London Transport

BRIAN SELLERS (1907–81)

Brian Sellers was one of the most successful county cricket Captains there has been. He led Yorkshire to six county championship victories between 1933 and 1948. He was named Wisden Cricketer of the year in 1940. Latterly, he was a Test team selector.

SIR FRANK SWETTENHAM (1850–1946)

Sir Frank Swettenham is regarded as one of the greatest British colonial administrators. He was the first Resident General of the Malay States 1896–1901. Port Swettenham (now Port Kelang) in Malaysia was named after him. There is an outstanding portrait of him in the National Portrait Gallery by John Singer Sargeant.

Norman Yardley

NORMAN YARDLEY (1915–93)

Norman Yardley was one of the outstanding cricketers of his generation. He captained Cambridge University, Yorkshire 1948–55 and England in 1947, 1948 and 1950. He played in 20 test matches, scored 812 runs and had a bowling average of 33.66 runs per wicket. Between 1956 and 1973 he was commentator for Test Match Special. Yardley was named Wisden Cricketer of 1948. In more recent times he served as President of Yorkshire Cricket Club.

169

Sir Frank Swettenham by John Singer Sargent, 1904
(National Portrait Gallery, London).

Roll of Honour 1914–1918

Name	Forenames	At St Peter's	Date of Death	Name	Forenames	At St Peter's	Date of Death
ALLEN	William Sproston	1909–14	14–Mar–18	LEONARD	Herbert Shaw	1895–1901	31–Dec–16
ALLENBY	Augustus Heathcote	1875–77	7–Aug–15	MACKAY	Donald Paley	1895–1901	9–Oct–17
BARTON	Bernard	1894–97	11–Aug–18	MAXWELL	James Watson	1904–08	14–Sep–18
BASKETT	Roger Mortimer	1906–13	14–Nov–16	McFARLANE	William Arthur	1916–17	7–Feb–19
BEAUMONT	Philip Fairclough	1906–08	9–Oct–17	McGUIRE	Brian	1906–07	14–Sep–14
BETHELL	Richard Carrington	1909–12	22–May–16	MORTIMER	James	1882–86	15–Sep–16
BINGHAM	Frank Miller	1885–93	22–May–15	NORTHCOTE	James Fitz Gaulfield	1907–11	9–Oct–17
CAMM	Bertram Cunliffe	1905–11	7–Jan–18	PATTINSON	Edwin Potter	1912–15	3–May–17
CLEMONS	Arthur John	1893–95	6–Feb–17	PENTY	Sidney Wallace	1903–07	10–Apr–18
COLLEY	John Francis	1908–10	2–Aug–17	PETERS	Gerard	1904–08	24–Feb–17
COOKSON	Bryan	1889–93	10–Apr–17	REYNOLDS	Guy Beresford Eaton	1909–14	18–Nov–16
DURRANT	Humphrey Mercer			RICHARDS	Peter Arthur Wilmott	1908–15	10–Sep–16
	Lancelot	1910–11	6–Jun–16	RICHARDSON	Tom	1913–14	3–Dec–18
FAIRBANK	Geoffrey Thurnam	1909–10	16–Apr–17	RIGBY	James Richard		
FERGUSON	Fritz Eberhard	1907–10	7–Oct–19		Anderton	1906–07	26–Sep–15
FERNANDES	Dudley Luis De Tavora	1908–12	23–Oct–14	ROBINSON	Charles Lawson	1882–86	8–May–15
FISHER	Thomas Wilfred	1904–08	21–Feb–17	ROY	Kenneth James	1888–94	23–Aug–14
FOSTER	John Cecil	1907–11	20–Aug–17	SCAWIN	William Neville	1895–1900	15–Apr–18
FOSTER	Robert Douglas	1901–09	7–Aug–15	SCOTT	George Jefferson	1888–90	25–Dec–15
GRAY	Oswald	1911–16	27–Aug–18	SHANN	Kenneth	1908–12	8–May–15
HARLAND	Eustace William	1913–17	18–Mar–18	SMITH	The Rev. Fred Seaton	1899–1902	15–Nov–18
HARPLEY	Robert Ableson	1909–15	5–Jul–16	STEPHENSON	Charles Lindsay	1898–1900	8–Nov–17
HAWORTH	Harold Stanley	1894–98	13–Aug–16	STORRS-FOX	Geoffrey Noel	1912–16	28–Mar–18
HAYNES	William Harold	1908–14	26–Sep–18	TATE-SMITH	Robert Ronald	1901–04	23–Feb–18
HEAP	Thomas Reginald	1894–97	25–Nov–16	TENNENT	Oswald Moncrieff	1906–13	16–Jun–15
HILLYARD	Noel Hardcastle	1901–02	23–Apr–17	THORNSBY	Robert Henry	1910–13	23–Dec–18
HORTON	Reginald William	1909–13	12–Nov–18	TROTTER	Alick Dunbar	1906–11	18–Sep–18
HUTCHISON	Alexander	1899–1900	25–Sep–14	WADSWORTH	Maurice Moxon	1904–07	9–Jul–15
JOHNSON	Richard Digby	1888–93	24–May–15	WATSON	John Peirson	1893–97	29–Jul–17
JOLLY	Benton Ord	1906–13	9–Feb–17	WEST	George Clifford	1910–15	12–Feb–17
JONES	Percy Barrett	1893–96	28–Sep–15	WHYTEHEAD	Hugh Richard		
KENNEDY	David Hew	1904–08	31–Jul–17		Augustin	1891–97	22–May–15
KING	Percy James Church	1897–1900	24–Oct–17	WILSON	William Victor Royal	1913–14	31–Jul–16
KNOWLES	Frank Henry	1901–05	3–May–17	WINDLE	Harold Edmund	1901–04	13–Sep–16
LAWTON	William Victor	1903–09	8–Jul–18				

Roll of Honour 1939–1945

NAME	FORENAMES	AT ST PETER'S	DATE OF DEATH
AMBLER	Thomas Denison	1933–37	13–Jun–43
AMOR	Henry Desmond		
	Fitzmaurice	1933–37	15–Dec–42
BENTLEY	Ronald Cameron	1903–06	25–Aug–41
BIGGIN	Michael	1930–34	15–May–41
BRITTAIN	John Athron	1927–32	31–May–40
BUCKLE	Michael John	1929–38	11–Jan–43
BUTLER	James Wilfred	1929–35	1–Nov–41
CARLTON	Maurice Quarton	1927–36	6–Jul–44
CARNEY	William John	1919–21	12–May–43
COOMBE	Antony Paul	1938–40	24–Dec–43
CROASDALE	John Deneys	1938–40	11–Jun–44
DALES	John Haverfield	1925–27	22–Dec–40
DEAS	John Browning	1930–33	1–Jun–40
DODDS	Stephen	1930–34	20–May–40
DOUGLAS	Angus Ward	1931–36	27–Nov–43
EVELEIGH	Thomas Brian John	1924–28	27–Feb–45
FARROW	John Paterson	1926–35	4–Oct–44
FERGUSON	John Mackay	1911–16	6–Feb–42
FINERON	Frederick William	1920–27	16–Jul–43
FOSTER	John Hope	1926–29	11–Jan–41
FOTHERGILL	John Miles	1929–32	27–Mar–41
GARNHAM	John Stephen	1936–40	4–Jul–43
GLAVES	John	1929–35	9–Sep–42
GREEN	Samuel Morris	1934–36	6–Jun–44
GRIFFITHS	Reginald Thomas John	1932–36	19–Jul–44
HANKS	Walter Henry Haydn	1928–35	24–Apr–45
HEYWOOD	Peter	1931–36	9–Nov–42
HOLLINGTON	John Raymond	1933–35	30–Sep–39
JACKSON	Brian Holroyd Watts	1920–24	4–Jun–42
JOHNSTONE	Peter Anthony	1932–34	17–Sep–44
JOHNSTONE	Paul Dootson Douglas	1932–35	9–Dec–40
LEE	Brian	1925–29	19–Jan–42
LYNCH	Richard Challenor	1933–40	17–Sep–42
MARRIOTT	Kenneth Edward	1935–37	15–Aug–43

NAME	FORENAMES	AT ST PETER'S	DATE OF DEATH
MILBURN	Harold Ashton	1935–40	9–May–42
MITCHELL	Ivor	1931–36	29–Jan–44
MOREY	Peter John	1930–37	9–May–43
MORRIS	Arthur James	1934–36	30–Apr–43
PARKIN	Leslie Hugh William	1924–27	27–Feb–42
PEXTON	Harold Cass	1926–28	30–Jul–43
POWELL	Edgar Alwyn	1926–30	24–Jul–44
RAINFORD	John Rawsthorn	1927–30	22–Feb–42
RICHARDSON	Horace William	1931–36	13–Jul–40
ROBSON	Charles Maurice	1935–40	12–Nov–42
SCOTT	Samuel Paley	1926–31	27–Jul–42
SHILLITOE	John Burton	1931–40	6–Nov–44
STEAD	George Sumner		
	[Master]	1935–39	22–Jun–42
STEAD	John Walton	1931–35	17–Feb–42
TAYLOR	Hugh Lister	1935–40	26–Mar–42
TELFOR	Lemuel	1931–37	29–Nov–42
WALTERS	John Ralph	1936–39	16–Nov–43
WALTERS	William Lucas	1931–36	26–Nov–41
WATSON	Gerald Featherstone	1919–23	31–Jan–42
WELLINGTON	Michael Alban	1930	15–Nov–42
WILLIAMS	John	1921–27	Unknown

171

Old Peterite Anecdotes

Memories from OPs have flooded in and it has been difficult to know exactly which ones to include. Ultimately, reasons of space became the main determinant. I have tried to select the memories which shed a light on the community and which have a general applicability. The memories have tended to come from older OPs rather than younger ones. It has not been possible to attribute all anecdotes.

LOCAL BOTHER

We had lessons five-and-a-half days a week and were also expected to attend matins in chapel on Sunday, and in what dress? Would you believe it, a cut-away Eton jacket with the two-and-a-half inch, stiff collar, and one can imagine the cat calls (and more) walking from Clifton Dale to the school on a Sunday morning. Uniforms meant that day-boys were something of a target for local youths. I remember being set upon by a street gang …

THE OPEN-AIR SWIMMING POOL

The swimming pool was a concrete hole in the ground … looking back it had no attraction whatever. The changing rooms were merely two boarded off areas … no such thing as lavatories existed. During the term … cleaning parties were organized because there was no circulation of the water, and after about two weeks it turned a dark green … when the water was let out of the pool it had to be scrubbed by hand.

WENTWORTH PING

Many memories about Wentworth Ping are recorded. Most speak with affection of him but there are those who record a darker side. Teddy Denison's memories of him are typical.

I remember him as a big, bluff man with a voice that is reputed to have carried instructions to the rowing crew from the steps of the White House. A keen and knowledgable countryman, he enthused generations with his knowledge of wild flowers and his lessons in natural history could startle many a class. It was not unknown for him to throw up the window of his bedroom, or elsewhere, and take a shotgun to a squirrel or other vermin on the lawn. He would then march into his first class, slam it on the desk and proceed with a fascinating lesson about the wretched animal or bird. Not the nicest side of Pingy was the two canes 'Hengist' and 'Horsa' which he wielded with great frequency upon miscreants actual or imagined.

THE SECOND WORLD WAR

Night-time fire-watching was organized on a regular basis and in the holiday time it was the day-boys who were used for this task. Fire-watching teams were based in the small ground-floor room to the left of the first entrance to the Queen's building, on the right of the archway. The room was fitted out with bunkbeds and roster times differed according to the time of the year. Somehow we survived the night, sleeping four or six in bunkbeds in that small room, together with a master who had the luxury of a bed. We had to patrol at irregular times, but as nothing happened the regimen slackened. Nevertheless, it was quite exciting for a young boy.

Other holidays in wartime included the farming camp. The camp was a collection of bell tents set up in a field near Hovingham. All ages were pressurized to volunteer for one, but preferably two, weeks' work during the summer holidays, and then potato-picking in the Christmas term. I am sure equal pressure was brought to bear on the members of staff to supervise and help … Those attending helped on the local farms, mostly in pairs or fours and we worked hard. Harvest seemed to be earlier in those days, and once started you could have quite long days stooking and stacking. Petrol was not available, so we were expected to take our bikes and cycle to and from the farms. If the harvest had not started we were put onto odd jobs like scything thistles … Senior boys were able to make regular calls at the local pubs, but nothing ever got out of hand.

Another constant reminder of the war was the digging and maintenance of air-raid trenches to the right of the swimming pool, running parallel with the bottom hedge, between the hedge itself and the touch line of the 1st XV pitch. To begin with, air-raid practices (which entailed the whole school going into the trenches) took place on most Saturday mornings, but as the tide of fortune turned in the war, these practices became less frequent and eventually the trenches fell into disrepair, but remained an attractive haunt for some time for adventurous Peterites and would-be Romeos or smokers.

Teddy Denison, St Olave's 1936–41, St Peter's 1941–46

Having done rather well in the end-of-term exams I was nevertheless called into Dronfield's study at the end of term. I was petrified and wondered what I had done wrong. In fact he told me we shared the same birthday, which was on that day and that it was his habit to share sherry with anyone else celebrating their birthday on the same day as his. This habit continued until I left in 1961.

Nigel Thornton, 1956–61

KENNETH CHILMAN

Kenneth Chilman was hugely popular in our day. A big, jowly man who, when playing cricket for the Staff, was always the schoolboy's favorite since he had a tendency to launch himself into hitting huge sixes on a regular basis. It was said that he hit one that smashed the clock on the top end of the outside wall of the (then much shorter) Big Hall building. Anyone who did it again was offered a huge prize by him. Few of us could loft the ball anywhere near the building, let alone get close to the mended clock. So Kenneth's prize money was always considered safe in his pocket, as he knew it was always going to be anyway, the canny devil!

'WIZZY' WISEMAN

Wizzy was unique among the staff for his tendency to wear his black gown and mortarboard to class. His habit was to enter the classroom for our Latin lessons, stride up on to the dais and bang his books on the table, before sitting down on its corner. He didn't need to tell us to shut up because he was such an entertaining teacher, even for Latin: we all quietened down and were glued to his oratorical gifts.

One day some bright spark set the table on the edge of the dais. Sure enough in came the unsuspecting bulk of Wizzy, who, as always, slammed his books down and sat on the table's edge. As planned, it collapsed, and we all sat there horrified as he loudly disappeared in a flurry of black gown and flying mortarboard, flat on his back on the floor. We jumped up to see him now in a sitting

position (thank God he was all right), red faced and flummoxed. But not for long. What came out of his mouth at that moment was brilliant, and remembered to this day by all of us lucky to have been there:

> 'Wizzybus sitibus on the deskioram,
> Deskibus collapsibus, Wizzy on the floorum.'

To this day that off-the-cuff answer at his embarrassing predicament was the most astonishing piece of repartee we had ever heard. Wizzy's reputation, already considerable, soared. We were dazzled. To us he became godlike, never again to be treated with anything less than awe.

Jim Knapton, 1949–57

FIRST DAY AT BOARDING SCHOOL

I was dropped off by my parents at Wentworth House one late afternoon in September, 1949. I was all of nine years old. In the evening the new boys were assembled in the common room for welcoming remarks from our new housemaster, David Blunt. At the conclusion, a small boy piped up 'Sir, why are we here?'. The main theme of the eloquent response to this unheard-of question (shades of Oliver Twist) was our good fortune in attending such an ancient and prestigious school. We would forge lasting friendships, be instilled with a sense of discipline and learn authority, such that when we went out into the world, be it to the colonies or here at home, we would be leaders of men. Heady stuff for eight- and nine-year-olds and all that was missing was the sound of trumpets and a drum roll.

THE GUY FAWKES AFFAIR

Just before 5 November 1956, I lent my cap to a day-boy. While he was cycling home a boy from Bootham snatched the cap from his head. The word was that my cap was destined for Guy Fawkes, who was sitting atop the bonfire on Clifton Green waiting for the big night. Rising to the challenge, I determined to retrieve my cap and on the evening of bonfire night, in the company of my friend, Charlie, set off under cover of darkness. We took a circuitous route and were soon on the Green, eyeing my cap set at a jaunty angle on Guy Fawkes' head. In a trice, I was up on the unlit bonfire and the cap was back in the owner's hands. As luck would have it, we were seen and reported. It was not long before our housemaster, Bob Harding, requested our presence. I went in first. 'What is this I hear about your being down in Clifton?'. I duly recounted the sequence of events and, much to my surprise, his face lit up with a big smile as he said, 'Well done, Laird'. Charlie did not fare so well. Denying the escapade did not help his cause and he finished on the receiving end of a little 'corrective action'.

173

In those days we were led to believe that suffering was good for the soul. It built character. Charlie had a lot of character …

John Maxwell, 1949–57

THE GHOST AND THE RED SLIPPERS

The Chaplain in my first years in the school was Canon Fawcett, who is supposed to have heard the sound of shuffling slippers in the chapel late one evening. I believe he never denied the story. Certainly it used to make the hairs on the backs of our necks stand up when, after lights-out, we used to elaborate on the story and frighten some of our more sensitive contemporaries and often ourselves.

Michael Kent, 1944–49

MEMORIES OF AN AIR RAID

It is amusing now, but during an air raid we had to grab our clothing, which was readied in a bundle, and our eiderdown and all go down to the morning room with the matron and Mrs Ping. Mr Ping would patrol outside the house with his double-barrelled shotgun, ready to defend us against the enemy. If air raids lasted a long time we were allowed to sleep in on the following morning. We rather enjoyed air raids because of the excitement of getting up; the search lights and bangs in the distance we thought were fun. We were quite convinced we were safe and that we would win the war soon. Most of the air raids would provide souvenirs of bits of incendiary bombs and shrapnel, sometimes dug out from one of the wooden buildings. The enemy also released silver strips to confuse the radar and these could be folded into Christmas decorations.

UNIFORM

In my first year at St Olave's I despised Sundays, because we had to wear Marlborough suits and highly starched collars, which we called 'tin collars' because that is how they felt. In the summer we had straw hats for Sundays and we got into trouble, because they made marvellous bats for pebbles and other small objects and then the top would be perforated.

R. John Gibson, 1938–49

PADDY POWER

Paddy was one of the great characters of the School and is remembered with great affection. He was SSI and taught swimming, boxing and fencing. I am sure many, many tales could be told about him, but this one catches the spirit of Paddy rather well. Paddy was a character full of Irish blarney and he certainly earned his name. He was a football league referee and he often came back on Mondays with tales of matches. On one occasion there was a dispute as to whether the ball had crossed the line or not for a goal. Paddy waved both teams to one side and strode over to the linesman. 'Are you all right for a cup of tea after the game?' he asked. As soon as the linesman nodded, Paddy pointed to the centre spot, confirming a goal.

TOYNE

At the start of the First World War the 1st XV pitch was dug up to grow potatoes, with Toyne (who had a supreme confidence in all his abilities) supervising. Shortly afterwards a government inspector arrived to vet progress and pronounced that the school was doing it all wrong. 'How strange that you should have such lengthy experience and yet I know so much better how it should be done,' retorted Toyne.

Pat Norwood, Denis Norwood's daughter

TRADITIONS

You had to learn what all the different school ties looked like and what they represented and you had to learn all the school captains of every sport and the result of every school team. You were regularly tested by the senior pupils and woe betide you if you got any answers wrong: more unpleasant punishments came your way.

CRAZES AT ST OLAVE'S

One of the most popular crazes at St Olave's were games of marbles, where you rolled your marble at an upturned box that had slits in it, and if it went into the box through one of these slits you got your marble back, together with the quantity number written above the slit.

David Quarrie, 1954–63

SCIENCE LESSONS: THE GUY FAWKES TRADITION CONTINUES

Mr Harris was a superb Chemistry teacher. His 'fog day' was justifiably famous. He had the entire chemistry class boiling two solutions side by side (I will not name them for obvious reasons) and very rapidly the classroom would fill with fog. He would then go round turning off the Bunsen burners and he would be followed round, in the fog, by a boy who was lighting them again. I firmly believe he well knew what was happening and expected it. He would then say, 'That is enough, boys' and we would then turn them off – he knew boys and we knew he knew boys! I do not know if he taught us how to mix iodine crystals and 'x', but it produces a super-sensitive explosive which will go off with the lightest touch, when it is dry. I made some and put it into a tobacco tin and put it into my warm trouser pocket. I was in the choir and processed into chapel. Because I was in my final year at St Peter's, I was at the back of the choir and behind me came only the 'The Man', Head Master John Dronfield, and Canon Patteson. All of a sudden there were loud bangs behind me, and then I realized what it was: the paste had dried to a powder, leaked out of the tin and fallen on the chapel floor as I had gone in. I kept very quiet while both CP and The Man looked down at their feet and of course could see nothing. Nobody ever discovered what caused the bangs.

Finally, I should tell the story of the test firing in the lecture theatre in the science block. One of the boys who was at school with me was Mike Gray. He was always interested in explosives and had constructed a cannon out of a heavy brass tube, which he had fixed solidly into a large gun mount made, I seem to remember, out of oak. He had made some explosive, probably gunpowder, and then charged his gun with some wadding and screws, nails and any other bits of metal he had found lying about. There was a firing hole through which he had passed electric wire. Firing was to be by passing a large current through the wire.

The gun was set up in the lecture theatre and we would retire to a safe distance and metaphorically press the plunger. The safe place was the signals room round the corner from the lecture theatre. The plunger was pressed and nothing happened. Mike went back and adjusted something and the plunger was pressed again, and again and again. Richard Shepherd and I got bored and went back to what we were doing. All of a sudden there was a tremendous BANG and Mike appeared round the corner covered in black powder with no eyebrows, but fortunately quite unhurt. We went into the lecture theatre and the front of the desk had a big black mark on it and there was nails and screws embedded in the stairs of the lecture theatre ... and they were STILL there when I went back to visit the school in 1987.

Looking back, I think the School must have heaved a sigh of relief when we left. Guy Fawkes was alive and well and went to school again 1949–54.

Malcolm McCallum, 1949–54

The Coronation, 2 June 1953

Earlier in the year I had won a Combined Cadet Force competition and was invited to represent the school CCF at the Coronation. RSM Paddy Power was to take a few boys from York. It was a special privilege and a wonderful experience. The following is my diary entry:

Up at 3am. Breakfast at 4.15am. Train to Victoria 5.20am (from Hounslow). Victoria Memorial by 6.30am outside the Central Gate of Buckingham Palace. RSM Power was brilliant; he got us on to the front row. Processions began about 8.40. There was constant rain before Princess Elizabeth came out but it then

stopped. The Coronation Service was relayed on speakers. Crowd outside the Palace shouted, 'We want the Queen'. Balcony appearance at 5.45pm. Went along the Corornation route, terrific, fireworks at Victoria Embankment. Large crowds. Train back to York at 12.55am. Home at 5.45am. Bed.

A.B. Sellers

I met the great Yorkshire County Cricket Club captain when he brought the Craven Gentlemen to play against the School in 1954. Whilst awaiting his arrival for tea during the interval, I was perched on the trestle tea table. As he walked in I politely rose to greet him. His first words were, 'Keep tha' face down there lad'. He was always a tough customer.

Richard Bough, 1949–54

Late for Dronfield

In 1955 I was batting for the 2nd XI against Bradford Grammar. After hitting the ball in the direction of the old squash courts, I called for two runs only to be run out by some tight fielding. Next morning I was late for my maths lesson with John Dronfield. No one was ever late for his classes. 'Sorry I am late, Sir', I stammered. 'You were late yesterday as well, Crane', he responded tersely, but I did feel there was a twinkle in his eye.

Peter Crane 1951–57

Air-Raid Duty

One master and two boys did this duty, which was great fun. We slept in turns in a room on the ground floor of Temple House, with buckets of sand and long-handled shovels for dealing with incendiary bombs at the ready. One of the main perks of this job was that one boy was allowed to go to the fish-and-chip shop in Clifton and bring back a late supper for all three. My dormitory in School House, before it was burnt out in the air-raid in April 1942, overlooked the quadrangle towards the chapel. It became the practice to order our fish and chips from the fire-watchers to eat in our dorm. We received them in a basket at the end of a piece of rope lowered from our window. We were discovered when too many people got in on the act.

Peter Leigh, 1939–43

Music

Without Freddie Waine's music appreciation option during my sixth-form years, my whole life would have been the poorer. Those double periods on a Friday morning spoke to my soul and kindled a deep love of music which has sustained me ever since. Whenever I hear a Beethoven symphony or a Schumann piano piece, I am transported fondly back to the old music room and gramophone, with the acoustic horn in the corner. Even extracurricular forms of musical expression found their way into

175

the Memorial Hall in those rock-and-roll years. I remember a Sunday night gig after chapel, with Mick Precious and Dave Kendall's unbelievably authentic rendition of Richie Valens' *La Bamba*. Mark Jesper did a great impression of Eddie Cochran and Buddy Holly with *The Casuals*. Tony Skiera, Norman Crumpton and Andrew Thompson sang in *The Trespassers*. Many of us 1960s children were formed by a new musical culture and St Peter's music had its influence, ancient and modern.

John Lacy

SCHOOL UNIFORM AND THE WAR

I was one of five boys from local council schools awarded City Scholarships in 1940. The transition from our free and easy clothing to the strict dress code of St Olave's was traumatic enough, but must have been more so for our parents. Clothes were severely rationed in those days and I am sure my parents must have sacrificed their own supply of coupons to kit us out. Two years later they had to do it all again when we moved up into the senior ranks. We did not take kindly to the regulation shirts of that time: thick, striped flannel with separate stiff, white collars (studs front and rear) and because they would have to last several years they were always bought several sizes too big.

Don Hardisty 1940–47

BEFORE RISK ASSESSMENTS AND HEALTH AND SAFETY LEGISLATION ...

The lower study was lighted by a double-branched gas bracket from the ceiling. We used to light one burner, fill our hands with gas from the other, light the handful of gas at the lighted burner, and by a sudden and adroit movement light the other. The gas taps in some of the bedrooms were controlled by a string passing round the walls to one of the beds, a piece of ingenuity that was not encouraged by the powers.

During Gilbert's reign as housemaster I slept in a room which had in the ceiling a vertical window opening to the roof ... I remember one gala night, when it was suggested that the roof would be a good place from which to view the fire-works. The key was obtained from the housemaster, a ladder brought and Mr and Mrs Gilbert climbed with us on to the leads. Some obtained a better view by climbing the chimney stacks. One chimney pot was hot.

John Atkins Easten, 1881–90

LESLIE CHARLES LE TOCQ, TD MA BSc (ECON), SECOND MASTER

Whenever opponents of the shooting sports try to paint shooters as in some way dangerous or undesirable, I think with the warmest gratitude of Leslie Le Tocq, an exemplary human being.

He set two whole generations of his pupils the finest example of calm self-discipline, integrity and humour, and above all had a knack of treating us as responsible adults, a challenge to which boys naturally responded. I suspect he began to learn that lesson as a teenager keeping watch for boats entering the very real danger area of the Guernsey rifle range in L'Ancresse Bay, where there was no stop-butt and all bullets headed out to sea, a responsibility which would horrify those who see in shooting nothing but danger, and who have no religion but 'safety'. How lucky we were to be taught by a man with a deeper grasp of life and of human nature.

David Harding, 1960–70

Leslie's colleagues remember him as an outstanding Second Master. His great qualities of integrity, calm, warmth and humour (which he carried throughout the School in his dual role of Administrator and Teacher) are most appropriately and eloquently described here.

MARK HEPWORTH ATTENDED CLIFTON PREP SCHOOL, ST OLAVE'S AND ST PETER'S FROM 1960 TO 1971. HE WAS MADE HEAD OF SCHOOL IN 1970.

At the time I entered the School, John Dronfield was Head Master. I knew that he had established for himself an authority and reputation, such that his retirement in 1967 was a significant event in the history of the School. I also became aware, certainly in my later years, that his approach to life in general and school mastering in particular, would not, in all probability, have co-existed easily with the rapid change in social mores that occurred during the second half of the 1960s. Had he remained in office, either he or the world in general would have had to change and in the event that neither felt so inclined, I can only wonder at what discord might have ensued.

However, Peter Gardiner was appointed as his successor and my recollection of him is a man with a clear vision of how the School should evolve in difficult times. He was a traditionalist in that he rigidly upheld the values of personal integrity, hard work and sporting endeavour but he was in tune with the times in that he recognised the need for individual expression and cultural diversity. One got the impression that there were those (and not only within the School) who hankered after a more authoritarian approach but PDRG recognised that to lead the School in such a way would have caused dissention and conflict between the School and the wider environment in which it existed. It is clear that Peter Gardiner was a far-sighted Head Master who succeeded in steering St Peter's away from the worst excesses that afflicted many other schools at this time.

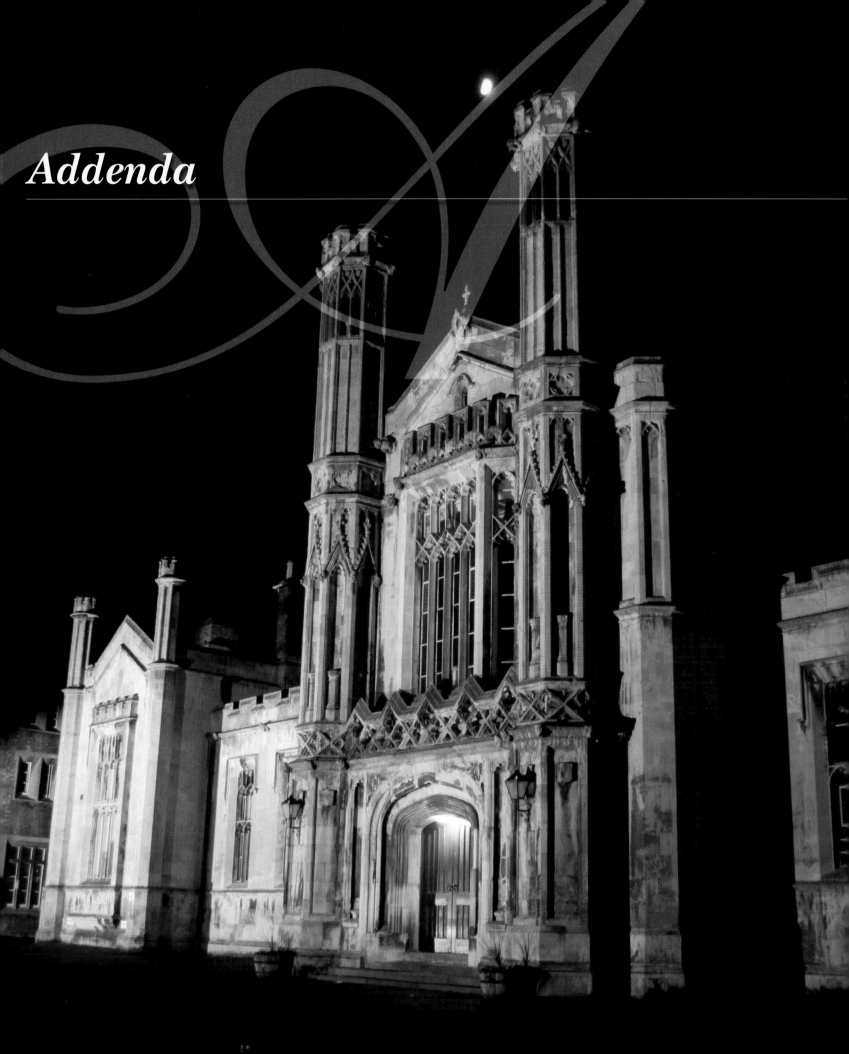

Addenda

Long-serving Members of Staff

John Dronfield served the School for 30 years. Those 22 members of the recent academic staff (17 of them appointed by him) who have also served for 30 years or more are:

B. Allen, 1964–99, Housemaster of The Grove and Head of Science

J.D. Blissett, 1964–2000, Senior Master, St Olave's

J.C. Brown, 1954–92, Housemaster of Alcuin and Head of Art

R.J. Bulcock, 1966–2001, Housemaster of Temple, Housemaster of The Manor, Contingent Commander CCF, Head of English

K.G. Chilman, 1920–65, Housemaster of Elmet

K.G. Coulthard, 1949–91, Housemaster of Dronfield, Head of Geography, Head of Careers

D.G. Cummin, 1949–80, Head Master 1984–85, Second Master, Housemaster of The Rise, Contingent Commander CCF, Head of History

M. Dawson, 1970–, Head of CDT

C.E. Field, 1950–82, Head of Classics, St Olave's

J. Gaastra, 1952–82, Head of Art

N. Gypson, 1950–82

R.F. Harding, 1938–74, Housemaster of The Grove, Head of Games

P.L. Harris, 1946–78, Head of Science

R.H. Hubbard, 1968–2002, Housemaster of Queen's, Head of Careers

D.P. Johnston, 1956–89, Housemaster of Wentworth, Senior Master, St Olave's

D. Kirby, 1962–2001, Housemaster of Queen's, Housemaster of The Rise, Head of German

Leslie C. Le Tocq, 1937–81, Housemaster of The Manor, Head of Geography, Head of Economics, Second Master

I.M.K. Lowe, 1972–2004, Head of Drama, Head of General Studies

M. Mason, 1943–67, Head of English, St Olave's

J.V. Mitchell, 1965–88, Head of History, St Olave's, Librarian 1988–92, Archivist 1992–2001

J. Nix, 1942–72, Senior Master, St Olave's

J.A. Owen-Barnett, 1976–, Housemaster of Dronfield, Housemaster of Linton (formerly School) House

K.R. Pemberton, 1954–94, Director of Music

A.W. Ping, 1921–55, Master of St Olave's

K.H. Rhodes, 1923–69, Housemaster of Temple, Head of History, Senior Master

C.A. Robinson, 1968–99, Maths Department, Housemaster of Fairfax and Beverley

G.M. Shuttleworth, 1957–89, Housemaster of Queen's and The Manor, Head of Maths

G. Yeld, 1867–1919, English and Drama

Three died in service, all of whom had also served for many years, died in service and I commend the relevant edition of *The Peterite* for further details:

A. Craven, 1946–67, Head of Modern Languages

R.B. Daniel, 1967–86, Housemaster of School House, Housemaster of Dronfield

P. Taylor, 1979–2004, Housemaster of School House, Housemaster of Dronfield, Head of Classics

Opposite page from top left clockwise: Kennelth Rhodes (portrait by Mick Arnup), 1923–69, Housemaster of Temple, Head of History and Senior Master; George Yeld, 1868–1919, the longest serving member of staff who was also a famous alpinist and renowned for hybridising day lilies; Senior Masters 1958–1997; Academic Staff 2005 and Academic Staff 1936.

Rugby, Cricket and Boating Honours

RUGBY

International Honours

1888	L. E. Stevenson (Scotland)
1895–96	F. Mitchell (England)
1901–02	E. J. Walton (England)
1905	R.F. Russell
1906	C. V. Crombie (Captain, Canada)
1933	C.L. Troop (England)

Schoolboy International Honours

1923–24	E.P. Sewell (English Public Schools XV)
1967	D.J. Emsley (England Schoolboys' XV)
1979	J.F. Ellison (England Schoolboys' XV)
1997	A. Drysdale (Scotland U15 XV)
1998	A. Springgay (England U18)
1999–2000	A. Springgay (England U19)
2002	T. Woolsey (England U16)
2004–05	P. Wackett (England U18 AER)
2004	J. Marsden (England U18)
2005	J. Wackett (England U19)
2005	T. Denton (England U18 AER)

Oxford and Cambridge Blues

1882–84	E.A. Douglas (Cambridge)
1884–85	L.E. Stevenson (Cambridge)
1893–95	F. Mitchell (Cambridge)
1886–87	W. G. Wilson (Oxford)
1888	J.H.G. Wilson (Oxford)
1900	E.J. Walton (Oxford)
1955	M. Kershaw (Cambridge)
1980–83	M. F. Gargan (Oxford)
1983	J.F. Ellison (Cambridge)
2006	T. Woolsey (Cambridge)

Oxford and Cambridge Rugby League

2004	N. Rusling (Cambridge Blue, man of the match against Oxford)
2005	A. Drysdale (Cambridge Blue, man of the match against Oxford, Hawk of the Year 2005), N. Rusling

CRICKET 1945–2005

Honours

	David Kirby (Public Schools XI, Captain of Cambridge University, 1961, and Leicestershire, 1962)
1968	Joe Richardson (Public Schools XI)
1973	Stephen Coverdale (Cambridge Blue)
1977	David Riley (MCC XI, England Young Cricketers, Kent 2nd XI)
1982	Shuan Gorman (HMC Schools XI, National Association of Young Cricketers, 1983, Cambridge Blue)

Bowling

Joe Yuill (144 wickets, 1951 season, 61 wickets for an average 7.78 runs. Peter James also took over 100 wickets.)

Bill Pickersgill (150 wickets, 1950, took all 10 wickets for 13 runs against Giggleswick, 1965)

Gordon Tait (63 wickets, 1977)

Tom Woolsey (183 wickets, 2000-04)

Batting

23 centuries were made 1945–75, whereas 47 centuries were achieved 1975–2005. In the 1963 season, Tom Mitchell and Peter Nettleton made a record stand of 272 against Worksop.

Mike Davies (5 centuries, highest score 169 not out in 1993, 2,344 runs in 84 innings)

Nick Kay (3 centuries, 200 not out in 1998, 3,026 runs in 77 innings, 1,076 runs in 1998 (the only Peterite to achieve this in one season)

Andrew Kay (4 centuries)

James Burdass (167 not out, 1984)

Richard Hutchinson (2,019 runs in 81 innings)

St Peter's School Boat Club Results 1992–2005
National Representation and Medals
National Schools' Regatta

1997	Women's Junior 16 Coxed IV Silver
1998	Women's Junior Coxed IV Bronze
1999	Women's Junior Double Scull Silver: H. Austin, G. Bentham
1999	Women's Championship Coxless Pair Gold: H. Austin, G.Bentham
2002	Men's Junior 16B VIII Silver
2003	Men's Junior 16B VIII Bronze
2004	Women's Junior 16 Single Scull Silver: R. Gaunt
2004	Women's Championship Single Scull Gold: K. Stiller
2005	Women's Championship Double Scull Gold: K. Stiller, H. Thomas

Boat Club – National Representation & Medals
Great Britain National Championships

1998	Women's Senior Coxless IV, Gold: H. Austin
1999	Women's Lightweight Coxless Pair, Bronze: G. Bentham
1999	Women's Junior 16 Single Scull, Bronze: V. Johnston
1999	Women's Senior Coxless Pair, Bronze: H. Austin, G. Bentham
2001	Women's Junior Double Scull, Bronze: V. Johnston
2004	Women's Junior 16 Single Scull, Gold: R. Gaunt
2004	Women's Junior 18 Single Scull, Silver: H. Thomas
2005	Men's Senior Coxless IV, Gold: A. MacLeod
2005	Men's Senior VIII, Gold: R. Robertson
2005	Women's Senior Coxless Quad, Gold: K. Stiller
2005	Women's Junior 18 Single Scull, Silver: H. Thomas

St Peter's School Boat Club – International Representation & Medals
Anglo-French Junior 16 Match

2004	R. Gaunt Great Britain WJ16 1X 2nd Vitre, France

Home International

1999	H. Austin England WJ 2, Gold, Cork, Ireland
2004	H. Thomas WalesWJ 1X, Bronze Nottingham, England
2004	H. Thomas WalesWJ 4X, Silver Nottingham, England
2005	H. Thomas Wales WJ1X, Gold, Cardiff, Wales
2005	H. Thomas Wales WJ2X, Gold, Cardiff, Wales

Munich Junior International Regatta, Germany

2004	K. Stiller Great Britain WJ 2X 7th, 4th
2005	K. Stiller Great Britain WJ 2X, 4th
2005	K. Stiller Great Britain WJ 1X, 5th
2006	R. MacLeod Great Britain MJ 4, 16th
2006	R. MacLeod Great Britain MJ 2, 6th
2006	R. MacLeod Great Britain MJ 4X, 12th

Coupe de la Jeunesse

1998	A. Dangerfield Great Britain MJ 1X, 6th, Bronze, Candia, Italy
1998	G. Bentham Great Britain WJ 2, Bronze, Silver Candia, Italy
1999	G. Bentham Great Britain WJ 2, Gold, Cork, Ireland
2003	D. Janes Great Britain MJ 4X, 7th, 4th Hazewinkel, Belgium
2004	D. Janes Great Britain MJ 4X, 4th, 4th Ravenna, Italy
2006	R. Macleod Great Britain VIII, Silver, Groningen, Holland

Junior World Championships

1998	H. Austin Great Britain WJ 4, 5th Ottensheim, Austria
2004	K. Stiller Great Britain WJ 2X, 9th, Banyoles, Spain
2005	A. MacLeod Great Britain MJ 4, Bronze Brandenburg, Germany
2005	R. Robertson Great Britain MJ VIII, 8th Brandenburg, Germany
2005	K. Stiller Great Britain WJ 4X, Bronze Brandenburg, Germany

181

List of Subscribers

Jonathan Abel

Peter Abel

Tom Abel

Nick Adams

Michael G.H. Adcock

Lorna Aiken

Jane Alexander

Alastair Alton

Edward Alton

Stephanie Atkinson

Dr Jeff Anderson

Thomas Darley Farrow Anderson

W.P. Anelay

Steve Angel

M.C.M. Anyan

Paula Arkley

Hannah Armstrong

J.O. Armstrong

John Armstrong

Richard Armstrong

Eloise Atkin

Brian J. Atkinson

D.P. Atkinson

D.S. Atkinson

Graham D. Atkinson

Richard Atkinson

Roger Atkinson

Helen Austin

Simon Austin

Alison Aveyard

Jason Ayers

Miki Ayton

Daniel Flitcroft Bailey

Guy Bailey

Mike Bainbridge

Chris Ball

Henry Ball

David Ballinger

Alexander Banerjea

Anthony C. Barker

Edward Charles Barker

Robert Barker

Lesley Barlow

Rachel Barnes (*née* Taylor)

Rich Barrett

Roger Barrett

Alastair Barron

David Barron

Sir Douglas Barron

Roderick Barron

Dr David Barton

N.R. Barton

Jon, Amanda and Joseph Bates

Vincent D.F. Bates

Alfred Battrick

Edward and Emily Battye

David Rothery Baxter

Robert Baxter

Tim Beaumont

Helena Bedford

Robert Bedford

Keith Beetlestone

Elliot and Lewis Bell

Nigel J. Bell

P.K. Best

Mike Bidgood

Susan and Chris Binks

John Birch

Stephen C. Blackman

Lawrence Bleasdale

Claire Blenkin

N.A. Blenkin

Mr J.D. Blissett

Kieran Alexander Bloor

Alex Bond

Julia Bond

Robert Boocock

C.P.G. Booth

R. Maxwell Booth

Tom Booth

In memory of R.G. Bough

Thomas B. Boulton

Kim Bowler

Mr Michael Bowstead

Nikki and Beth Bradley

Professor Paul Brenikov

John Brewer

J. David Brewin

R.A. Brindley

Clive Broadbent

Captain J. Michael Brook

Paul G. Brooke

Mr and Mrs Byron Brown

Gary Brown

Hugh Brown

Mr and Mrs S.J. Browne

Mr and Mrs R.R. Buchanan

Danielle Henrietta Buckley

James Burdass

Steven Mark Burn

N. Burnett

Paul Burnett

David A. Burns

Amy Burrell

Henry and Ellie Burton

Prof. Robin Butlin

J.A. Bygate

Murray Bywater

Harry Caley

Stephen Caley

A.A. Camfield

P.C. Campbell

Joshua Cantrill

Neil Carmichael

Neville W.M. Carr

Simon David Carr

Samantha Carter

Ciara and David Cecil

Christopher Chadwick

Mr Jonathon Chambers

Tom E. Chambers

Charles C.S. Chapman

P.W.G. Chilman

Mrs Sally Chilwell

Faye Elizabeth Clark

Charles Clarke

184

Chris J.L. Clarke
Stuart Clarke
Kevin Clarkson
G.R.H. Clemons
Roger Coates
Katie A.L. Cockill
Richard Anthony Cockroft
Charles Burton Code
Harriet Code
Clifford J. Coggrave
D.P. Coles
J.R. Coles
Lucy Collier
Peter Collins
Ian Collinson
John Nigel Collinson
David, Jane, Tom, Sam and Katy Colthup
Edward F. Contreras
Harry R. Contreras
James A. Contreras
William G. Contreras
Valerie Cook
Scott Cooper (Kipper)
Timothy E.J. Cooper BSc MBA
William J. Cordingley
Keith and Margaret Coulthard
Richard Craig
P.A. Crane
B.W.A. Craven
David R. Cross
Alex Crossley and Joe Crossley
J.B. Crossley
J.A. Crowther
R.G. Crowther
Dr James P. Curley
Marie-Sophie Dalglish
John R. Dalkin
The Rev'd Jeffrey Daly
Gillian Daniells
Robert Davidge
Charlotte Davies
Mark Davies
Dr Peter Davies
Nigel Dawkins
A.J. De Mulder
John Dean
Nikki Dean
Christopher C. Dee
Kevin Dell
J.D. Dench
E.A.K. 'Teddy' Denison
Tom and Oli Denton
Miss F.E. Devlin
Nicholas A.J. Devlin
Andrew V.A. Dickie

Ben Dickson
Drs C.J. and T.M. Diggory
R. Dingwall
Anna Dixon
Anthony John Dixon
John B. Dixon
Mike Dixon
R.S. Dixon
Philip and Joshua Dobbins
Lucy Dodgson (née Evans)
Philip Andrew Dodman
Matthew R. Doncaster
P.A. Dornan
S.R. Dowding
Duncan W. Downes
Claire and Mike Downie
Nicholas and Sally Doxey
The Drever-Smith Family
Dr Michael Drucquer
Euan Drysdale
Charles Duke
Georgina Duke
Oliver Duke
Dr N.P. Durham
Edward Eaton
James Edgecombe
Adam Tom Walton Edwards
John Eggleshaw
Mr and Mrs P.N. Elkington
Mr and Mrs M.H. Elliott
Richard Ellis
Lorna Emery
Robert Ende
S.J and D.M. England
A.C. and M. Evans
John Fairclough
Mr and Mrs A. I. Falconer
Vanessa L. Farr
Hugh Fawcett
Philip Fawcett
J.N. Fenton
Alistair Fernie
Sybille Fiaux
Paul and Jenny Firth
John Fishley
Emma Fitton
Doug Fleming
Adam Floyd
Michael J. Foley
Matthew Ford
Samantha Ford
Jonathan David Forsyth
Catherine Fort
Jonathan Fort
Colin F. Foster

Michael and Charlotte Foster
Luis John Gordon Temple Fox
Benjamin France
Michael Frank
Andrew and Jenny Frazer
Julien French
Cherry Fricker
Joe Fricker
Nicholas P. Frost
Martyn Fry
Edward Fulbrook
Grant S. Fullerton
R.K. Gabbertas
Peter Gardiner
Bobby Gardner
Dave Gardner
Sophia Gascoyne
Philip Gaunt
Rosie Gaunt
Sorrel Gaunt
Steven Gaunt
Marc C.S. Gee
Andrew George
Dylan George
Iuan George
R. John Gibson
Laura Gilding
Nick Gillgrass
Andrew and Abigail Gisbourne
Paul Gittins
M.J. Glen
C.G. Goodlock and J.D. Goodlock
Joanna, Ian and Clare Gordon
James Gossow
Cameron W. Gough
Andrew Grace
Justin Grace
Sue Grace
Theo Grace
Dr G.E.L. Graham
J.M. Graham
W. (Bill) Graham
Matthew Grant
Alexander Gray
Helen Gray
Quentin Gray
John Greaves
Claudia and Isabel Green
David Green
J.H.D. Greener
Miss Anna Greenwood
Mr Johnnie Greenwood
Peter Gregory-Jones
David Grice
Colin G. Grieves

Sheila Groves
Jonathan M. Hall
Michael E. Hall
Simon D.V. Hall
Andrew R.J. Halstead
Jack Hamilton
Dr D.J. Hanly and Dr F.M. Forsythe
Mrs Fiona Hannah
Richard Harding
Don Hardisty
Bryan Harnby
Jack and Katie Harrison
Graham Hart
John B. Hart
Mrs P.A. Hartley
The Rev'd Steven Harvey
Nazeeha Hasan
K.W. Headlam
Charlotte Emma Heads
Felicity Hearn
Clive, Susan, David and Richard Heaton
Nicky Hemsworth
Mark Hepworth
Mitchell and Callum Hernaman
Olivia and Victoria Herrenschmidt
John Herring
Robert T. Hey
Abigail Hickman
Justin Hill
Helen Hilliard (née Stringer)
Jamie P. Hockin
David and Veda Hodgin
Clive I. Hodgson
Laura Hodsdon
Jenny Hoggard
Julian Holdsworth
J.M. Holt
Dr and Mrs Hopkinson
Anne M. Hopper
Martin Hornby
John and Sheila Houghton-Brown
Henry W. Houseman
Jeremy N.T. Howat
R.H. Hubbard
Dr C. Keith Hudson
Mr Leslie R. Hudson
William M. Hudson
Aleksander Hughes
Richard J. Hugill
C. David Hunter
Ian T. Hunter
Sarah Hunter
John N. Hutchinson
Richard E. Hutchinson
James Hutt

David Hutton
Matthew J.K. Hyde
Mr W.R. Ibberson
Magnus Inness
Richard Iveson
Donald C. Jack
Edward J. Jackson
Hannah L. Jackson
J.A. Jackson
Jonathan Jackson
R.A. Jackson
Freddie Jagger
Giles Jagger
Robert Jaques
B.L. Jarvis
G.M. Jobling
Mrs Anne Johnson
C.D. Johnson
Chloe Johnson
Felicity Johnson
J. Andrew Johnson
D.P. Johnston
Matthew and Susannah Jones
David Joy
Alexandra Kaars Sijpesteijn
Casper Kaars Sijpesteijn
David Kaner and Amanda Rigby
Andrew L.T. Kay
Jordan Edward Simon Kay
Michael G. Kay JP
Nicholas J.C. Kay
Fleur Keith
Michael Kent
Maurice Kershaw
The Ketteringham Family
Steve Kettlewell
Guy King-Reynolds JP M.A. LRAM
David Kirby
Ian Kirkus
Jamie, Angus and Lucy Knox
Christine and John Lacy
Winnie Kong Lai-Wan
Professor Peter Lamarque
G.D. Lambert
R.F. Lambert
Dr James Larcombe
John Adrian Gordon Latimer
Mr Chris Lawrie
Henry Richard Lee
Joo Hyun (Maria) Lee
Mark Yuk-Ching Lee
Peter Leigh
Ben Lenighan
Ben Les
Bruno Les

Carl Les
Michael W.H. Leung
Hannah Lewis (née Fowler)
Simon Lewis
Caroline Liddle
Alice L.M. Lindley
Edward R. Lindley
S.R. Lister
Thomas Lloyd
Annabel Long
Briony Long
John Lowe
Mark J.G. Lucas
John Ludley
Stephen and Susan Lum
Andrew Lyall
Morag Lyall
James Challenor Lynch
Iain and Stuart Macalister
Brian MacDonald
J. Crawford B. MacKeand
Caitlin J. Mackellar
Iain MacLeod
Dr James and Dr Joan MacLeod
Duncan Macpherson
Alison Tracy Magson
Ian Magson
Nicholas Magson
Clare Maguire (née Summers)
The Mahon Family
Alan Mak
Shyam Mallen
David and Michael Mallinson
N.C.P. Marsden
P.S. Marsden
Philip W.F. Marsden
Charles C. Marshall
Valerie Marshall
T.E. Martindale
Mr M.C. Mason and Mrs J. Mason
Patrick K. Masser FHCIMA
P.G. Matthews
John Ronald Maxwell
Malcolm J. McCallum
Michael N. McCulloch
Alistair McGrath
Charles McGregor
Sally McLaren
Alex Mellor
Katie Mellor
Lydia Mellor
Mr Graham Metcalf
Karl R.O. Midhage
Christopher and Alexandra Millard
Andrew J. Miller

185

Kevin and Sue Miller

Stuart Milne

Maurice A. Monteith

Charlotte Morgan

Anthony Morris

Ian E.F. Morton

Charles Ashton Moseley

Richard I. Moss

P.B. Mullaly

Martin Muncer

Keith Murray

Richard Musgrave

Tracey and Allan Nadian

Gabriella Naismith

Jonty Naismith

D. Naylor

Mr Michael Naylor

Tony Neal

B.M. Nendick

Peter Netherwood

James D.H. Newbound

Dr Frederick Newton

Garry and Lizanne Newton

Tom Nichols

Sara Nicholson

Mr and Mrs A. Noble

Aleida Florence Norman

D.P. Norwood

Captain Guy O'Donnell, Royal Navy

Peter Oglesby

R.G. De H. Oldham

David Oldman

David Outhwaite

Michael Oxley

Nicholas G. Pace

Michael R. Pallant

Alistair Palmer

Kai and Neils Pampus

Edmund Pang

Elizabeth A. Pang

James Pang

Mr S.N. Park

Charlotte Parker

Ed Parker

Michael Parker

Edward Parkin

Ellis Parry

Chris Patchett

D. Mc I. Patchett

Graham Pattie

Steven Pattie

John Pearson

John A. Pease

Tim and Will Peet

Daro Peeters

Thomas Henry Perrin

Oliver Willem Pettigrew

Alison Pike

John Pike

Richard Pike

Stephen Pike

Robin Pittman

Geoff Plews

Brian Potter

Andrew Powles

John R. Precious

Toby, Bryony and Annabel Pring

Nigel G. Pritchard

David Procter

Stephen Proudley

John Prowde

George B. Pullan

Mr and Mrs J. Punnett

Mark Pyrah

D.N. Quarrie

Colin J. Quickfall FRICS

Nicholas Waud Quinlivan

Lt Col D.M.A. Quirke JP

M.A. Rawnsley

Christopher Elsworth Rawson

John Rayson

Paul J. Reah

Phil Reaston

The Rees Family

A.G. Reynolds

Jason C. Rhodes

John J. Rhodes

Simon J. Rhodes

Sam Richards

C.J. Richardson

Alistair F. Rigby

Jamie D. Rigby

Nicholas Riggall

Peter Rivers

Charles Roberts

E.S.T. Roberts

Nick Roberts

Annabel Robertson

Holly V. Robertson

Jane and Ian Robertson

Kirstie V. Robertson

Rory Robertson

Charles A.H.S. Robinson

Clive Robinson

Ian Robinson

Tobias R.H.S. Robinson

M.E. Robson

Rev'd Dr John Roden

M.G. Roe

Sally Roper youngest daughter of S.M. Toyne

Margaret M. Rounding

Mr E. Rowland

Emma C.R. Rowley

Peter J.D. Rowley

Gerald F. Ruddock

Paul D. Rushbrooke

David Rusholme

Mark Rusling and Nicholas Rusling

Benjamin Russell

Diana M.F. Russell

Phil Rutherford

Keith H. Sargeant

Benjamin Schonewald

Christopher Schonewald

David Scott

Jennie Scott

Richard Scott

Tom Scott

Anthony Scott-Brining

Alice Scruton

Anthony C. Sears

Peter Semper

Mrs E. Sewell

R.J. Sharp

Alexander Shaw

Katerina Shaw

G.E. Shepherd

Pat Shepherd

Emma Sherbourne

Rebecca Sherbourne

Edward Sheriff

J.M. Shirtcliffe and J.R. Shirtcliffe

Guy and Tanya Shuttleworth

Neil Shuttleworth

D.L.W. Sim

D. Neil Simmons

David H.K. Simpson

N. Sirotine

Filan Slater

James Anthony Sleight

John I. Sleight

Martin N. Smallpage

Richard Smalman-Smith

N.J. Smith

Major Peter E.H. Smith

S.G. Smith

Sue Smith

William R.H. Smith

J.M. Smithson

Richard and Nicole Smyth

Alan and Digger Spencer

R.A. Spilman

Alastair Paul Springgay

Stuart Stark

Felicity Stasiak

186

R.L. Stead
J.I. Stephenson
Dr T.J. Stephenson
Tim Stephenson
Robert Stevens
Emma Louise Stone
Christopher W.G. Storer
Lauren C. Storer
Robert J. Storer
D. Streather
Sqn Ldr J.E. Stuart MBE
Peter Stuttard
Jonathan and Oliver Suckling
James Sugden
Victoria Sugden
Timothy Summers
M. Sunley
Dr Rosemary Suttill
The Sweet Family
Peter and Moira Tait
Joseph Man Fung Tang
Andrew Graham Lyle Taylor
Ben P.O. Taylor
Claire Taylor
Edward Charles Taylor
Jennie Taylor
Jessica C. Taylor
N.D. Taylor
Nicholas P. Taylor
Rebecca K. Taylor
Robert James Taylor
S.A.A. Taylor
William Taylor
Derek Taylor-Thompson
Daniel Telfer
Gareth D. Thomas
Mr J.E.K. Thomas
Rhiannon E. Thomas
Alison Kate Thompson
David W. Thompson
Eric G. Thompson
Michael John Thompson
Richard J. Thompson
Robert Michael Thompson
Sarah E. Thompson
Marcus Andrew W. Thomson
William David B. Thomson
E. David Thornton
Nigel Thornton
Dr Russell Thorpe MB ChB
Sally and Paul Thrussell
Josh Tindell
Leo Tindell
Sophie Tompkins
Raymond B. Tonkinson

Clare Toole-Mackson (*née* Cooper)
Edmund Toomey
Col and Mrs P.R. Towers
Dr Eoin W. Trevelyan
Andrew Trotman
Douglas G.F. Tulley
Claire Tully
John Turner
Lara and James Turner
Marcus J. Tyson
Michael Veal
Jennie Wade
Emma L. Walker
Richard W. Walker
J.D.C. Wall
Simon Charles Wallis
Keith M. Walter
Mr J.R. Ward
Matthew M. Ward
Dr Stuart Ward
Thomas, Emma and Ruth Ward
Major J.A. Ware
F.F. Watson
Sarah Waugh
Mr B.G. Way
Adam Webster
Mrs Doreen Webster
Robyn Webster
Colonel (Ret'd) Peter Weighill
Emma Wells-Cole
Malcolm Welsh
Helena Westcott-Weaver (Bould)
James Wetherell
J.K. Wheatley
Dr Jeremy C.G. Wheeler
Nicholas Whincup
Lewis White
Melanie Whitehead (*née* Haslam)
David Whitfield
John Whittle
Claire Wike
Trevor Wilkinson
Heather R. Williams
Jack A. Williamson
Laura J. Williamson
Alasdair Wilson and Hannah Wilson
Kristina and Matthew Withers
Paul Withers
James M. Wood
Kathryn, Margaret and Jeremy Wood
Peter Wood
Philip A. Wood
Richard Wood
Alexander Woodrow
M.W. Woodruff

Christopher John Woolley
Bob and Elizabeth Woolsey
Matthew Wootton
Chris, Alex and Tim Wordie
Mr and Mrs M.R. Wroe
Gavin Edward Hokland Yardley
Kellea J. York
D.G.M. Young
Timothy J. Young

187

Index

Bold text denotes authorial contributions.
Italics denote illustrations

Adams, Matthew **82–3**
Aelberht (Albert), Archbishop 10, 96
Aislabie, John *165*
Albany House 70
Alcuin (Head Master 778–82) 10, *11*, 96
Alcuin House School 68
Alcuin House, St Olave's 66, 70, 77
Alcuin Library 56, 57, 70, 96–8, *97*, 162
Alcuin Lodge, The Avenue 70, 75
Allbutt, Sir Thomas Clifford 22, 88, 162, *165*
Allen, Bruce 176
Alton, Edward 152
Amateur Dramatic Club 126
Amor, H. 43
Anderson, William B. 71
Andrew, HRH Prince *59*, 60 79
Appleby, Mrs 65, 66
Arkley, Paula 66
Arnold, Thomas 14, 54
Aspinall, Ron 146
Athorne, Tom Beverley 126
Atkins Easten, John **174**
Atkinson, Oswald 12
Austin, Helen 150–1, *151*, 179
Austin, Simon 174
Avenue Terrace 64

Bader, Douglas 147
Badgely, Jasper M.C. 68
Badger, Thomas 162
Bagnio, The *12*, 13, 163
Baillie, James 163
Bainbridge, Dionis 16
Bainbridge, Julie 110
Bainbridge, Michael 134
Baird, Mrs A.N. 40, 41

Bairstow, Jonathan 146
Baker, Peter 144
Baldry, Natalie 151
Barlow, Charlie 150
Barry, John (John Barry Prendergast) 70n.,
    165, 166
Bartram, Tom 146
Basu, Indraneil 147
Battrick, Alfred 71
Bede, The Venerable 10
Bedern, York *11*, 12
Bedford, Julian 65
Belchamber, Harry C. 71
Bell, Peter 138
Bell, Simon 125
Bentham, Gemma 150–1, *151*, 179
Best, Paul 89
Beverley House, St Olave's 70, 75, 77, 79
Big Hall 29, 35, 46, *82*, 163, 171; *see also*
    Memorial Hall
Birch, Alistair 150
Blake, John (Head Master 1757–84) 14
Blake, Zachariah (Head Master 1726–57) 13–
    14, 96
Blaydes, Frederick H.M. 14
Blisset, J. David 176
Blood, Christopher 119
Bloomfield, Herbert 21, 162
Blunt, David 70, 171
Boat Club 150–2
Boat house 31, 44
Boddy, William 122
Bollands, Penny **102–3**
Bolton, P.H. 127
Border, Gerorge P. 71
Bough, Richard **173**
Bowring, Ceri 125
Brockbank, James 40, 163
Brown, David **84**
Brown, John C. 49, 150, 176

Buckler, Frederick N. 71
Bulcock, Anne 91
Bulcock, R. John **91**, 104, **104–5**, **138**
Bulletin, The 55, *94*, 95, 115
Bulmer, John 41
Bundy, Prudence 92
Burdass, James 178
Burgess, Leslie ('Bung') 41
Burroughs, Edward (Bishop) 162
Butler, James 14, 150

Calder, Gordon A.R. 71
Cannons, Andrew 80
Centenary Hall, CPPS 65
Chapman, Nigel 154
Charity Commissioners 21–2, 156
Charlemagne, Emperor 10, *11*
Cheney, Christopher 99
Charles I 12–13, 72
Charles II 72
Chilman Building, The 56, 61, *66*, 77, 78, 156
Chilman Scout Troop 69
Chilman, Kenneth G. ('Chilly') 40, 42, 43, 56,
    69, 74, 77, 153–4, 156, 164, 171, 176
Civil and Military Dept 19
Clarendon High School 57
Clarke, Stuart 150
Clegg, Marcus 163
Clifton Garth 22, 68
Clifton Grove 31
Clifton Manor 31, 35
Clifton Pre-preparatory School 58, 61, 64–6,
    65, 156, 159
Clifton Rise *29*, 31
Clitherow, Margaret 16, 167
Cloughton, Bill 154
Coggan, Archbishop *58*
Colin Shepherd Language Rooms 61, 86
Collegiate School, The 18–19

Collett, Miss 40
Collis, Major 43
Conaghan, Dan 115
Coode, Ed 152
Cooper, J. Scott 43, 70
Cottingham, John 112
Coulthard, Keith G. **90–1**, 93–4, 102, 176
Coverdale, Stephen 144, 145, 178
Craine, Gordon D. 50, 154
Crane, Peter **173**
Craven, A. 176
Creer, Hugh L. 164
Crews, Denys K. 43
Creyke, Stephen (Head Master 1827–38)
    14, 18
Cribb, Flt Lt 43
Croft, Peter G. *83*, 105, 115
Crombie, C.V. 178
Crossley, Sophie 124
Crumpton, Norman 174
Cummin, David G. 47, 49, *53, 101, 105,*
    128, 176
Curley, Carlo 119
Curry, George 146
Cuthbertson, Sophie 142

Daly, Jeffrey **87, 112–13**
Dangerfield, Andrew 150–1, 179
Daniel, Cindy 56, 92
Daniel, Gael 56
Daniel, Lindsey 56, 150
Daniel, R. Barry 51, 55–6, 92, 115, 136,
    138, 176
Darmody, John 122–3
Davey, Jo
Dawkins, Professor Richard 88, *89*
Dawson, Mike 105, **125**, 150, 176
Dench, Dame Judi *65*
Dench, Jeffrey D. 41
Dench, Simon 105
Denison Building, The *66*
Denison House 69, 156
Denison, Louise A. **51**
Denison Teddy 80, **156**, *156*, 158, **170–1**
Denton, Tom *149*, 178
Dining hall 35, 44, 45, 48
Discipline card 94, *95*
Dixon, John B. 99
Dobson, Christopher 12
Dodd, Captain 45
Dodds, Alan 154
Dodds, Richard 154
Douglas, E.A. 178
Doyle, Ian 150

Dronfield House 35, 37, 58, 62, 90–1, 92, 93,
    159, 164
Dronfield, John (Head Master 1937–67) 17,
    33, 34–7, *34*, 38–41, 44, 45, 46, 47, 48, 49,
    93, 102, 108, 127, 163, 171, 173
Dronfield, Patrick 17
Dronfield, Sheila 34–5, 40, 49, 90, 114, 164
Drysdale, Alex 147, *149*, 178
Drysdale, Richard C.G. **18–23, 24–5, 26–32,**
    33, 42–5, 47–50, 52–3, 54–9, 85, 93–5,
    100–1, 105, **108–9, 134**
Duffy, Michael
Durham, Nigel 145

Eastwood, William 151
Edgar-Hunt, Kat 128
Edward I 16
Elizabeth I 16
Elizabeth II 76
Ellis-Davies, Arthur 150
Ellison, John 147, 176
Elwyn, Richard (Head Master 1864–72) *18*, 19
Emsley, D.J. 178
England, Alex 122
England, Archdeacon 70
Etruscans House, St Olave's 70
Eusden, Laurence *166*
Everingham, John 11

Fairfax House, St Olave's 75
Fawcett, Canon 172
Fawkes, Guy 16–17, *16*
Field, C. Edmund 176
Finney, Jacqueline 150
Fletcher, John (Head Master 1564–75) 16
Fletcher, Pat **140–3,** 140
Foster, David 69
Fowler, John Henry 97
French, CSM 28

Gaastra, John 105, 122, 176
Gardiner, Peter D.R. (Head Master 1967–79)
    47–50, *47*, 51, 94, 114, 115
Gargan, Martin 147, 178
Gatiss, Howard 159
Gaunt, Rosie 151, 179
George VI 69
Gepp, Major General 44
Gibbs, Lara 142
Gibson, R. John 172
Gilbert, Mr 174
Gildener, Gordon 154

Gill, Ben 152
Gillingham, Tory 158
Goode, H.W. 71
Goolden, Richard O. 68
Gorman, Shuan 178
Gowland, A. 71
Grant, Matthew **106**
Gray, Jeffrey 119
Gray, Mike 173
Greenwood, Jean 66
Griffith, Stephen **115**, *115*
Grove, The 32, 35, 140; *see also* Clifton Grove
Guy Fawkes Boat Club 152
Gymnasium 70, 72, 98, 162
Gypson, N. 176

Habgood, John (Archbishop) 52, *53*, 116
Hague, James 150
Halifax, Lord 32, 163
Hall, Chris **150–2**, 150
Hall, Mike **132–3**, 152
Hall, Sam **132–3**
Hamilton, Cynthia
Hamilton, Don H.
Handford, George (Head Master 1887–1900)
    21, 22, 126
Harcourt, Sir William Vernon 166
Harding ??? 43
Harding, David 105, **174**
Harding, John 163, 164
Harding, Richard D. **164–4**
Harding, Robert F. 47, 144, 147, 163, 176
Hardisty, Don **174**
Harland, Maurice H. (Bishop) 10, 37, 163
Harris, Philip L. 105, 114, 173, 176
Harrison, Cuthbert 13
Harrison, G.G.T. 71
Harvey, Stephen *115*, **115–16**
Hazelrigg, Antonia 142
Henderson, Sally 142
Hepworth, Mark G.B.
Herbert, Sir Thomas *72*, 166
Herriot, James 120
Hewson, William (Head Master 1838–44)
    14, 18
Hey, William (Head Master 1844–64) 19, 21
Heywood, Peter 71
Hill, Christopher *167*
Hill, David *167*
Hindhaugh, Ian 145
Hitler, A. 46
Hodd, Murray 144
Hodgson, Ann 150, 152
Hodsdon, Clive **86**

Hoggard, Jenny 142
Hoggard, Karly 142
Hoggard, Lynsay 142
Holgate, Archbishop 12, 14
Hollington, John R. 42
Hope, David (Archbishop) 79
Horsefair School 12, 14, 16, *17*, 98–9, 126
Hough, Ben 146
Houghton, Jenny
Howat, A. Tudor 70, 75

Howard, Ken 171
Howman, Stewart 106
Hubbard, Richard H. *102*, 116, 128, 154, 176
Hudson, William M. 134, 154
Hughes, Allan 79
Hughes, D.E. Peter (Head Master 1980–84)
    52, 52–3, 114, 115
Hughes, David J. 92, 114, 116, 129, **136–7**, 150
Hume, Basil (Cardinal) 116
Hutchinson, Richard 178

Incubator, The (dormitory) 45

Jackson Recital Room 118
Jackson, Andrew 154
Jackson, Anne 66
Jackson, G.F.
Jackson, Mr ('Wheeze') 46
James I 12
James, Peter 178
Janes, Daniel 151, 179
Jasper, Dean 114, 115
Jelbert, Brian 56
Jenkins, David (Bishop) 116
Jentoft, Captain 44
Jesper, Mark 174
John of Beverley, St (Head Master 705–18) 10
John of York (Head Master 1368–79) 11
Johnston, D. Peter 176
Johnston, Mike **153–4**
Johnston, Victoria 151, 179
Jones, Mike **85–6**
Jones, Nick 150

Kallis, Jacques 146
Kay, Andrew 178
Kay, Nick 178
Kemp-Welch, Noel H. 51, 114
Kendall, David 174
Kent, Duchess of *56*, 120, 156
Kent, Michael **172**

Kershaw, Maurice 147, 178
King, Colonel John C.R. 68
King-Reynolds, Guy E. **38–41**, *38*, 53, 70, **71–4**, 95
Kinnell, Pamela 142
Kinnell, Sarah 142
Kirby Hall 31
Kirby, David **144–6**, *145*, 164, 176, 178
Kitchener, Lord 28
Knapton, Jim **171**

Lacy, John **174**
Lamb, Maggy 119 'MAGGIE' IN TEXT
Lang, Cosmo (Archbishop) 162
Lang, Wai Hong 123
Langley, William 13
Langstaffe, Rex 41
Lawrence, Craig 105
Le Tocq, Leslie C. 43, 47, 105, 174, 176
Leach, A.F. 10
Leigh, Peter **174**
Lennon, John 114
Lewis, Tom 163, 164
Lightwing, Daniel 86
Linton House 61
Linton Lodge 56, 92, 156
Lloyd, Chris 150
Lloyd, Sophie 142
Lockey, Claire *51*
Long, The (dormitory) 45
Lowe, Ian K.M. 49, 115, 128, *129*, 130, 176
Lowther, Arbel 128
Lynch, Richard C. 42–3
Lyon, Alex, MP 76

Macalister, Ian 125
Mackenzie, John 105
Mackie, Mrs 40
MacLeod, Alistair 148, *151*, 179
MacLeod, Jamie 150, 152
MacLeod, Rory 151, 179
Mann, John 68
Manor, The *28*, 32, 39, 45, 46, 68, 90, 91, 93, 94; *see also* Clifton Manor
Marrick Priory, Swaledale 114
Marsden, J. 178
Marsh, Joanna 116, 119
Martin, Mr 44
Martin House Hospice 159
Mary I 12, 37
Mason, M. 176
Mathis, Robert 85
Maxwell, John **172**
Maw, John 105

McAllister Hall, Emma 142
McCallum, Malcolm **173**
McDermid, Norman 164
Meaby, Miss Phyllis 58, *64*, 64–5
Medhurst, Charles *167*
Mellor, Katie 142
Memorial Hall 51, 54,87, 115, 128, 163, 164, 174
Merchant Adventurers 158
Metcalfe, Sarah 142
Middleton, Robert 17, 167
Milburn, Harold A. 42
Milne, Alfred 28
Milner-White, Dean 37, 114, 163
Mirfield 116
Mitchell, Frank 144, 178
Mitchell, John V. **67–70**, 70, 98, 176
Mitchell, Tom 145, 178
Mohan, Keith 146
Monteith, Maurice 148
Montgomery, Field Marshal 37
Moore, Albert 122, 123, *168*
Moreton, Thomas 17
Morris, Connelee 149
Moxon, Neil 105
Mulryne, Trevor **78–80**

Natural History Society *88*, 89
Naylor, Murray 80, **156–7**, *156*
Nettleton, Peter 178
Newman, David
Newman, Debbie 141
Nix, J. 176
Nokes, Mr 13, 14
Northfield, Peter **88–9**
Norwood, A.B. (St Olave's c.1883–1901) 67
Norwood, Pat **172**

Oak Leaf Day 72
Ogden Trust 158
Ogden, Rachael 142
Oldcorne, Edward 17
Oliver, Richard 12
Orford, Father Barry 116
Outhwaite, Emily 124
Owen, Edward C. (Head Master 1900–13) *19*, 22, 23, 67–8, 126, 162
Owen-Barnett, Ann 92
Owen-Barnett, John **92**, 176

Pandas Hockey Club 154, 164
Pankhurst, Mrs 17

Parkinson, C. Northcote *168*
Paterson, Derek **84**, 140
Patteson, Canon 154, 173
Paulinus, St (Head Master 627–30) 10
Pedley, Avril **10–14**, **16–17**, 57, **96–9b**, 104, 126–**8**
Pemberton, Keith R. 115, 116, 119, 176
Penty, Frederick T. 31
Philip of Spain 12, 37
Pick, Frank 123, 168
Pickersgill, Bill 144, 154, 178
Pike, Richard 147
Ping, A. Wentworth 68, 69, 70, *71*, 73, 74, 93, 170, 172, 176
Ping, Mrs 70, 172
Pinyer, Harold 49
Pittman, Laura 58
Pittman, Robin N. (Head Master 1985–95) 50, 53, *54*, 54–8, 80, 92, 115, 140, 156, 157
Platts, M.G.G. 71
Pope John 11
Porte, Liz 152
Porte, Mike 152
Powell, Kenneth T. 71
Power, Paddy 105, 172, 173
Precious, Andrew 154
Precious, John 154
Precious, Michael 174
Prendergast, J.X. 70
Price, Aubrey J. (Head Master 1936–37) *33*, 38
Procter, Mr 68
Proprietary School, The *15*, 18–19
Pulleyn, James P. 71
Pulleyn, John (Head Master 1576–91) 16, 26, 126
Purey-Cust, Dean 68

Quarrie, David **172**
Queen Anne School 39, 46, 49, 61, 78–9, *79*, 87, 88, 122, 157
Queen's Building 87, 98, 170
Queen's House 49, *104*, 140, 159, 163, 164

Raine, Angelo 6, 21, 22, 76
Ranson, Michael 154
Rayson, John C.M. *75*, 76–7, *144*
Rayson, Sally 76
Reid, Buff **158–9**, *158*
Reynolds, Anthony G. **46**
Reynolds, Guy, **see under** King-Reynolds
Rhodes, Kenneth H. 37, 46, 47, 164, 176

Richard of Beckyngham 10
Richards, Tiffany 120
Richardson, Horace W. 42
Richardson, Joe 145, 178
Richardson, Thomas (Second Master) 18, 19
Riddolls, Dr (fl. 1942) 64
Rigby, John 85
Riley, David 178
Riley-Smith, Captain 36
Rise, The *29*, 40, 45, *46*, 70, 92, 93, 115
Robertson, Alistair 147
Robertson, Jane (*née* Shepherd) 158
Robertson, Rory *151*, 179
Robinson, Anna
Robinson, Clive A. **75–7**, 79, 176
Robinson, Jennifer
Robinson, Ruth 65
Roden, John M. *114*, **114–15**
Rowland, Chris 150
Rowley, Peter 86
Royal School *19*
Rusling, Nick 142, 178
Russell, R.F. 178

Sanatorium 90, 160
Sargeant, Elizabeth 142
Sargeant, Joanna 141, 142
Sargeant, Kevin 79
Sargeant, Linda 79
Scargill, F.M. 104
School House 40, 45, 46, 51, 57, 58, 62, 70, 85, 90, 92, 115, 174
Science Society 41, 49, 89, 108, 116
Scott, Colonel H.C. 32
Scott, Henry 164
Selborne College 57
Sellers, Brian 144, *145*, 169, 173
Severn, Andrew **82**, **83–4**, **135**
Sewell, Betty (*née* Toyne) 69, 74, 164
Sewell, E.P. 178
Shang, Shuo 86
Shanks, Ken 150
Shepherd family 158
Shepherd, Patrick 158
Shepherd, Richard 173
Shepherd, Sir Donald 158
Shepherd, Wendy **140–3**
Shillitoe, Pilot Officer 43
Shuttleworth, Guy M.S. **90**, 91, 116, 176
Shuttleworth, Tanya 91
Simpson, Peter **160**
Sinclair, Meghan 124
Singleton, Gertrude 64
Singleton, Susan 64

Skiera, Tony 174
Slingsby, Jackie 79
Slingsby, John 79, 149
Smalley, Amelia 141
Smalman-Smith, Richard 150
Smith, Bethany 124
Smith, Erica 142
Smyth, Richard (Head Master 2004–) 62, 80, 157
Southgate, John (Dean) 80, 156
Spartans House, St Olave's 70
Spaven, Greta **64–6**
Spencer, David **86**
Sports Centre 49
Springgay, Andrew *149*, 178
St Catherine's (11 Clifton) 35, 55
St Helen's, Clifton 68, 70n.
St Leonard's Hospital 11
St Maurice's Church, Monkgate 64
St Olave's House 22, 32, *67*, *69*, 70n., 163
St Olave's School, Ripon 69
St Peter's Grove 35, 52, 58
St Wilfrid's, Clifton 68, 70n.
Stanley, Irene 119
Stead, George 41, 42, 43
Stephen, Elizabeth
Stephen, Paddy 92, **147–9**, 154
Stephenson Room 21, 98, 163
Stephenson, Alfred R. 98
Stephenson, Henry M. (Head Master 1872–87) 21, 98, 126, 162
Stevenson, Louis 162, 178
Stiller, Kristina *151*, 179
Stirling, Penny 119
Strickland-Constable, Charles 86, 89
Sunderland, Alice 142
Swettenham, Frank *169*
Swimming pool 31, 35, 162, 170, 171
Sykes, P.H. ('Pizzie') 74

Tait, Gordon 178
Taylor, Claire 142
Taylor, James 145
Taylor, Joby 150
Taylor, Paul **85**
Taylor, Peter 58, 62, 92, 176
Taylor, Sue 58, 92, **92**
Temple, William (Archbishop) 32, 39
Temple House *36*, 40, 43, 102, 174
Tessimond, Oswald 17
Thatcher, Margaret 108
Thebans House, St Olave's 70
Thomas de Farnilow 11
Thomas of Bayeux 10

191

Thomas, Hannah *151*, 179
Thomlinson, William (Head Master 1679–1711) 12
Thompson, Andrew 174
Thompson, James E. 41
Thompson, Paul 115
Thornton, Nigel **171**
Tommy Card 19
Tooms, H. Alan 105, 106, 138
Tosdevin, Mrs (of CPPS) 65
Toyne Library, The *97*, 98, 163
Toyne, Betty, *see under* Sewell, Betty (*née* Toyne)
Toyne, Mrs 32, 127
Toyne, Stanley M. (Sam) (Head Master 1913–36) 23, *26*, 27, 29, 30, 31, 32, 38, 74, *88*, 98, 104, 126–7, 144, 153, 163, 172
Trojans House, St Olave's 70
Troop, C.L. 178
Trotman, Andrew F. (Head Master 1995–2004) 58, *59*, 59–60, 80, 156, 157
Trott, Group Captain 43
Turton, L 71

Wackett, James 146, 178
Wackett, Katherine 142
Wackett, Peter *149*, 178
Waine, Freddie 43, 105, 174
Walker, Revd *21*
Walker, Robin 49
Wall, M. Philip L. 45
Wallace, Richard
Wallace, Suzanne
Walter, Douglas 147
Walters family 43
Walters, John R. 43
Walters, William L. 43
Walton, E.J. 178
Wandesforde, Christopher 12
Wandesforde, George 12
Ward, Gill 152
Ward, John 150
Warrington, Tim 105

Weatherill, Enid 73
Wellburn, Hamilton 71
Wentworth House, St Olave's 35, 70, 77, 79, 171
Whalley, Stephen 116
White House, The 77, 170
Whitestone Gallery 61, 122, 159
Whitmore, Bernard G. 41
Whitney, Pilot Officer 44
Wilkes, Mr 153
Wilkinson, J.G. 153
William I 10
William Rufus 10
Williams, Esther 141
Wilson, Benny 146
Wilson, Emily Annie 67, 68
Wilson, Revd Henry A. (Founder of St Olave's) 67, 69
Wilson, J.M.G. 178
Wilson, W.G. 178
Wise, Greg **130**, *130*
Wiseman, Freddie ('Wizzy') 6, 171
Wombell, David 105
Woodrow, Alex 119
Woodruff, Malcolm 145
Woods, Sarah 142
Woolsey, Tom 146, *149*, 178
Wright, Andrew 57, **87**, 116, **118–21**, 128
Wright, Charles J. 24–5
Wright, Christopher 16
Wright, David H. 71
Wright, John 16
Wright, Robert A. 71

Yardley, Norman 75, *144*, 154, *169*
Yeld, George *23* 126, 176
York College for Girls 71, 76
York Pageant 1909 21, *127*
Yr Hafod, Snowdonia 136–7
Yuill, Joe 178

PHOTO ACKNOWLEDGEMENTS

Every effort has been made to credit photographs correctly but in some cases this has not always been possible.

Mark Pickthall pages 2, 63, 66, 77-79, 80-1, 84, 87, 104-107, 117, 119, 121, 139, 141-3, 146, 149, 151-2, 154-5
Dave Morris pages 4, 7-8, 15, 60-2, 89, 91, 97, 102-3, 110, 112-3, 118, 120, 128, 129, 135, 148, 151, 158, 160, 172, 175 and the front coverpages
"The Evening Press" pages 49, 51, 55-7, 60, 121, 142-3, 148-9, 150-1
John Armstrong pages 99, 134, 16
Matt Wilson pages 34, 61, 111, 150
John Davidson page 114
Sam and Mike Hall page 133
John Bulcock page 138
Mike Dawson page 125
Dave Hughes page 137
Erica Town page 159
Ian Lancaster page 99
KL Photographs pages 143 and 177
John Darmody pages 122-4
Paul Hughes page 161
Terry Berry pages 92 and 106

192